IMAGES
of America

SHARONVILLE

AND ITS PEOPLE

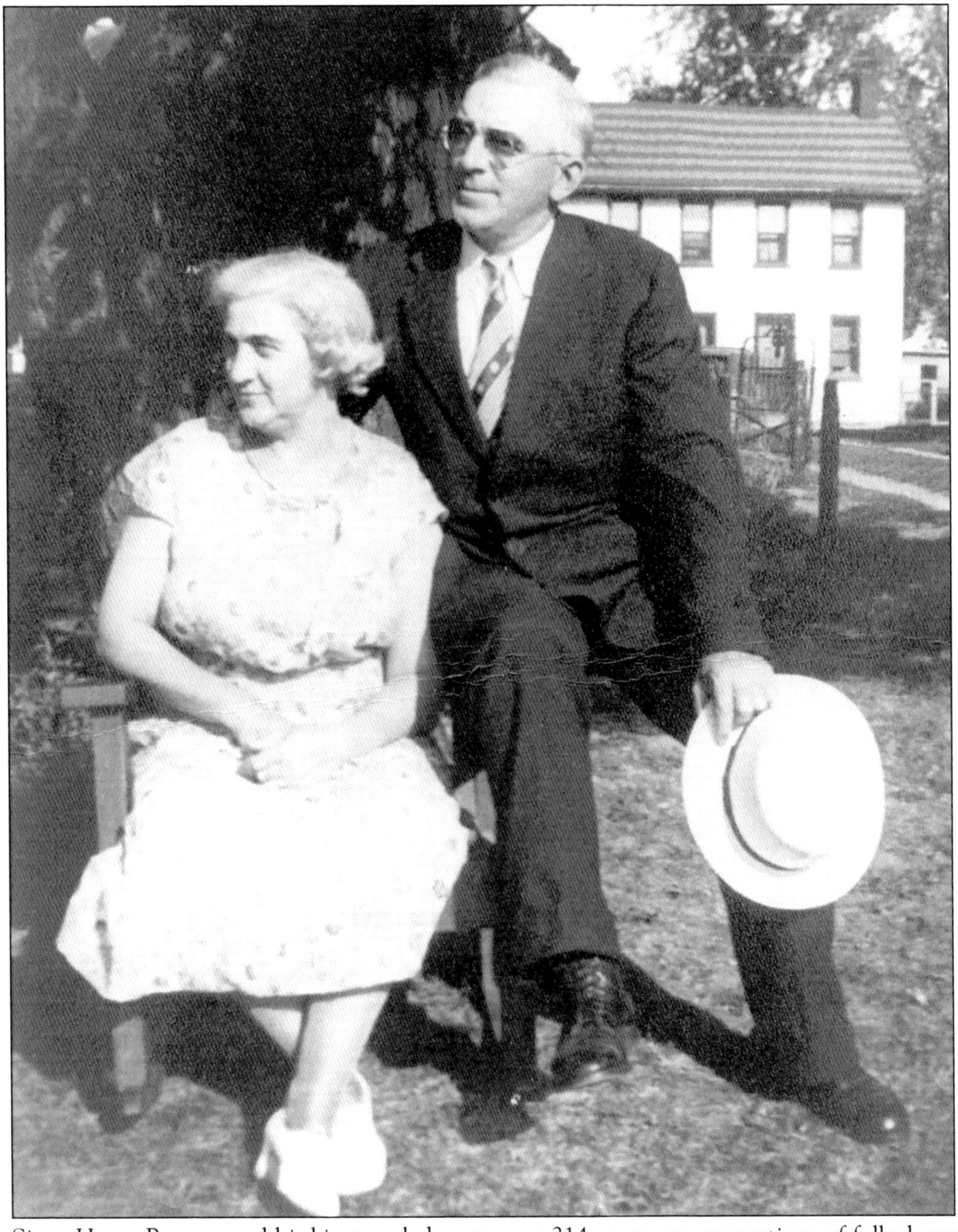

Since Henry Runyan and his kin traveled west some 214 years ago, generations of folks have called Sharonville home. On the occasion of their 50th wedding anniversary, Bessie and Thomas P. Donohoue sat outside for this photo. They moved to Sharonville from Springfield, Ohio, in 1923. Bessie Shoaf Donohoue was the mother of 11 children: Charles E., Thomas E., Stephen R., Theodore E., James R., Raphael F., Theresa J., Beatrice L. (Grant), Marjorie D. (Spellmire), Katheryn I. (Painter), and Mary E. (Muennich). Bessie passed away in 1970 at the age of 83. Her husband, Thomas P., was a fireman and engineer for the New York Central Railroad from 1911 to 1958, a total of 47 years. He left this world in 1962 at age 74. Many of their descendants still live in the Sharonville area.

IMAGES
of America

SHARONVILLE

AND ITS PEOPLE

Maria R. Eckhoff

ARCADIA
PUBLISHING

ISBN 978-0-7385-1963-0

Published by Arcadia Publishing
Charleston, South Carolina

Printed in the United States of America

Library of Congress Catalog Card Number: 2002107470

For all general information contact Arcadia Publishing at:
Telephone 843-853-2070
Fax 843-853-0044
E-mail sales@arcadiapublishing.com
For customer service and orders:
Toll-Free 1-888-313-2665

Visit us on the Internet at www.arcadiapublishing.com

This book is dedicated to the people of Sharonville, past, present, and future.

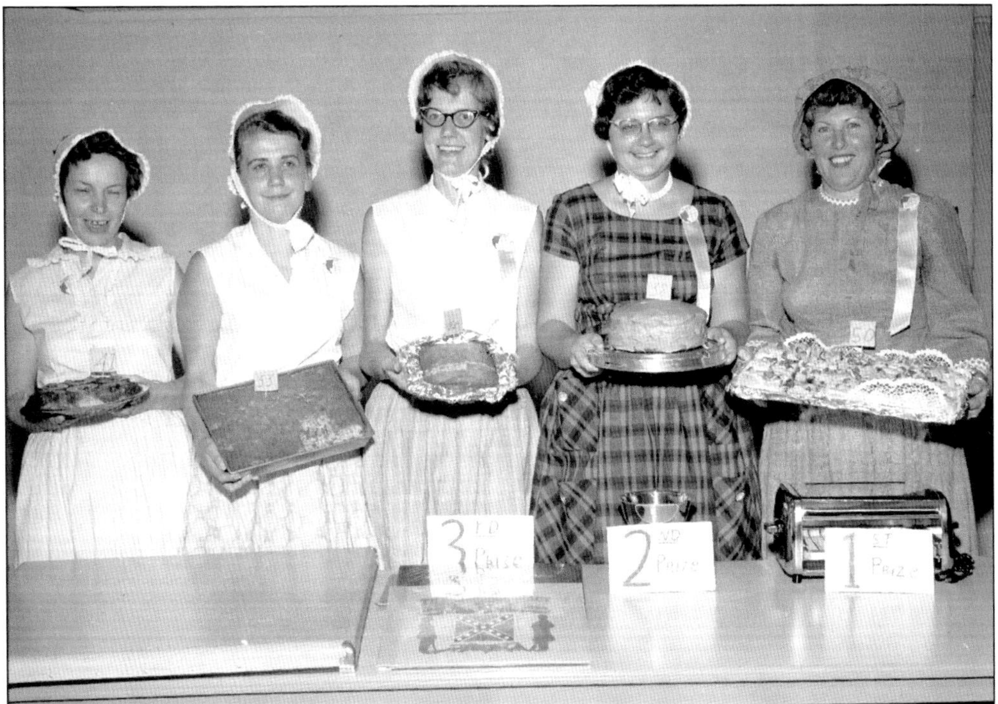

A baking contest was held during Sharonville's Semi-Centennial Celebration the week of August 20-26, 1961. Displaying their baked treats are, from left to right: Helen Kucharchuk, Shirley Carden, Carol Weaver, Peggy Yohn, and Rose Neumeister.

Contents

Acknowledgments

While the author is the person most likely to hear the cheers and complaints after a book is published, she can't function in a vacuum, especially if she's a first-time author. I want to thank the many people who helped me through this endeavor. Without their advice, help, and support, the "Sharonville and Its People" book would still be just another idea. In particular, many thanks go out to the following individuals for lending their technical help and professional expertise: Dan Burke, Chopper Eckhoff, Nick Giordano, Kevin Hutzel, Tom Keating, Pat Larson, and Eric Lefebvre. Thanks also to the members of Sharonville City Council, who trusted me enough to let me run with this project.

Lastly, but perhaps most importantly, I want to thank a group of people, some I know quite well, some I've met briefly, and some I've never met at all, whose creativity, spirit, works, and personal support inspired me and kept me going from writing the proposal, through hours of staring at photos and computer screens, to finally publishing this book: Marilyn Koenig Eckhoff (mom, cheerleader, and my "biggest fan"), Arthur and Charlotte Hanes Koenig, Bob Houston, Jim Borgman, Howie Dorough, Julia Cameron, Karen Shaw, Marcia, Carmen, and Lisa who kept me balanced and laughing; and William Shakespeare, "This above all: to thine own self be true."

The following people donated or loaned photos and provided their memories for this book. I'm sorry I couldn't use everything. Thank you for your encouragement and for your willingness to share.

Ray Asbrock, Ray Baxter, Marts Beekley, Beulah Boone, Gail Williams Burg, Melvin Burg, Pauline Roth Chambers, Don Clark, Ken Cork, Theresa Donohoue, Maria Eckhoff, Joyce Gruber Feltz, Mary Louise Ferrell, Harry Finley, Bob Foster, Don Glaser, Jim and Dorothy Gorman, Susan Hawkins Graham, G. Richard Hagee, Bill and Mary Haines, Dorothy Nuss Hargy, Martha Hauenstein, Yvonne Hicks, Martha Jean Marquardt Hill, Marlene Smith Holley, Bob and Ernestine Houston, Paul Kattelman, Al Krick, Elaine Duermit Krick, Lynn Lemen of the Sharonville Recreation Department, William K. Lewis, Helen Hubbard Lovins, Joyce Lovins, Thomas Floyd (Bub) Mehaffie, Carl Miller, Alfred Mohrfield, James Muchmore, Carol Penson; Jim Rahtz, Communications Director, and Al Winstel, Julie Herzog, and Amy Smith, Naturalists, with the Hamilton County Park District; Mark Adams, Park Ranger; Tracy Crawford of Heritage Village Museum; John Powell, Doug Prenatt, Mary Jo Dyer Richardson, Delphine Robbins, Rita Robertson, Gene Rosselot, Joe Roth, Jr., Pat Madyda of the Sharonville Chamber of Commerce; the Sharonville Fire Department, especially Chief Dale Duermit, and Assistant Chiefs John Mackey and Ralph Hammonds; the Sharonville Police Department, especially Chief Mike Schappa, Lt. John Cook, Lt. Joe Witzman, Lt. Bobby Fisher, Sgt. Paul Healey, Officer Bob Menth, and Auxiliary Officer Chet Doverspike; Mike and Reva Schwan, Karen Shaw, Tony Shaw, Jane Muchmore Simpson, Ruth Hines Slaughter; St. Michael Parish, Mary Jane Fuller, Archivist; Judy Surface Taylor, Sara Lou Teets, Robert C. (Bucky) Walters, and Joe Wright.

Introduction

This book is about the people of Sharonville, 1788 to 2002. These are the folks you might read about in the "Neighbors" column of the local paper. These are the people who take pictures at family outings and send you a copy in a letter or card. These are your grandparents, great-grandparents, and even great-great-grandparents. They're the human beings inside the uniforms. The book shows how different we are from the people who lived here 50, 100, or 150 years ago; and yet, how much we have in common.

Sharonville was founded in 1788—at least the first settlers at Runyan's Station came back then. The town was for some time called Sharon. We have tried to find out where the name came from with no luck. I don't know if one of the founding families had a relative named Sharon or if it was a phonetic change of something an immigrant called it, such as "Shawan." This is a good guess as the area was home to many Indian tribes, particularly the Shawnee people (Shawandassee), prior to the influx of pioneers. Legend has it that the "ville" was added in the 1800s after a body being taken home for services by train wound up at the wrong Sharon (there is at least one town called Sharon northeast of here). After the mix-up, our town became Sharonville. The original geographic area ran between Runyan's Station on the north (basically the Hamilton/Butler county line) and Cunningham's Station on the south (in what is now Evendale). The original town was located in the center of an area now bound by State Route 42/ Old Route 25 on the north, Reading Road (formerly Rose Street), Main Street (running north and south), and by what is now Sharon Road to the south. Many details about the founding of the town, its leaders, and what the town looked like over the years were covered in a previously published book called *Sharonville, Then and Now*. Though out of print, you can find it in local Hamilton County, Ohio libraries and in our historical society library.

People have asked me: "What was the hardest thing about creating this book?" My answer is always the same: "Getting people to contribute to it." It only reinforced my resolve to put together a book like this. I can't tell you how frustrating and disheartening it is to hear people say, "Well, my family has only been here (fill in the number of years)." It could have been 80 years or 8 years but the story was always the same: ordinary people don't think their lives are worthy of being remembered in a book. That's sad. So many of these same people spend hours in musty old libraries searching for some shred of information on a tattered yellow page that gives them a clue to who their great-grandmother was. Whole Internet sites are devoted to "Missing Ancestors"—trying to identify the face of a person in a photo long lost or sold in a penny garage sale box; or trying to match up descendants of families with a well-worn bible containing pages of thoughtfully inscribed records of life events, purchased at an antique mall.

One of my goals in doing this book is to change that perception of unworthiness. Who knows, maybe so many people will see their friends and neighbors in the book that they'll be moved to say, "My family counts too," and send me their pictures and stories. Maybe I'll get so many that I'll have to put together another book "Sharonville and Its People II: The People Who Didn't Think They Were Worthy Enough the First Time." Okay, so I'll drop the second part, but you get the idea.

Some of my Native American friends believe that before a decision is made, one should consider the impact it may have on the next seven generations. While that sounds like a heavy burden to bear, think of what a different place the world would be if everyone took that advice to heart. My hope is that seven generations from now, someone searching for a long lost ancestor in Sharonville will find them in this book, thanks to the generosity and forethought of some individual contributor. My hope is that seven generations from now, some student in a high-tech school who wants to know what Sharonville was like "back then" will pick up this book (or an electronic facsimile thereof) and see more than bricks and mortar, more than streets and buildings and dates, but the heart and soul of a people.

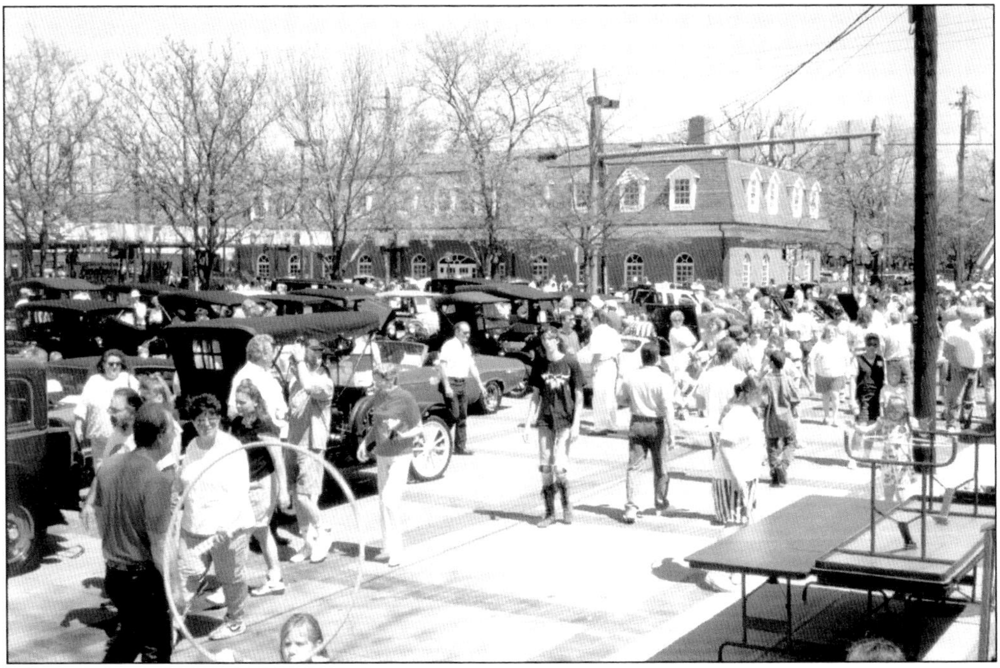

The crowd seems to build at the Sharonville Car Show every year. Created in 1978 by the old Sharonville Businessmen's Association, this annual community event typically draws 700-800 entries of vintage vehicles. This is "the one they block the streets for." It has grown to be one of the largest car shows in southwestern Ohio. The late April weather challenges the organizers every year—temperatures can range from "jacket weather" to the balmy 80s, with ominous storm clouds or brilliant sunshine and deep blue skies. This 1994 crowd enjoyed a picture perfect day.

One

More Than Storefronts

A town is more than just establishments with signs hanging out front. People run those businesses. In the days before large corporations, families ran the businesses and often passed them down from one generation to the next. For decades, the largest employer in Sharonville was the railroad. A check of one street in the early 1900s yielded at least one family member from each home working for the railroad. Not every man who passed through Sharon Yard lived in Sharonville but a lot of them did. Even today Sharon Yard is an integral part of the town. An old red caboose sits behind a replica of the old depot in the center of "original" Sharonville. The area has even been given the official name of "Depot Square." You'll find the train on city welcoming signs, the historical society logo, tote bags, and other items easily identified as representing Sharonville.

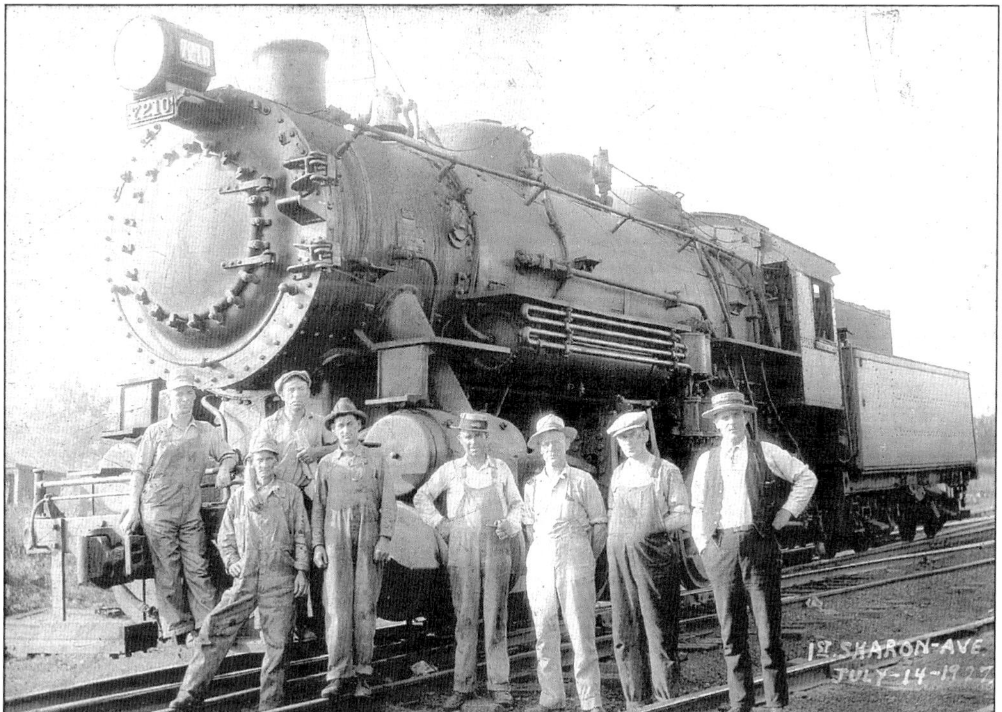

Men from Sharon Yard gathered next to the enormous Engine 7210 for this photo on July 14, 1927. Pictured, from left to right, are (front row) Jim Brogan, Unidentified, Lou Procter, Joe Wright, Sr., Unidentified, Unidentified; (back row) Unidentified, Unidentified.

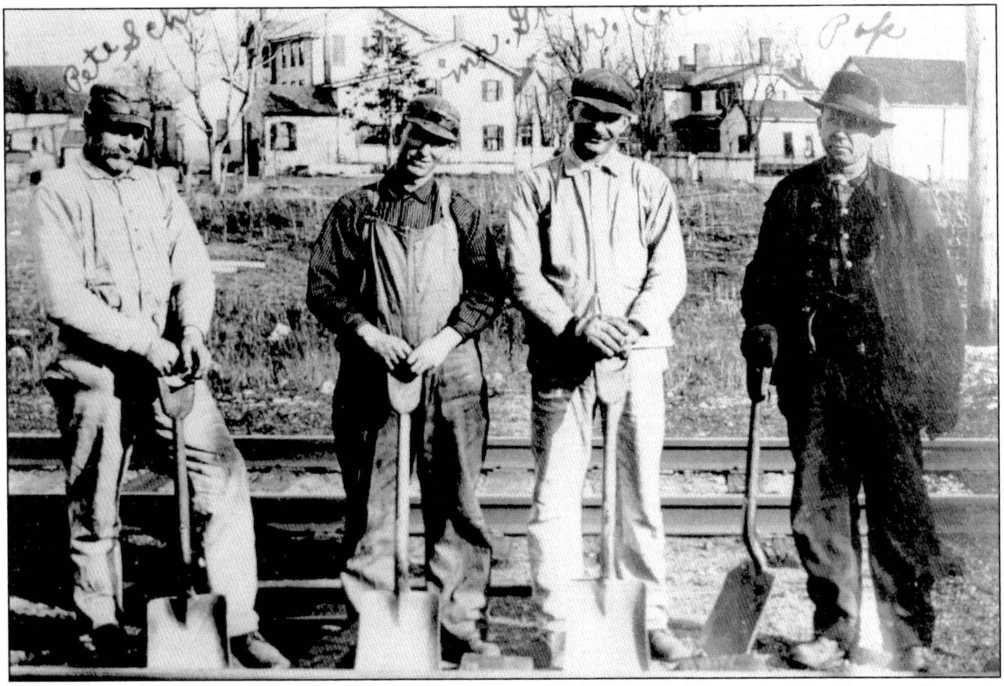

Across the tracks at Sharon Yard, these men were probably shoveling coal or cinders in the early 1900s. Pictured, from left to right, are Pete Schriever, Mr. Green, Mr. Cork, and John Prenatt, Sr.

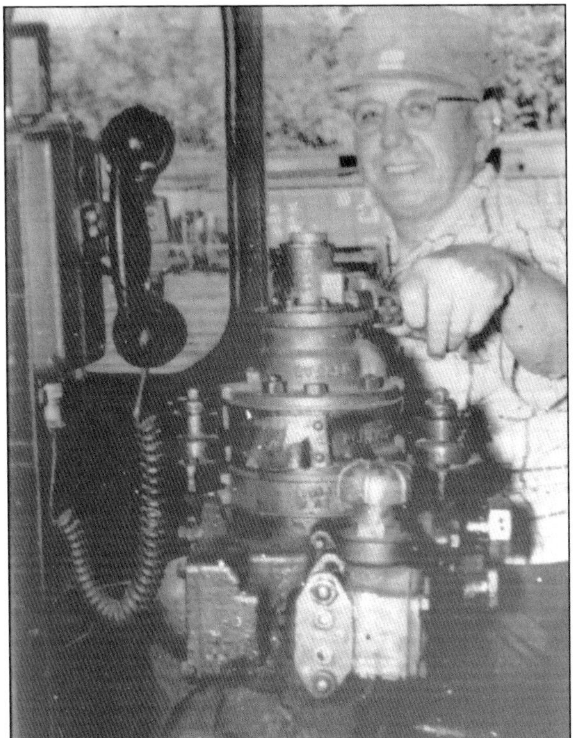

This man's photo was printed in 1988 on page 77 of the book *Sharonville Then and Now* in the chapter about Sharon Yard. He was unidentified. That man is no longer a mystery. He is Joe Roth, Sr. who worked for the railroad for 52 years. An engineer, he was the father of two of our historical society members, Pauline Roth Chambers and Joe Roth, Jr.

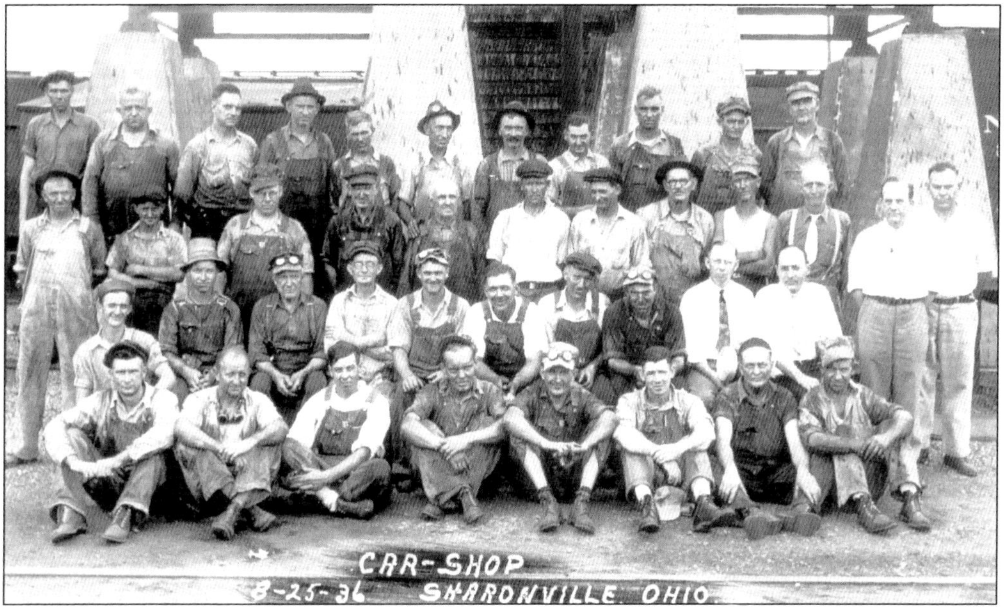

The Car-Shop guys stopped work long enough to pose for this photo at Sharon Yard August 25, 1936. Many of these men are presently unidentified but no less appreciated. Those who can be identified are, from left to right, (front row) the third man is Bob Surface; (third row) the third from the end of the row is Mr. Hager, the last man in the row is Harry Vaughn; (back row) the fourth man is Walter Brockman, the fifth man is James Robbins.

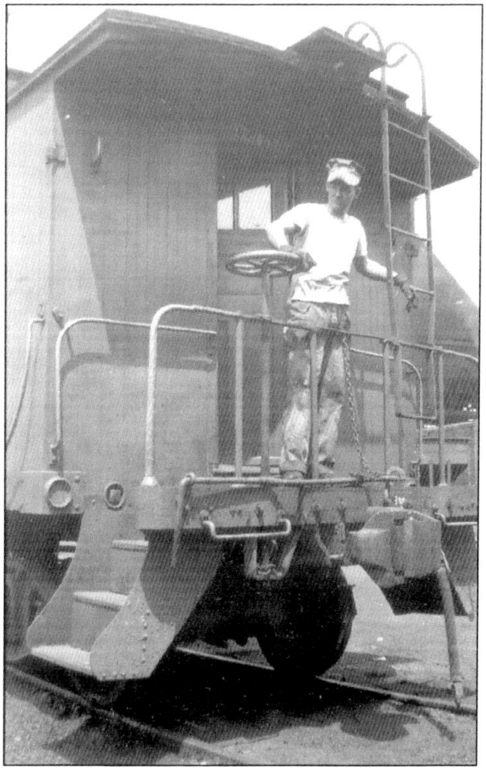

Gene "Skeeter" Hanna, a resident of Maud, was an air brake repairman and a buddy of Bill Lewis. Skeeter is pictured on a New York Central caboose at Sharon Yard in 1948.

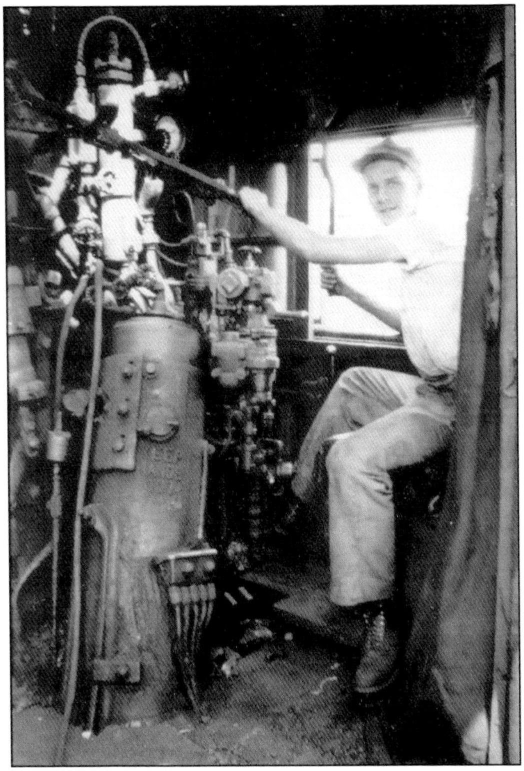

Bill Lewis was an air brake repairman at Sharon Yard for two years, around 1948–1950. Bill, Skeeter Hanna, and "Duke" changed train wheels, couplers, and doors when the work was light. They played around with pipes, too. It seems they became experts at creating small whistles from 3/8-inch pipe. They'd hook them up to the air brakes on the caboose by request. This enabled the guys working the back of the train to take a little break and still be able to make it back onto the train when they heard the brakes whistle. Apparently no one ever questioned their "retrofitting" activities. Bill is pictured pretending to be an engineer in 1948.

Many railroad companies run trains through Sharon Yard. The Penn Central Railroad had the Franklin Switch Run. Pictured on June 27, 1972, from left to right, are Conductor J.R. Roberts, Engineer Jack Moran, Fireman Charlie Carlier, Flagman Bill Surface, and Headman Bill Malie.

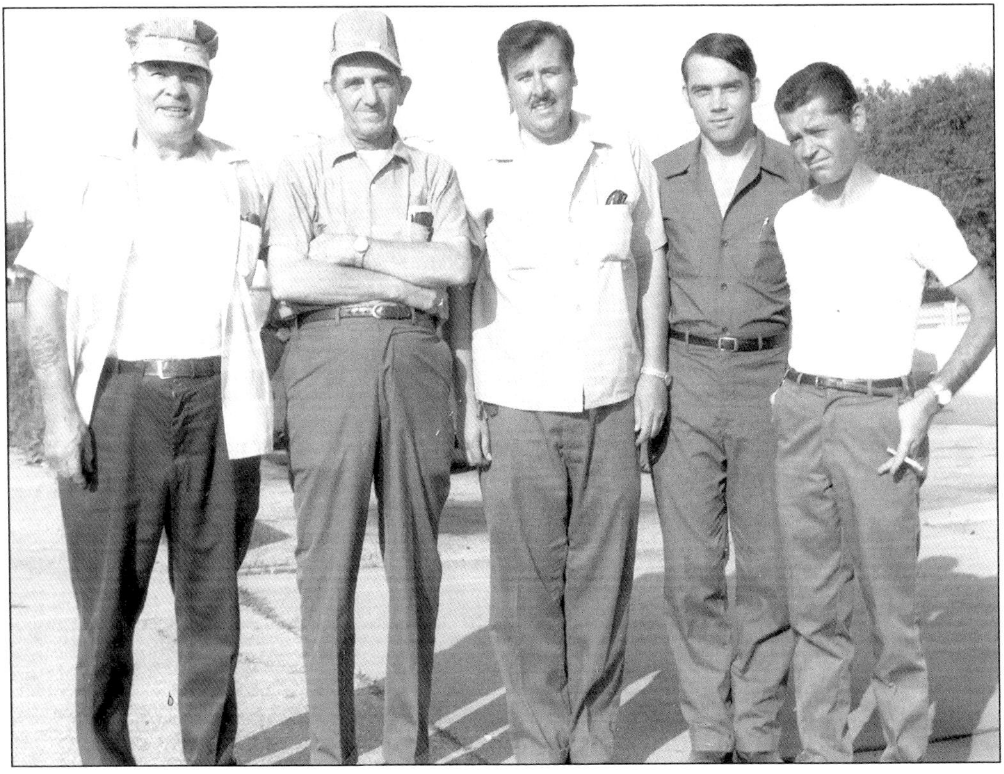

Pictured is the Prenatt family's first boarding house at 315 Main Street, c. early 1900s. The man on the porch is a boarder named Bill. John Prenatt often hired men to work for him but they had no place to stay. His wife, Elizabeth, made room for them and they would eat with the family. Soon after, other railroad men came seeking room and board. Notice the cross in the window. This was a way of letting people know that the woman of the house belonged to the Red Cross. The women knitted mittens, socks, and sweaters for the servicemen during World War I.

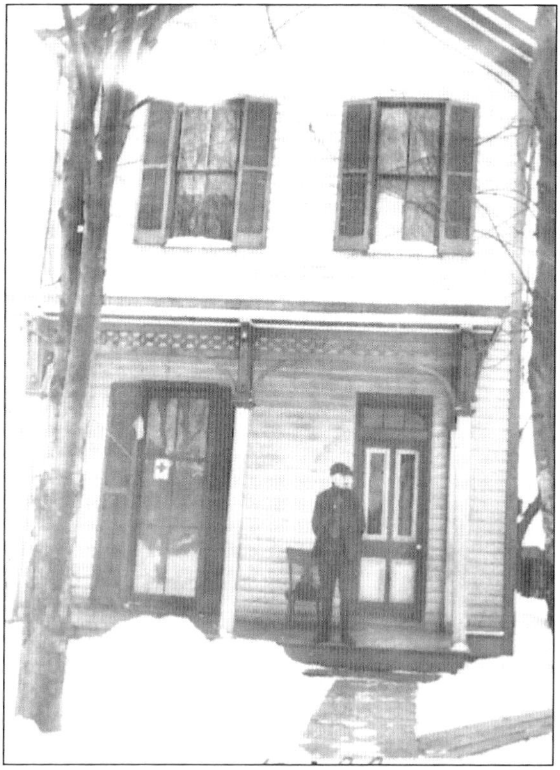

A police cruiser was parked at the tree-shaded intersection of Reading Road and Lebanon Road (Route 42) on July 14, 1959. Across the street is the Tower Gas station, where you could purchase fuel for a mere 28¢ per gallon. The view is west and slightly south.

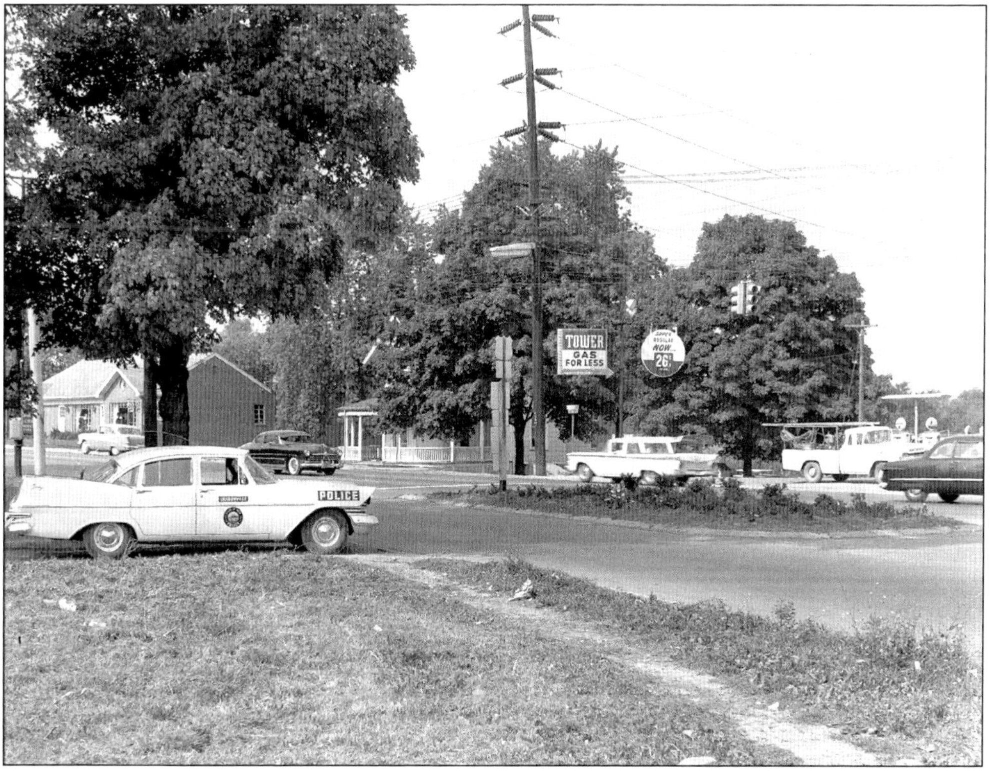

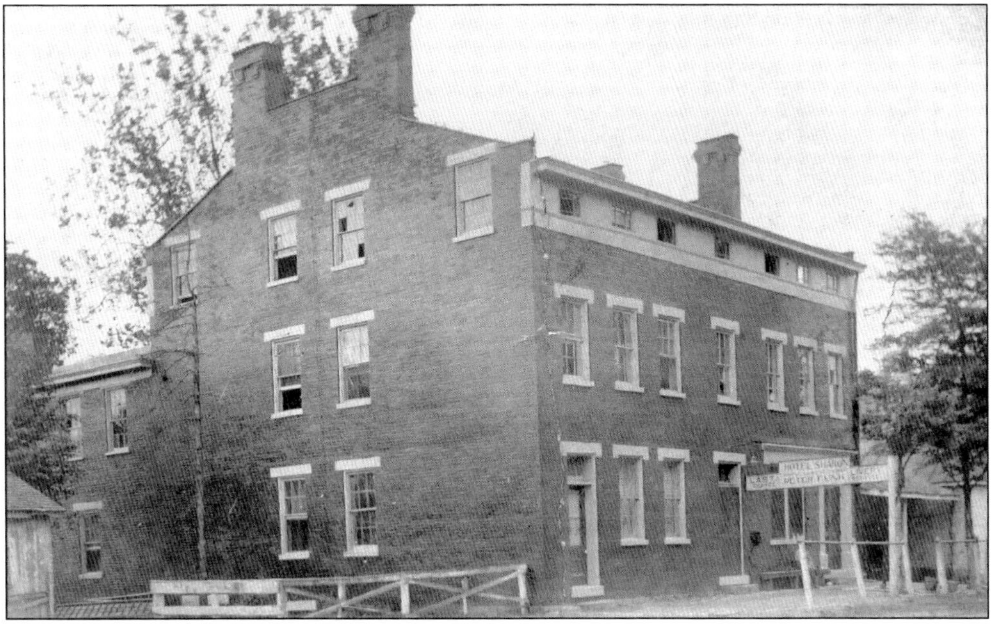

The Hotel Sharon was owned by Peter Funk from 1900 to at least 1912. The sign above the door says: "Hotel Sharon, Sample Rooms—Restaurant, Last Chance, Peter Funk, Livery." The 1911–1912 Williams County Directory also lists the following for the Hotel Sharon: "Headquarters for horsemen; Horses bought and sold." There was also a saloon on the premises. Today, the Twelve Mile House is Sharonville's contribution to the National Register of Historic Places and its rooms serve as offices for a variety of entrepreneurs.

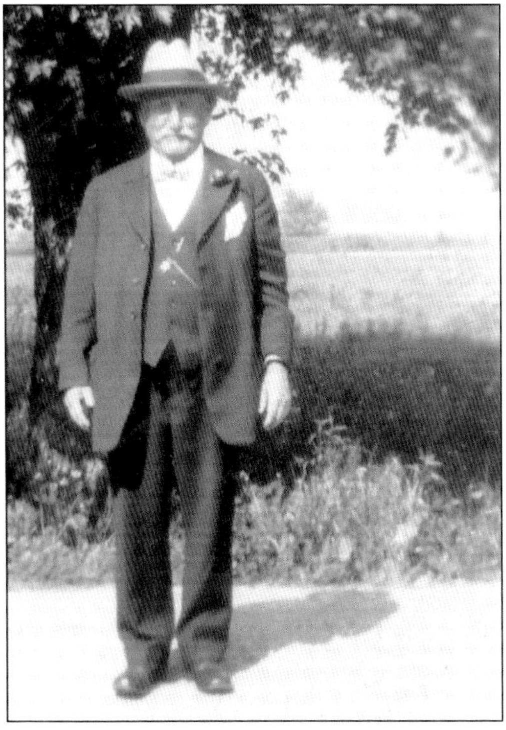

Peter Funk, the proprietor of the Hotel Sharon, stands beneath the trees that lined the main thoroughfares of Sharonville, *c.* the early 1900s.

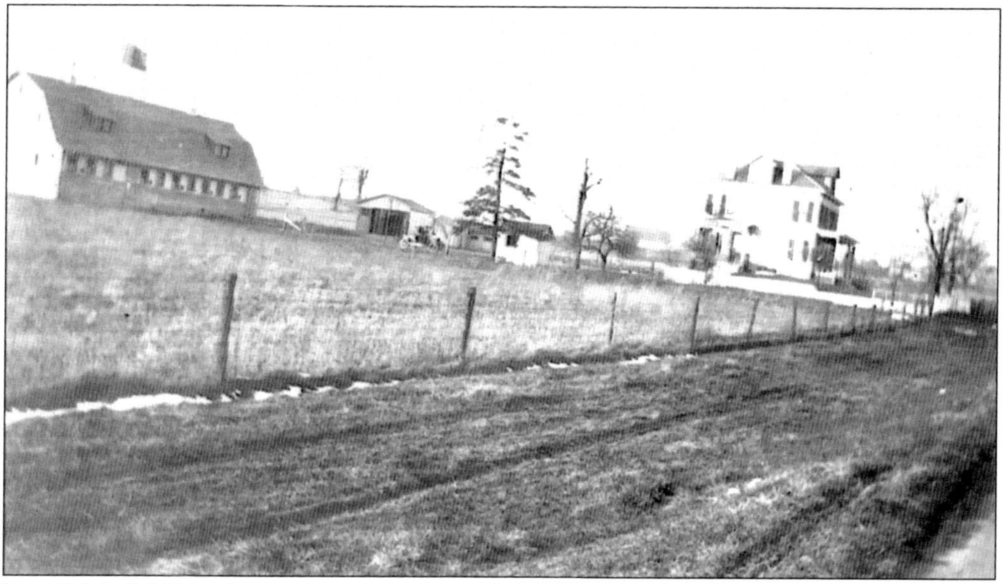

Louis Mohrfield bought this farm on Lebanon Road (State Route 42) from native New Yorkers Corwin B. Van Pelt and his wife on March 26, 1906. The barn was built about 1920. Mohrfield owned at least 100 acres of land (combined) on both sides of the road until the 1950s. The home has been in the capable hands of Louis' grandson Alfred for many years.

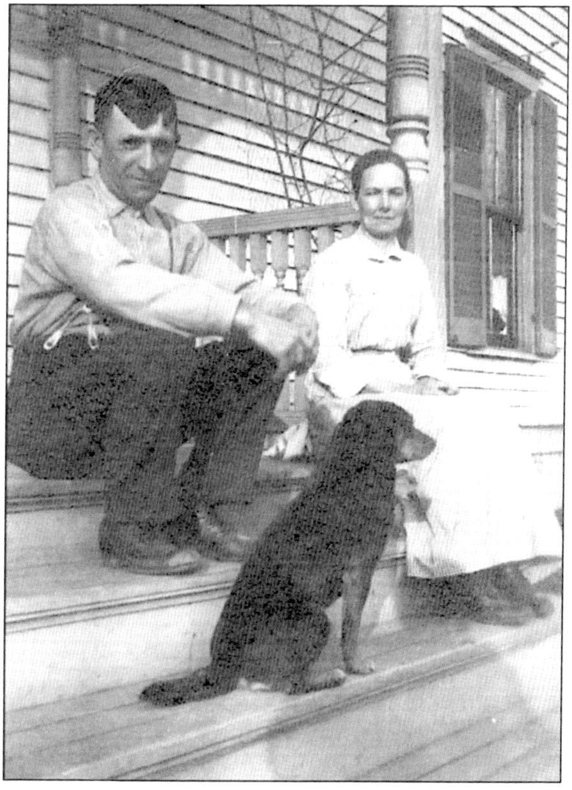

The Mohrfield farmhouse still stands at 12181 Lebanon Road not far from the Hamilton/Butler County line. Louis and Louise Mohrfield sit on the side porch steps with the family dog, *c.* 1923. Louis was born in Reading, Ohio, on October 8, 1871, while Louise Tacke Mohrfield hailed from Carthage, having been born May 29, 1874.

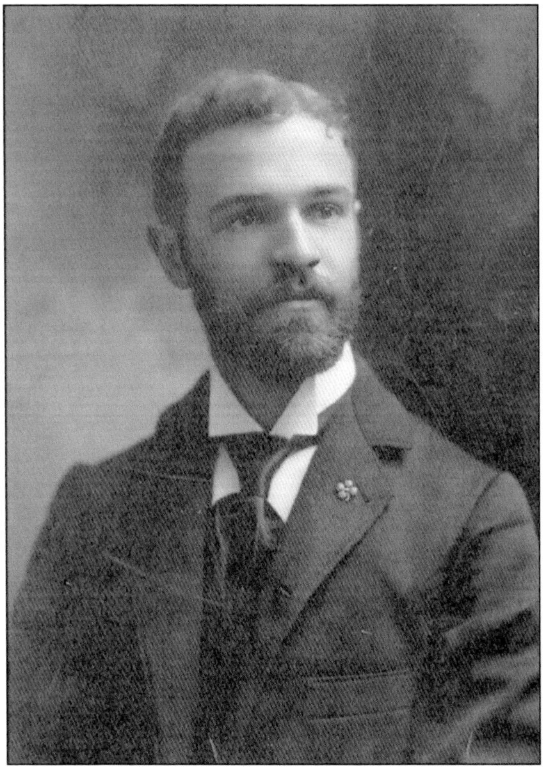

Dr. Herbert F. Beins was more than a well-known physician. Born in Evendale on June 20, 1875, he graduated from the University of Cincinnati in 1898. He truly cared about Sharonville and served on the town Council and the Board of Education at the time the new Sharonville School on Maple Street was built. He died June 14, 1930, the day before the new school was dedicated. The doctor was also a member of the Sharonville Masonic Lodge and other fraternal organizations.

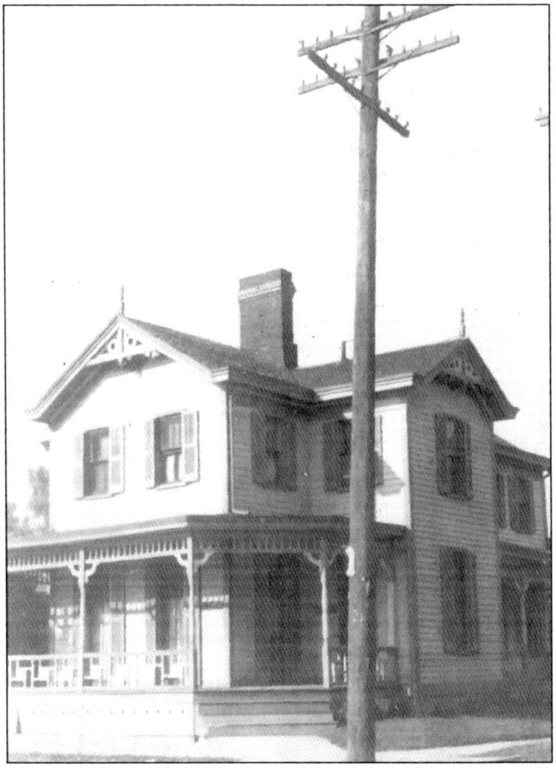

Many Sharonville residents were delivered and taken care of by Dr. Herbert F. Beins. His home and office was located on the southwest corner of Reading Road (Rose Street) and Walnut Street. It was at that corner for many years, and then at some point after 1929, his wife, Edna Whallon Beins, had it moved to the back of the property and a gas station was built on the corner. At the time of their marriage in 1903, Mrs. Beins taught all eight grades at Runyan School.

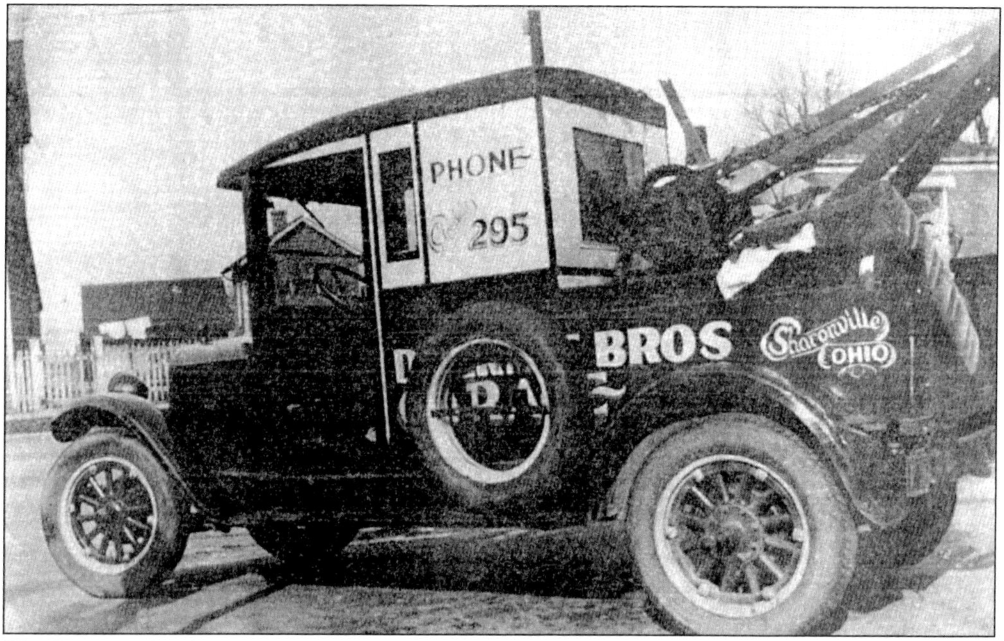

The Duermit Brothers' Garage was a staple in Sharonville for many years. Located just north of the Twelve Mile House, they provided more than just gasoline for your vehicle. Pictured is the Duermits' tow truck, emblazoned with their name and phone number: "Glendale-295."

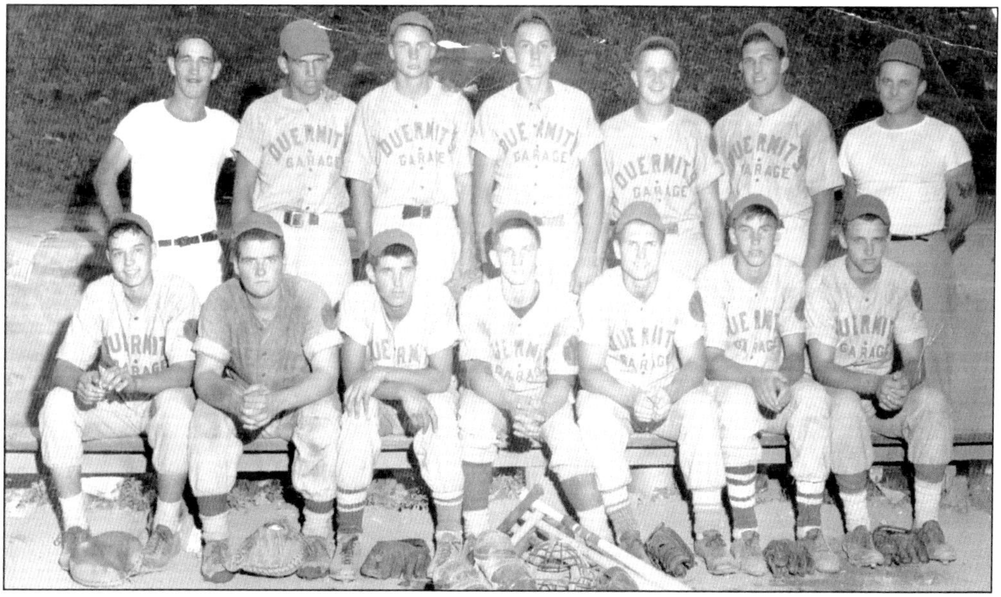

In August, 1948, the Reading Youth Organization Municipal Baseball Team sponsored by Duermit's Garage fielded many Sharonville residents. Team members, from left to right, are (front row) Bill Burke (catcher), Tommy Powers (catcher), Jerry Nickly (shortstop), Dan Danbury (second base), Marts Beekley (third base), Dave McGinnis (pitcher), Ken Cork (left field); (back row) Mike Haeffy (manager), Bob Hutchinson (first base), Ronnie Unger (outfield/pitcher), Bruce Flickenger (center field), Dick Muir (outfield/first base), Jerry Briggs (pitcher), and Howard Ply (coach).

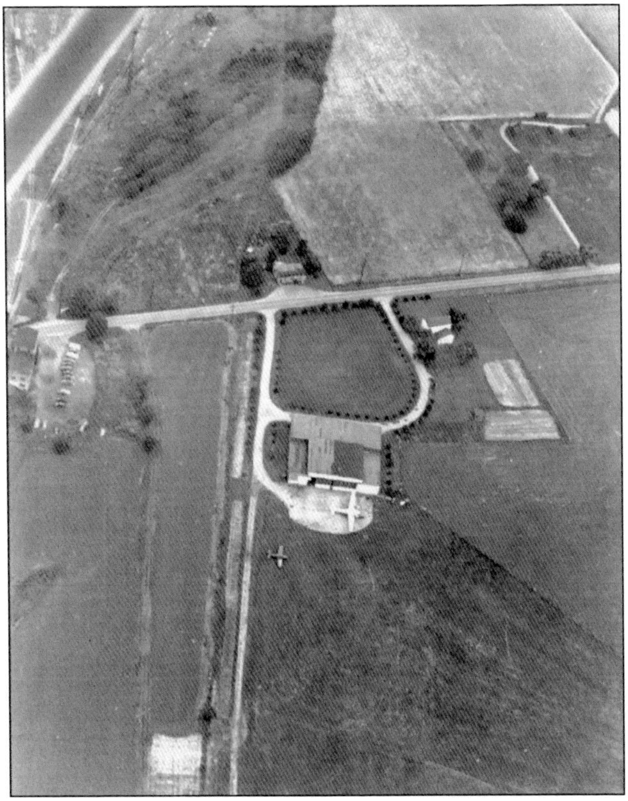

In the late 1940s, Sharon Avenue west of Sharon Yard was mostly populated by farm families. The one exception was the Crosley Airport property, which, in addition to the farmland, consisted of a home, airplane hangar, and private runway. It was owned by Cincinnati Reds' owner Powell Crosley, Jr.

Ann and Betsy Baxter had some fun with this old Navy landing craft in the summer of 1952. During the 1950s, the Baxter family lived in the white farm house on the Crosley Property and raised corn in the fields. The old Crosley airplane hangar is visible in the background.

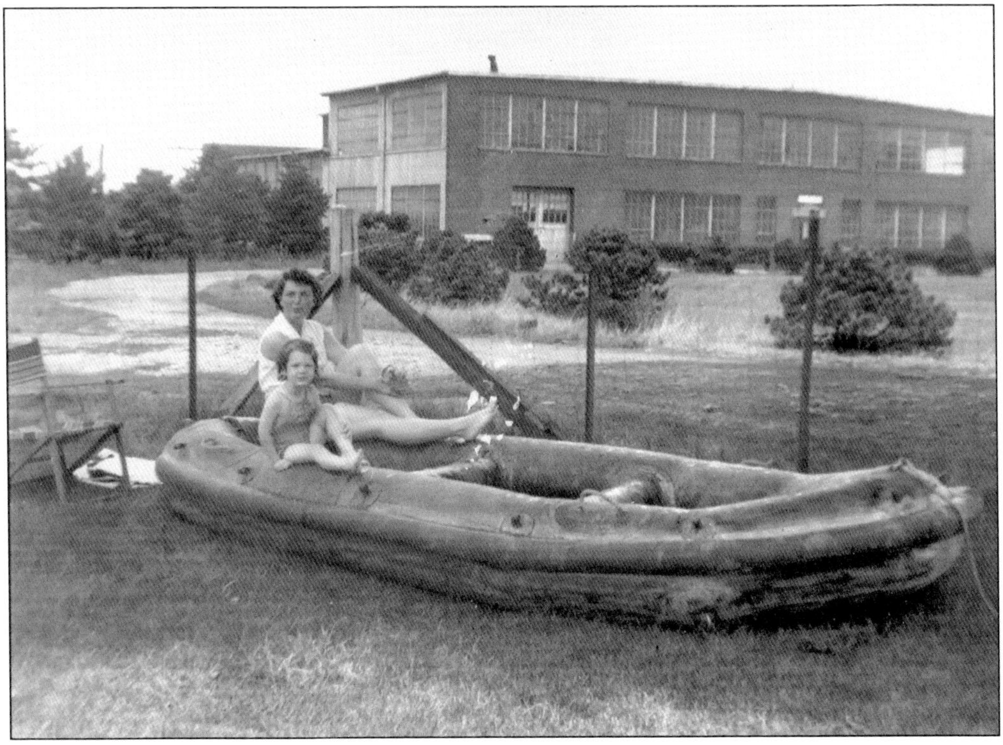

Powell Crosley, Jr.'s Le'sgo III airplane sits in the Crosley Airport hangar, c. 1954. In May of 1929, Mr. Crosley originally purchased the property in portions from the following individuals: Mary Rieck Bramble (who inherited about 50 acres from her mother, Celestine Bramble, in 1916); John R. Gano, his wife Grace A., of Danville, Illinois, and his brother Charles H. Gano, of Pittsburgh, Pennsylvania, (who inherited about 143 acres from their mother Emma Gano in 1927—Emma was willed the land from her father, John Rieck, in 1892).

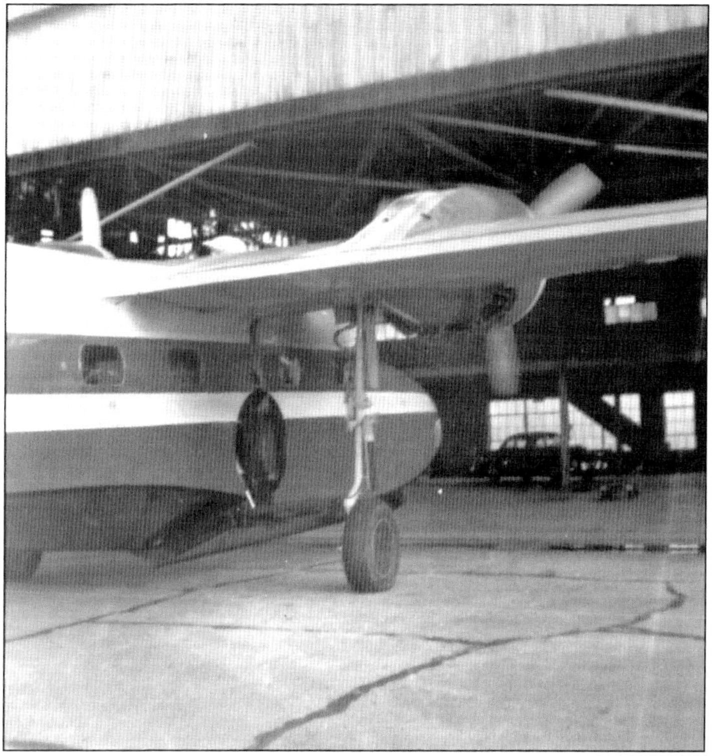

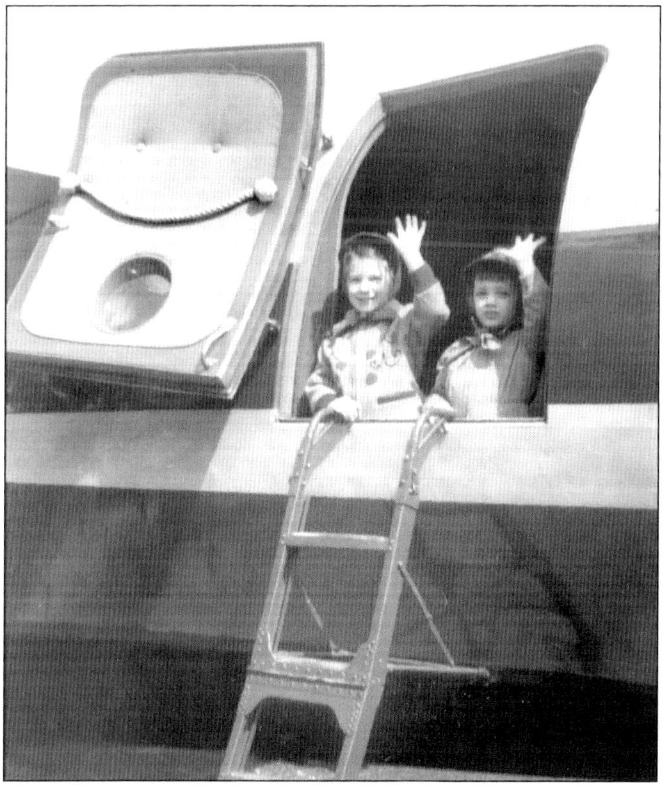

Betsy and Judy Baxter wave from the doorway of Powell Crosley, Jr.'s Le'sgo III airplane in May, 1954. Powell Crosley generally didn't pilot his own planes on the many business trips he took, although he was qualified. His pilot was usually Captain Eddie Nermaier, a local Cincinnati flier.

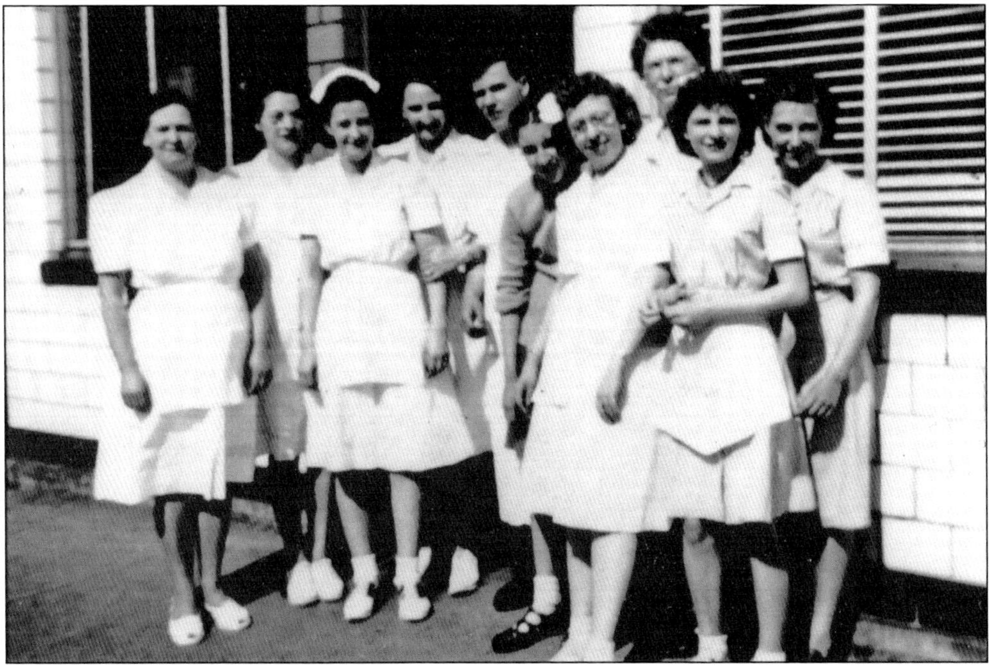

Cork's Sharon Grill was a popular Sharonville icon for a long time, particularly the 1940s. Mrs. Rose did most of the cooking—delicious pies, chops, and steaks. Pictured are some of the ladies who helped make the grill a pleasant experience, from left to right, Ann Redman, Frankie Locke, Louise ?, Salinda Cork, Unidentified, Charlotte Rose (Mrs. Rose's daughter), Golda Ball, Mrs. Alice Rose, Reva Kidd, and Dolly Stout.

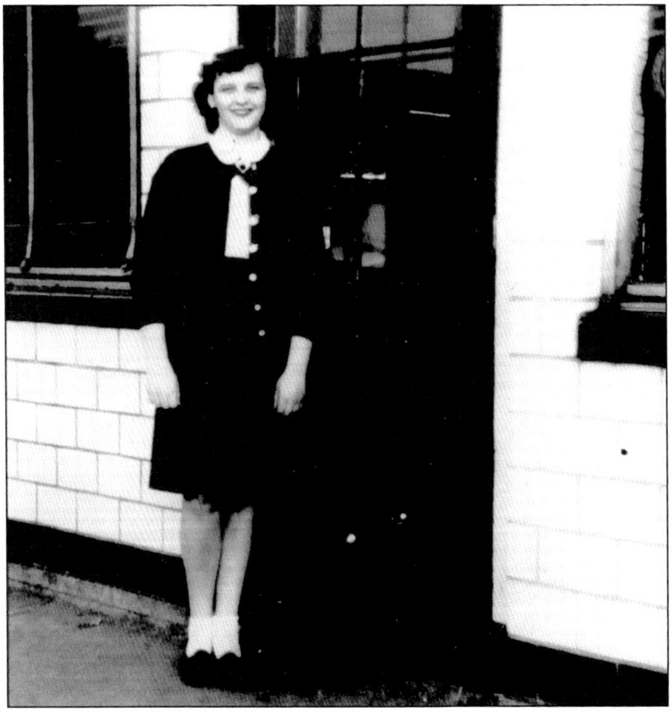

Joyce Gruber Feltz worked at the Sharon Grill for most of her high school years, probably from 1946 to 1948. While working there, she "met this nice young man from Wisconsin who was working on smoke stacks and had a job in Gano. He lived at Mooney's Motel and ate some of his meals at Sharon Grill. We met on September 13, 1947 and were married at St. Michael's Church on September 25, 1948." Joyce is pictured in front of the Grill.

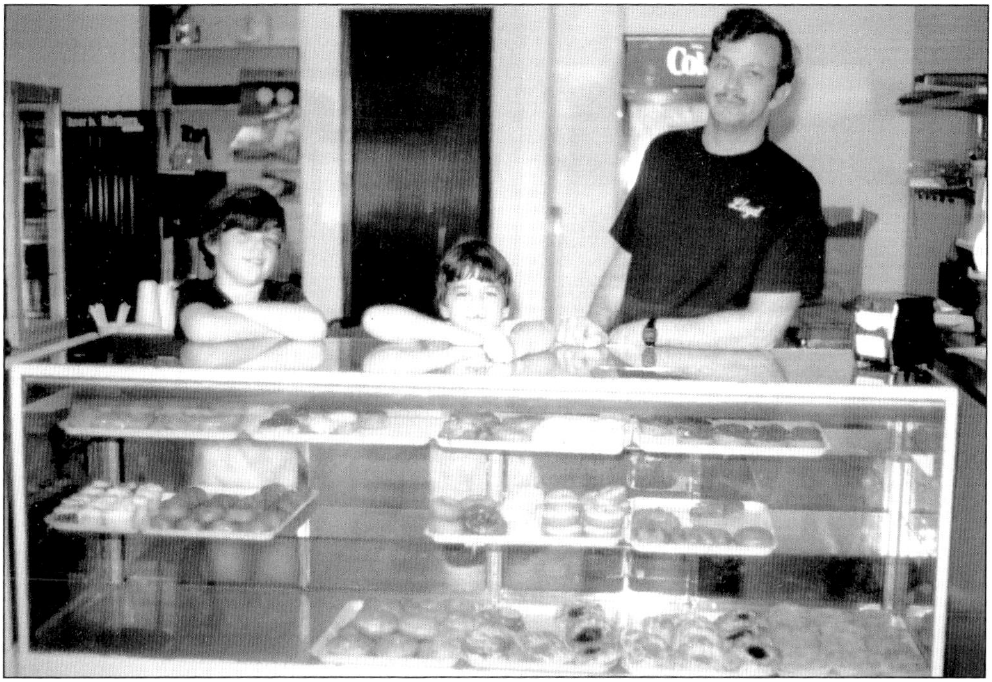

In September, 1984, Karen and Lloyd Shaw opened Pastries and More, featuring doughnuts and pastries along with luncheon sandwiches and soups. A year later, the business was purchased by employee Donna Fallon and her husband Bob, who continued at that location for several more years. Pastries and More was located at the corner of Creek Road and Main Street. Pictured, from left to right, are Tony, Ryan, and Lloyd Shaw.

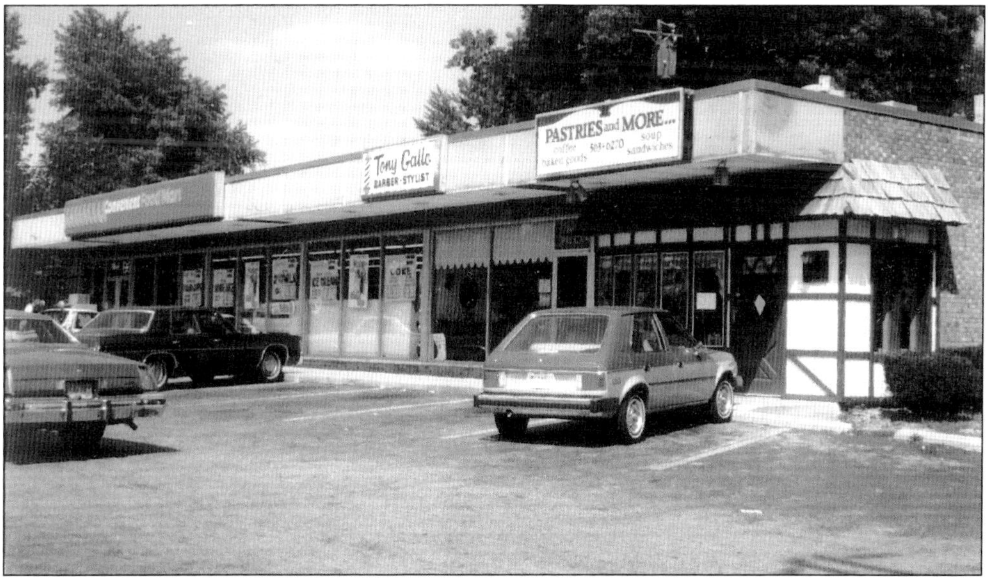

Convenient Food Mart and Tony Gallo's Barber Shop were mainstays of the shopping center located at the corner of Creek Road and Main Street for many years. The third storefront in the complex saw a number of small businesses. Arthur Treacher's Fish & Chips was there in the mid-1970s, Pastries and More in 1984, and in 2002, it is home to Angilo's Pizza.

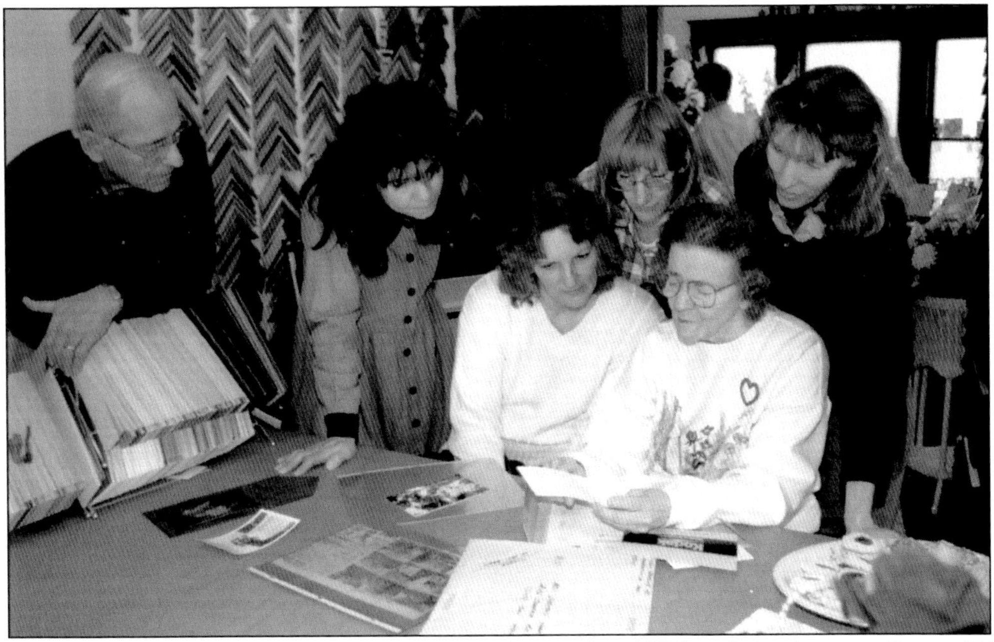

As Keepsakes Framing and Floral was setting up shop in the old Edward Nuss home on Route 42/ Lebanon Road, Ray Hils and daughter Barbara were treated to a trip back in time by Dorothy Nuss Hargy, daughter of Edward Nuss, who grew up in the house. Pictured, left to right, on February 14, 1998, are (seated) Dorothy's niece Tara Sue Jeffery and Dorothy Nuss Hargy; (standing) Ray Hils, Barbara Hils, Dorothy's nieces Todd Anna Harding, and Trudi Fricke.

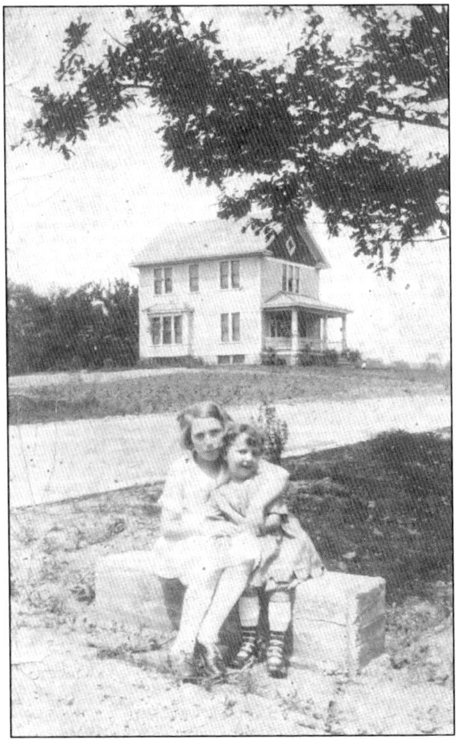

This picture of the Edward Nuss home was taken on a nice June day in the early 1920s, soon after the family moved in. Edward and Vivienne lived there the rest of their lives, he for 50 years and she for 53 years. The photo was taken across the street and south of the home. The people in the picture are unidentified.

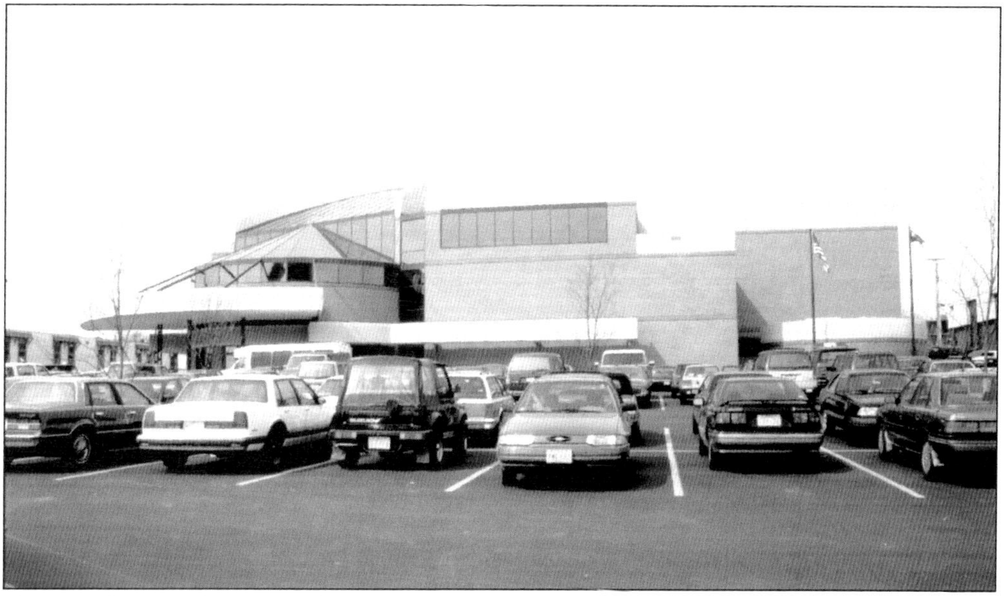

Sharonville amazed everyone by opening its own convention center on March 26, 1994. Built with the intention of bringing events to Sharonville that would also benefit local hotels and restaurants, it has exceeded original expectations. The convention center, with its packed opening day parking lot, became the newest jewel in the Chester Road business district.

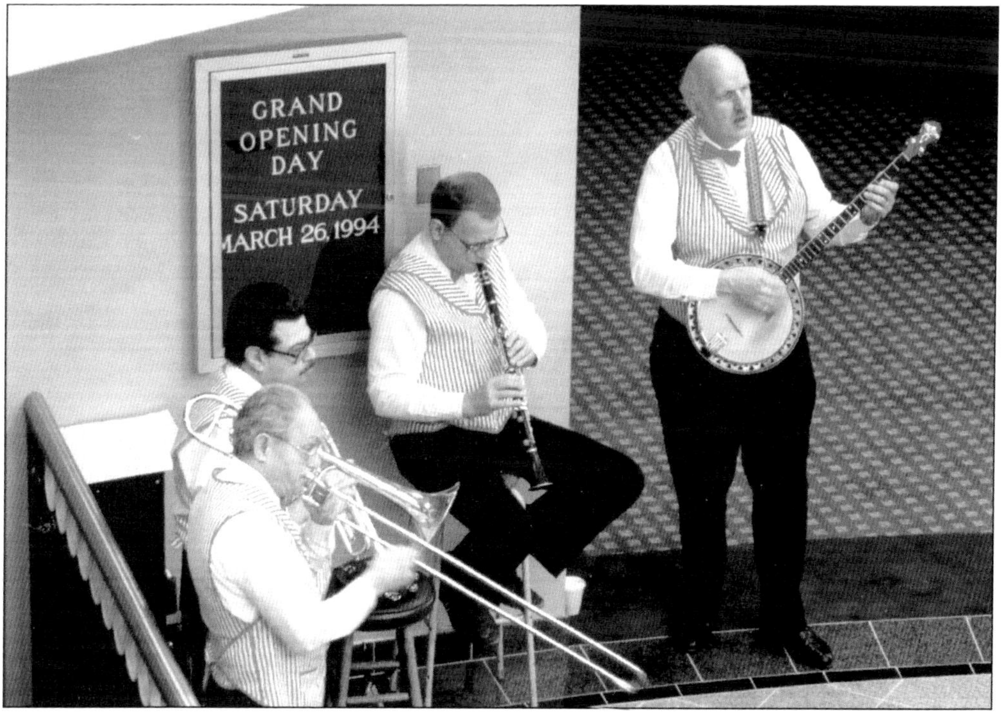

Visitors entering the main lobby at the new convention center were entertained by the Basin Street Dixieland Jazz Band.

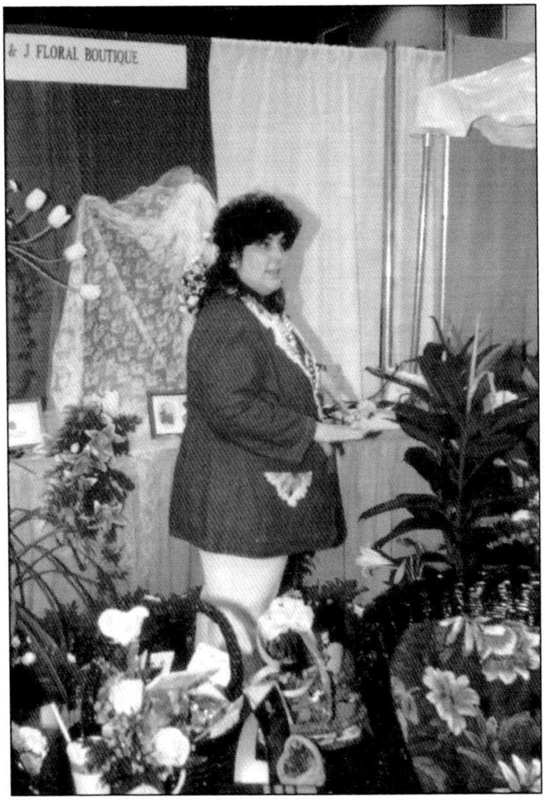

Many local businesses had booths set up in the convention center ballroom for the grand opening. Pictured is Alma from A & J Floral Boutique, a long time Sharonville business located at the corner of Main Street and Cornell Road.

Few good photos of the old Sharon Theatre exist. This one was shot in 1954. Dan O'Sullivan remembered the Theatre being built after a fire in the early 1920s destroyed the hall next door to Wheeler's Hotel and the adjacent store room: "Naturally, kids will be kids, and they all sat down in front. Mrs. Wheeler would go up and down the aisles with a flashlight seeking troublemakers. She earned the name 'Flashlight Sadie.' " The newly created Sharonville Fine Arts organization is planning to renovate the still-operating Act I and the adjacent building.

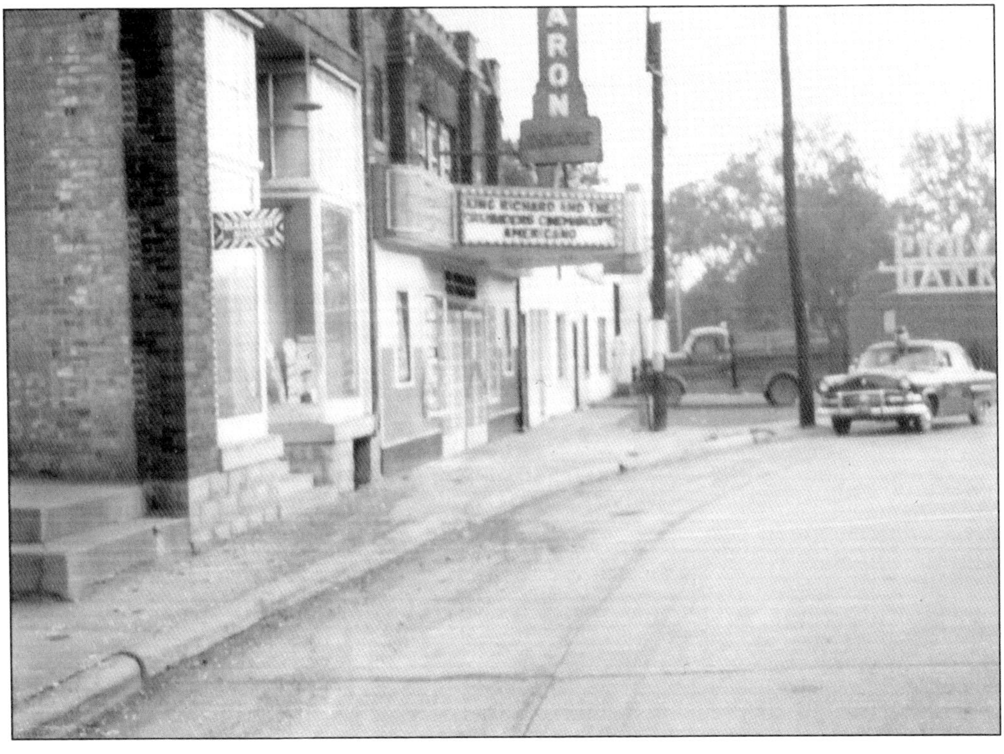

Two

LOCAL CHURCH PEOPLE

Since Sharonville was founded, it has been home to many different denominations of church-going people. It still boasts congregations of Baptists, Methodists, Presbyterians, and Roman Catholics. Only two of those groups submitted photos for publication but that does not diminish the importance of the others in the community. Two of the oldest buildings in Sharonville were originally built by the Presbyterian Church and the Methodist Church. The first is still in use by St. Gertrude the Great at the corner of Walnut Street and Reading Road. The second, at the corner of Main Street and Creek Road, has found new life as headquarters for the Salle du Lion Fencing Center.

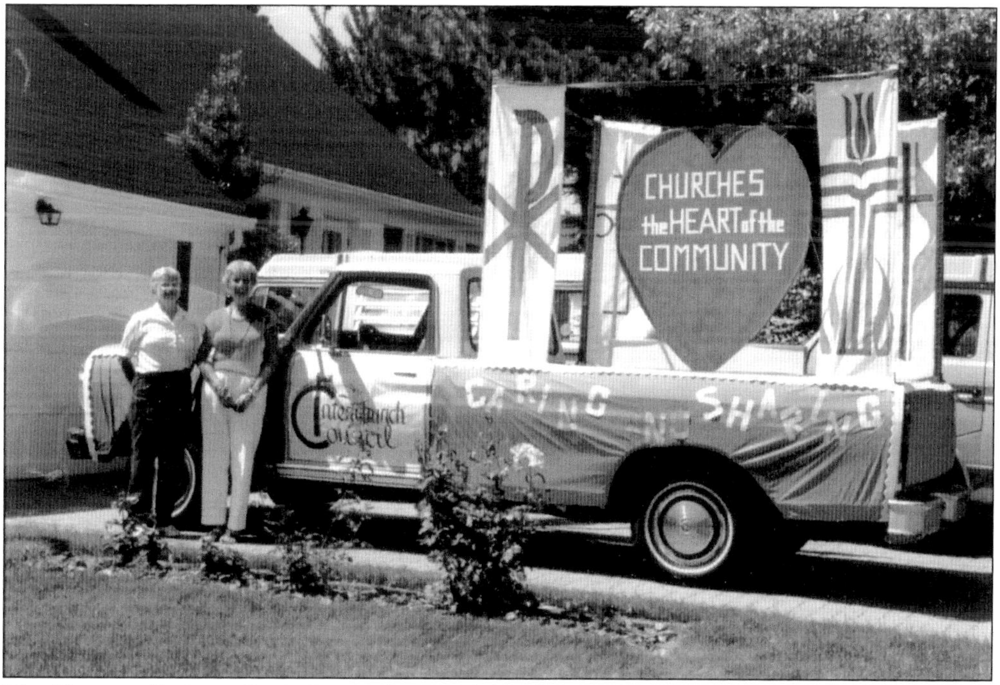

The Sharonville Inter-Faith Council entered this float in the 1987 Independence Day Parade. Their theme was "Churches: The Heart of the Community." Pictured are Jean Scott (left) and Rita Robertson.

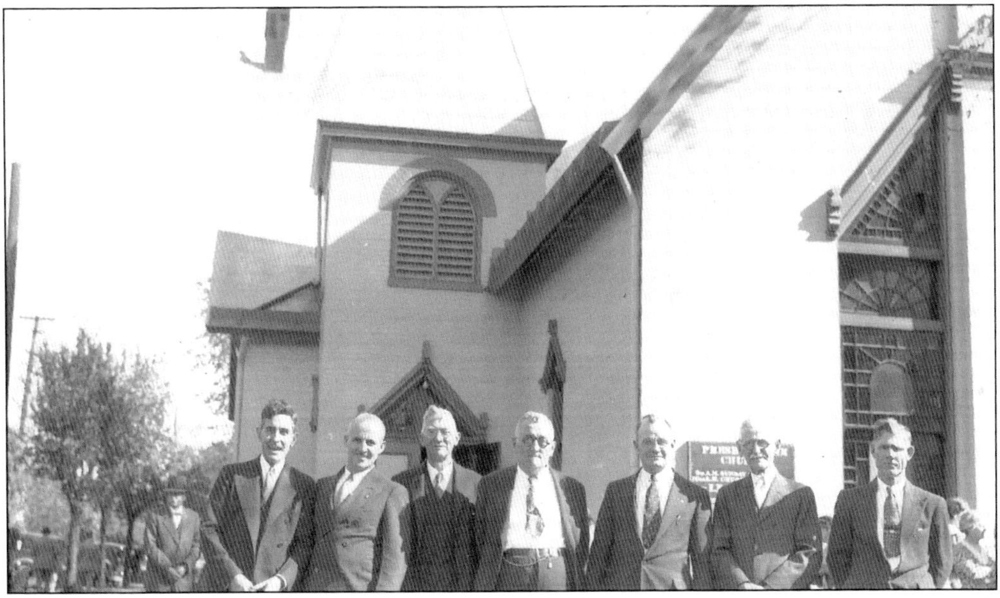

The S.K. Holtsinger Presbyterian Church once occupied one of the oldest buildings still standing in Sharonville, at the corner of Reading Road and Walnut Street. Pictured, from left to right, are Reverend Ira Stock, John Gallagher, Jr., ? Lindner, Logan Riker, Charles Sanger, John Gallagher, Sr., and Manaen Bartholomew, Jr. Based on the row of old cars parked under the trees on Walnut Street (they appear to be Model A Fords), the photo may have been taken in the mid-to-late 1920s.

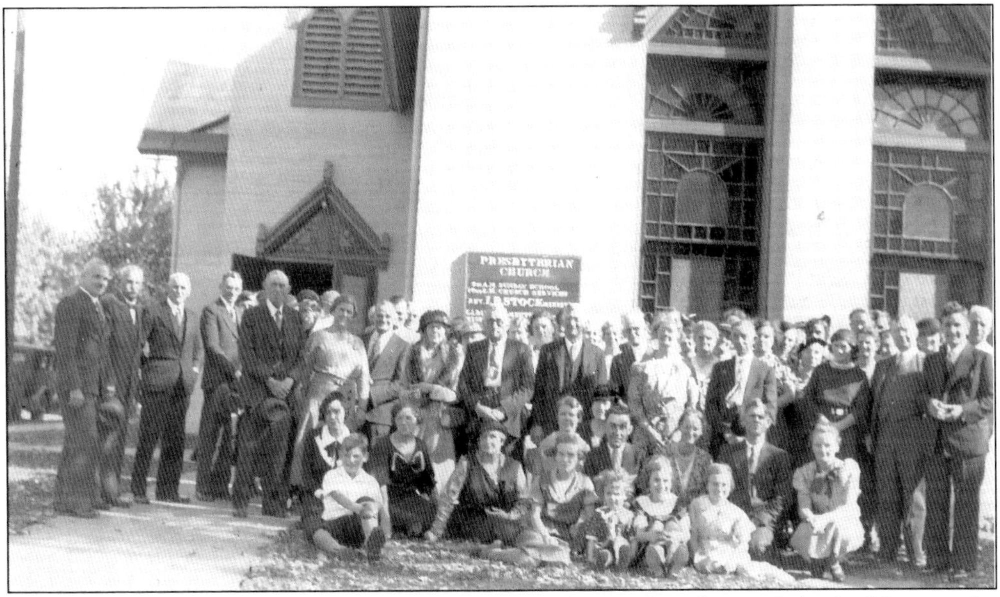

Members of the S.K. Holtsinger Presbyterian Church posed in front of the building at the corner of Reading Road and Walnut Street, c. mid-to-late 1920s. The ground for the church was originally purchased for $25.

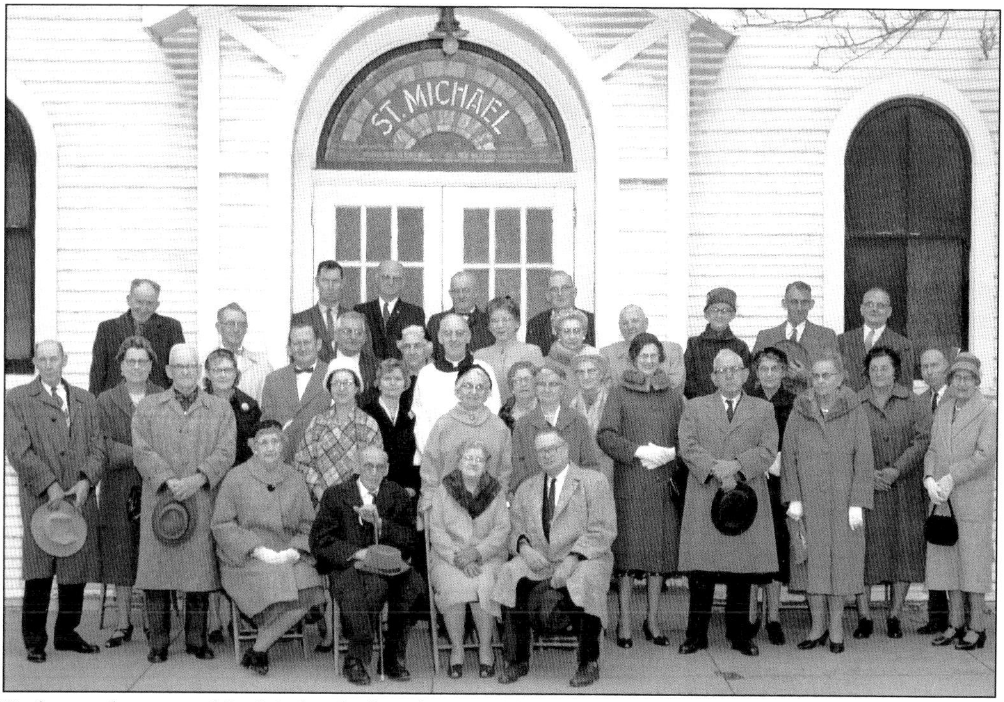

Early parishioners of St. Michael Church assembled in front of the little wooden church during the groundbreaking ceremony for a new church in 1963. Pictured, from left to right, are (first row sitting) Gertrude Crotty, Vincent Spellmire, Margaret Powers, and Bill Powers; (second row) Francis Hansman, Lucille Hansman, Tom Crotty, Helen Schmitt, Loretto Horner, Jeanette Finley, Matilda Roth, Mrs. Levesay, Mrs. Burwinkle, Mayme Honerlaw, Gertrude Schatzle, Joe Roth, Anna Knueven, Mrs. Tom Byron, Louise Huening, George J. Hagee, and Loretto E. Hagee; (third row) Bill (?) Horner, Ed Hansman, George Schmitt, Alfred Roth, Mrs. Thomas Donohoue, Mrs. Alice Rose, Gertrude Derrenkamp, Edward Derrenkamp, Mrs. Hawickhorst, Albert Schatzle, and William Huening; (fourth row) Herbert Hansman, Robert Hirschauer, Frank Schatzle, and William Nelson.

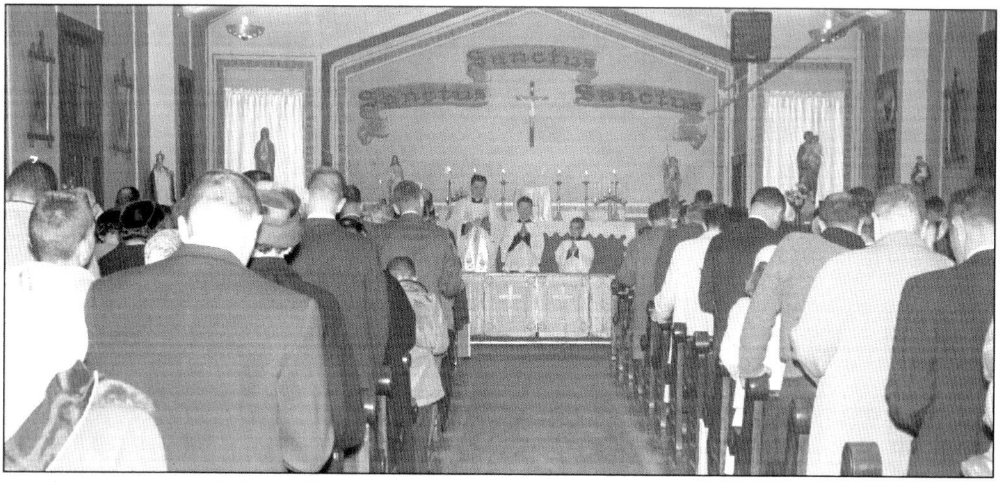

Parishioners at St. Michael Church prayed at a mass inside the old church in 1960. The pastor at the time was Father James Scanlon.

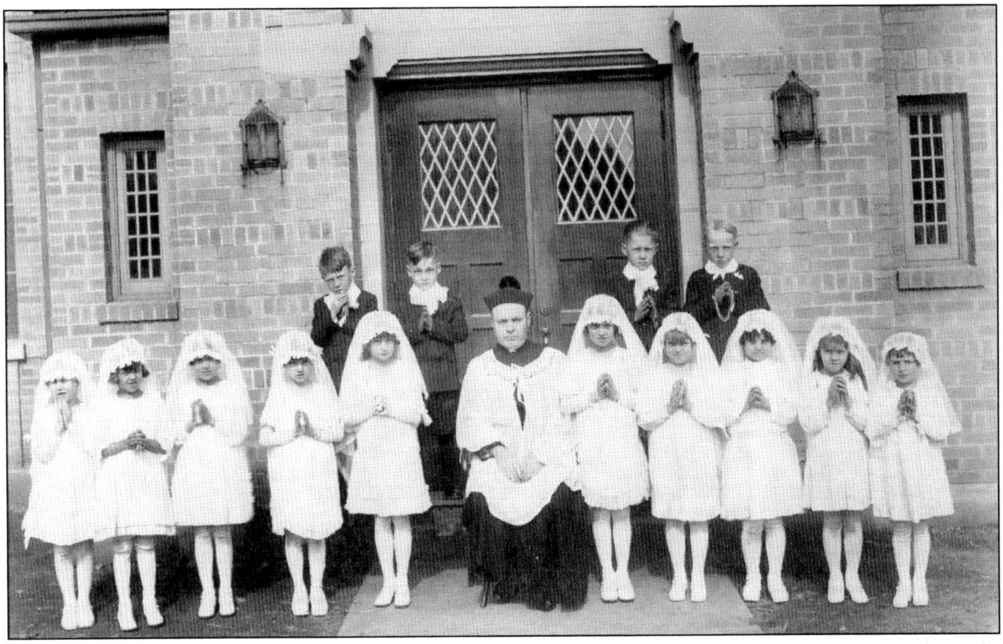

This group of students at St. Michael School made their First Holy Communion on May 15, 1927. Pictured, from left to right, are (front row) Frances Even, Dorothy Geohagan, Mary Casey, Kittie Donohoue, Mary Spellmire, Reverend James J. Conroy, Unidentified, Unidentified, Amelia Donisi, Phyllis Hallarn, and Unidentified; (back row) Hermie Winters, Eugene Honerlaw, Robert Knueven, and Robert Schatzle.

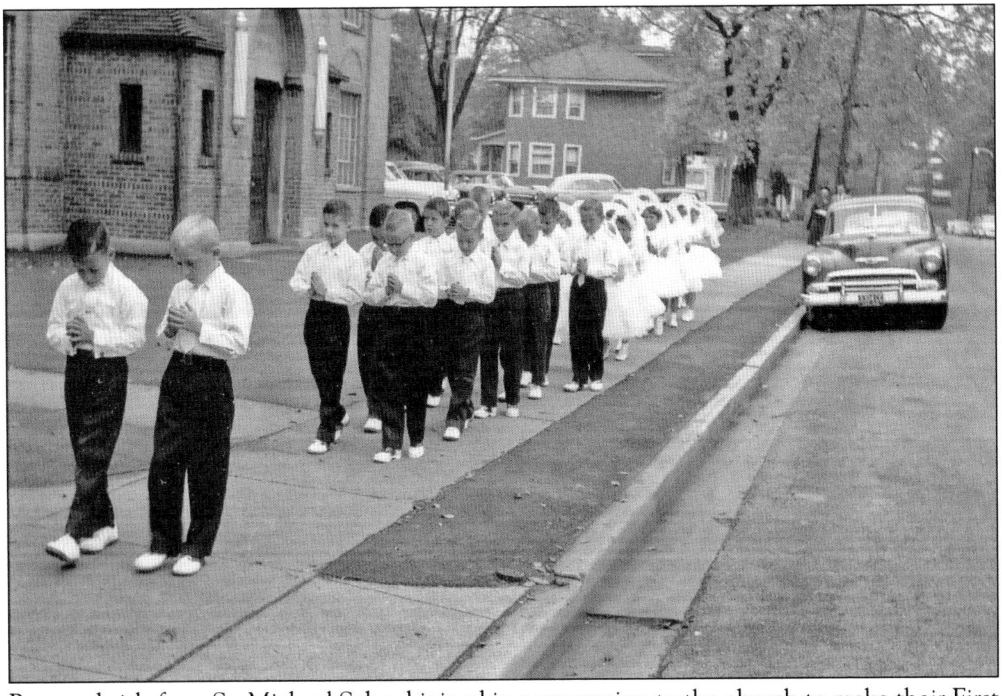

Boys and girls from St. Michael School joined in a procession to the church to make their First Holy Communion in November, 1958.

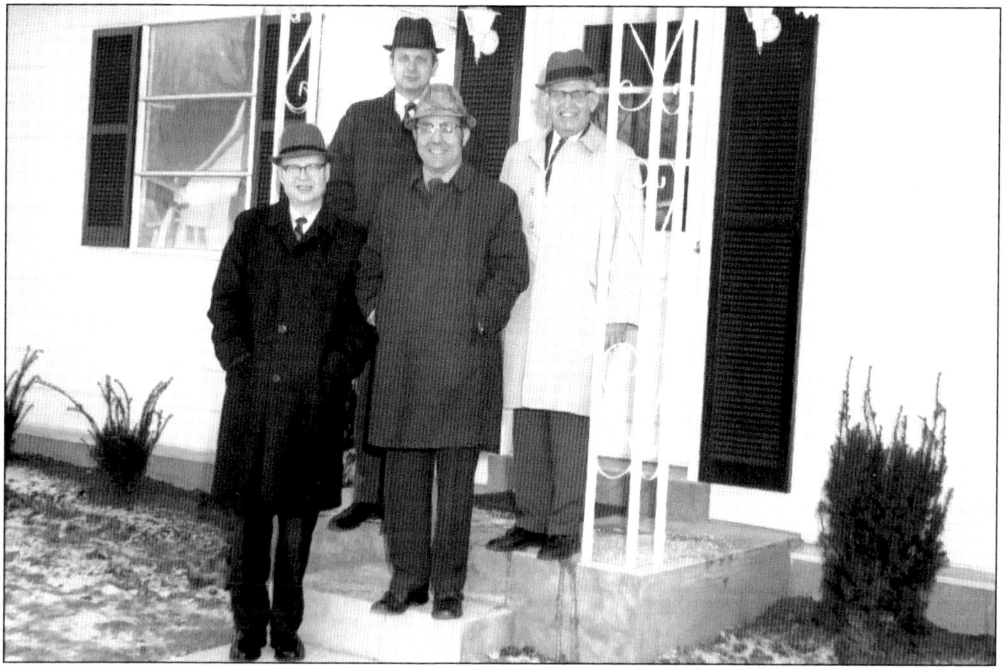

The officers of the St. Michael Parish Credit Union gathered for a photo in 1970. Pictured, from left to right, are (front row) George Heitker (Credit Committee Chairman) and John MacArthur (Treasurer); (back row) Ray Asbrock (Secretary) and Frank Weis (President).

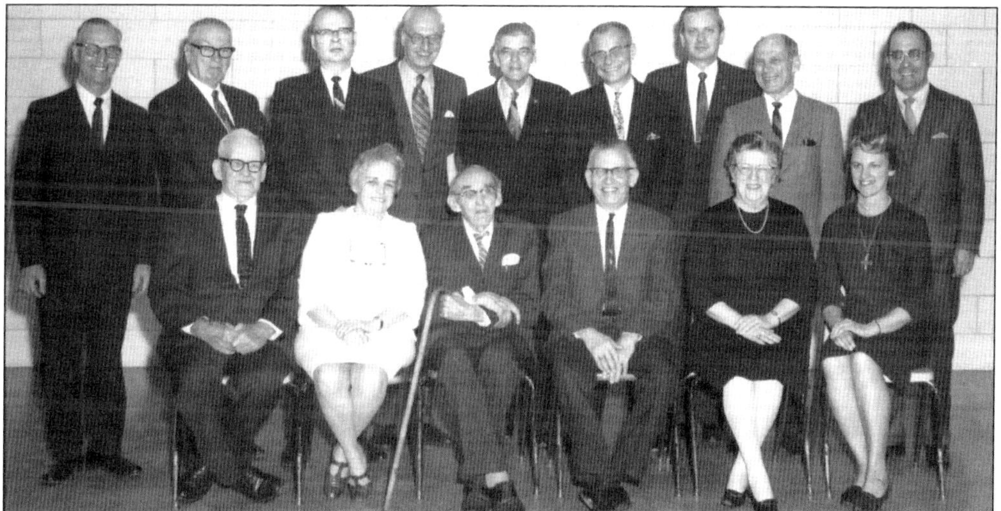

St. Michael Parish Credit Union held their 30th Anniversary Annual Meeting in 1971. Pictured, from left to right, are (front row) Tom Crotty, Louise Herring (Founder of St. Michael Parish Credit Union), Vincent Spellmire, Frank Weis (President St. Michael Parish Credit Union), Mary Burns (Cincinnati Division Ohio Credit Union League), Sister Rosemarie (St. Michael Parish School Representative); (back row) Earl Roth, Bill Powers, George Heitker, Grant Wilson (Superintendent Ohio Credit Unions), Bob Spellmire, Bob Kloss (Executive Secretary Ohio Credit Union League), Ray Asbrock (Secretary St. Michael Parish Credit Union), Bob Beck (Field Representative), and John MacArthur (Treasurer St. Michael Parish Credit Union).

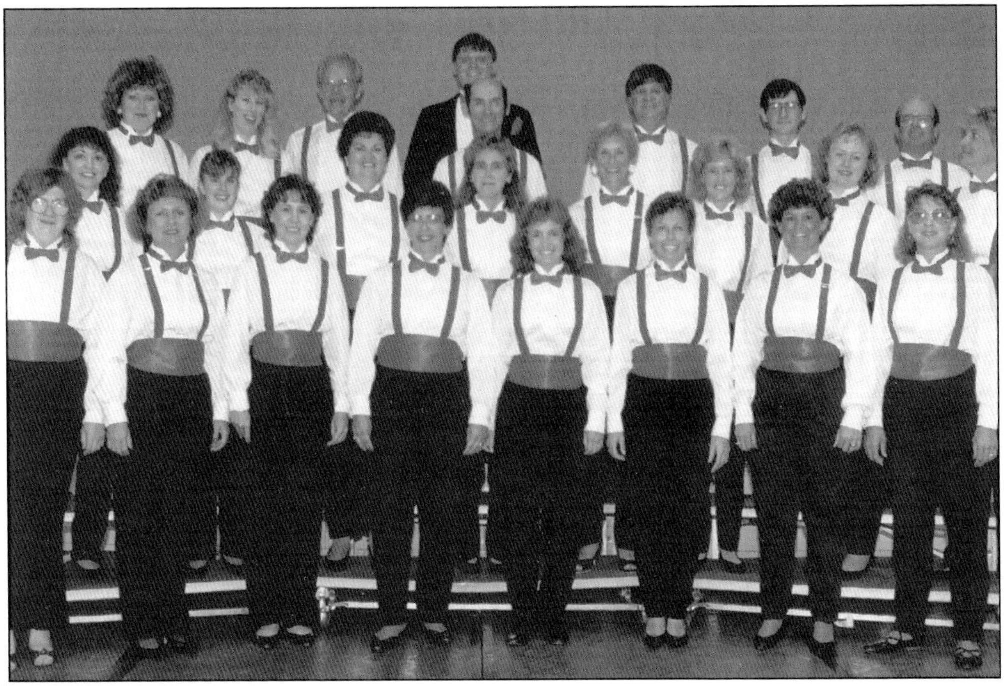

The St. Michael Singers were a vital part of the music department at St. Michael Church in the 1980s and 1990s. Under the direction of Michael Sayers, and later by Bruce Kotowitch, they performed throughout the city. Over the years, many different persons were involved. This picture was taken in 1989, shortly after the formation of the group. Pictured, from left to right, are (front row) Gayle Hall, Sue Finn, Maryann Schroeck, Marie Klaban, Karen Merkl, Judy Maitre, Linda Planes, and Donna Barkalow; (middle row) Dottie Kron, Julie Bockhold, Jan Settelmayer, Teresa Asbrock, Rita Robertson, Jane Fiely-Holtgrefe, Sharon ?,and Diane Pickering; (back row) Nora Posge, Beth Engel, Robert Rack, Bob Goeppinger, John Taylor, Erik Goeppinger, and Jerry Bockhold. Michael Sayers, the Conductor, is standing in the back rear. Not pictured was Donna Monahan.

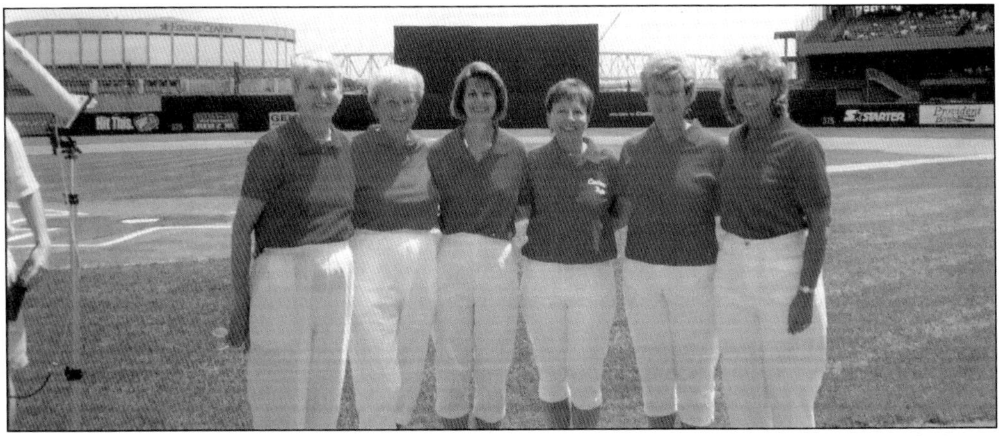

The "Perfect Blend" singing group from St. Michael parish sang the National Anthem before a Cincinnati Reds baseball game at Cinergy Field (formerly known as Riverfront Stadium) during the 2001 season. Pictured, from left to right, are Kathy Barnhorn, Rita Robertson, Kristi Gerbus, Judy Maitre, Donna Monahan, and Jeannine Hagee-Eaton.

Three

STUDENTS AND TEACHERS

During its history as a town, Sharonville can claim no less than nine schools within the city limits. The original Runyan school was built in 1879 on the farm of Henry Runyan, then north of Sharonville. The school still stands on Hauck Road (formerly Symmestown Road). All of the schools are represented here except for original Runyan, Stewart Primary, and Robert E. Lucas Middle School. There is one class photo from old Runyan in the Society of Historic Sharonville museum collection but none of the students have been identified. Old Sharon Road Elementary and the second Runyan Elementary were both torn down in the 1970s.

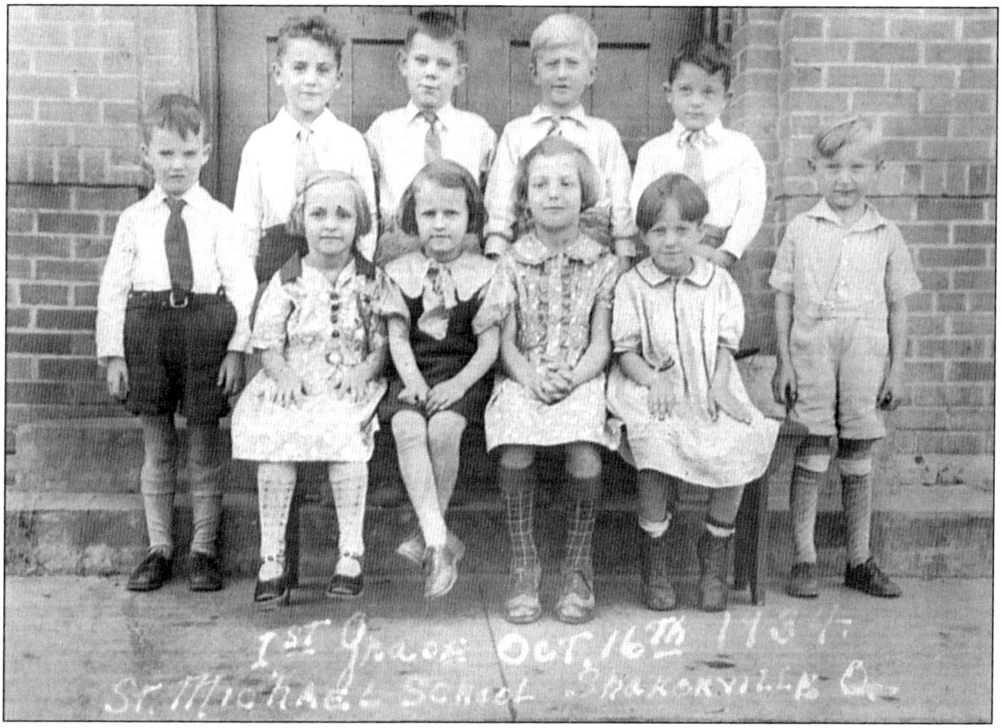

Students in the first grade at St. Michael School gathered for this photo October 16, 1934. Pictured, from left to right, are (sitting) Dorothy "Dottie" Roth, Jacqueline "Jackie" Brogan, Betty Siebenberg, and Mary Browne; (standing) Joe Wright, Robert "Bobby" Hagee, Jim Honerlaw, Unidentified, Harold Vetter, and James "Jimmy" Schatzle.

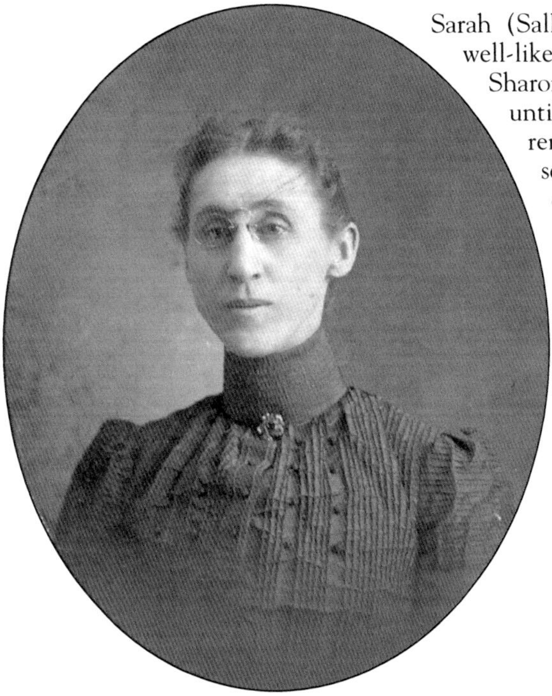

Sarah (Sallie) Williamson was a well-known and well-liked former teacher and principal at old Sharon Road Elementary School from 1896 until her retirement in 1925. Tom Crotty remembers Miss Williamson teaching seventh and eighth grades. Outside the classroom she was fondly referred to as "Sibby," but never in her presence. She lived with her parents in a home that was on Reading Road, near the site of the present Schmidt-Dhonau funeral home.

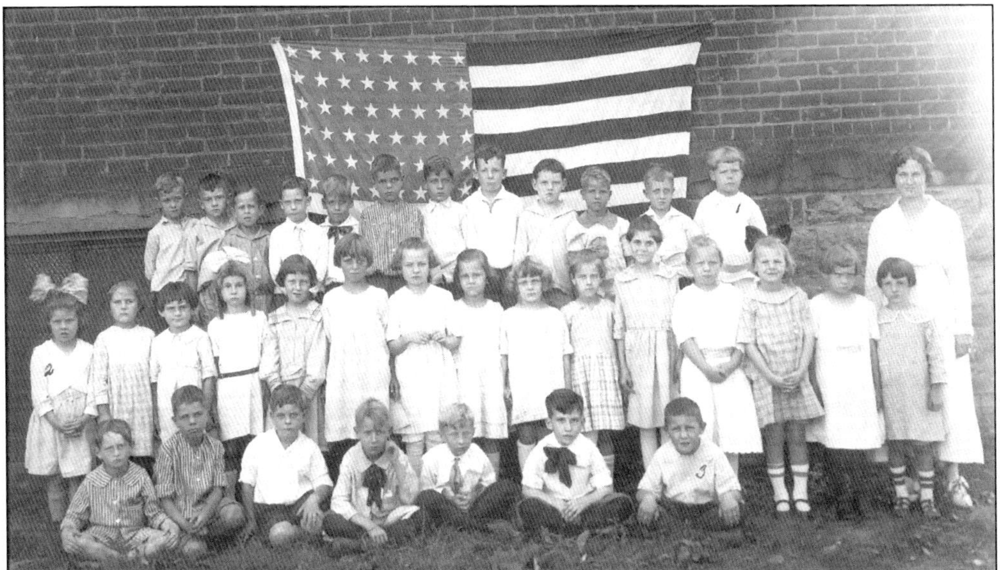

First graders at the old Sharon Road elementary school posed for the 1921–1922 school photo. Pictured, from left to right, are (front row) Herman Rittger, Frank Weider, Albert Eichenhorst, Edward Riouff, Kenneth Hanna, Robert Drake, and Raymond Bartholomew; (middle row) Mary Benson, Edith Barr, Dorothy Haney, Anna M. Levesay, Ruby Flannery, Harriet Gruber, Marie Vail, Ruth Yarbrough, Marjorie Coleman, Mildred Gorsuch, Mary Patrick, Ruth Potthoff, Alice Gallaher, Katherine Helrigle, and Pollyanna Haines; (back row) Frederick Rahe, Arthur Dillon, James Keith, Woodrow Butler, John Vail, William Rose, Herbert Drake, Curtis Whitaker, John Even, James Benson, Frank Gorman, and Stanley Morgan. The teacher is Miss Erhardt.

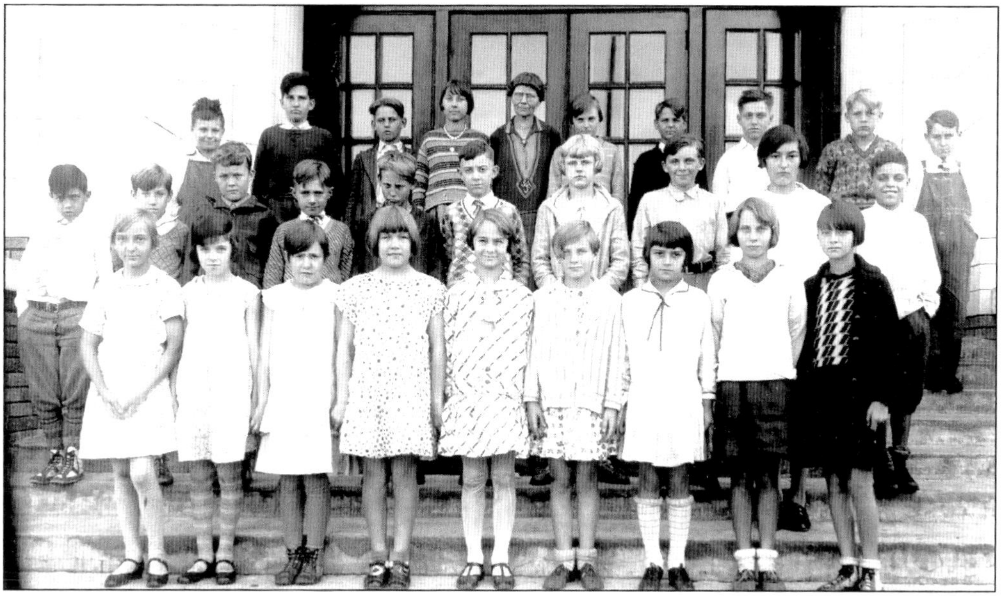

One of the highlights of the fifth and sixth grade at Sharonville School in 1929 was photo day. Pictured, from left to right, are (front row) Dorothy Ellis, Gail Williams, Helen Hill, Eileen Ward, Wilda Corrigan, Florence Dillon, Margaret Young, Gloria Dodds, and Betty Jones; (middle row) Dale ?, Orrin Long, John Mulcahy, William Deyhle, Oscar Bartholomew, Molor Duff, Doris Shape, Frank Yeager, Elise Potthoff, and Dale Smith (?); (back row) Jack Ryan, Frank Weider, Unidentified, Martha Wilker, Miss Cook (teacher), Gertrude Riouff, William Smith, Floyd Elix, William Rieck, and Charles Barr.

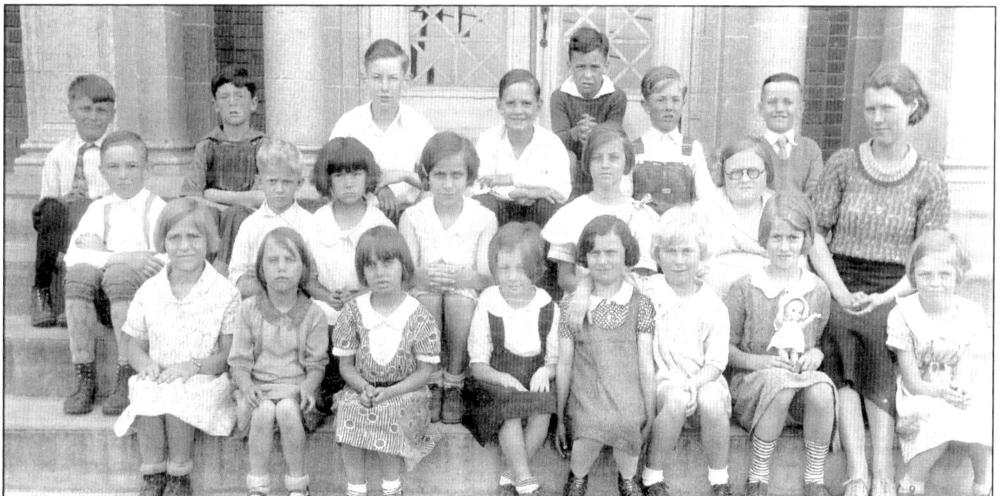

Merle Gorman (Cradler) and her young students paused from their lessons to have a class picture taken on the front steps of "new" Runyan School, c. 1931. Pictured, from left to right, are (front row) Gertrude Nuss, Unidentified, Unidentified, Unidentified, ? Jones, Unidentified, Unidentified, Unidentified; (middle row) Glen Mohrfield, Unidentified, ? Jones, Gladys Goldrainer, Unidentified, Jean Gaker, Merle Gorman (teacher); (back row) Edward Nuss, Huey Jones, Unidentified, Hubert Ball, G Richard Hagee (top looking over shoulders), Jim Goldrainer, and Unidentified.

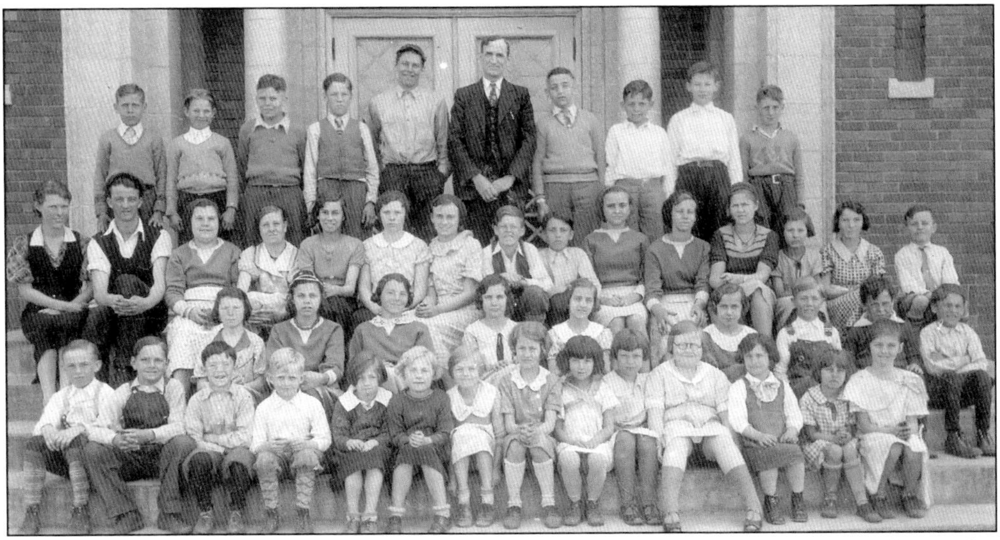

This photo was taken in about 1932 at the new Runyan School. Pictured, from left to right, are (first row) Glen Mohrfield, Hubert Ball, Huey Jones, Unidentified, Unidentified, Marshall Friend, Unidentified, Unidentified, Irene Gaker, Unidentified, Jean Gaker, Unidentified, Unidentified, and Unidentified; (second row) Ollie Jones, Edna McGee, Zeuloh Jones, Marie Mink, Dorothy Nuss, Gladys Goldrainer, Unidentified, Richard Hagee, and Omar Lindner; (third row) Merle Gorman (teacher), Jack Emmons (janitor), Dorothy Rieck, Helen Puckett, Irma Bates, Marie Stewart, Ernie Smith, Delmar Lindner, Margaret Young, Alma McGee, Jeanette Fahrenbrook, Beulah Jones, and Jim Goldrainer; (fourth row) Edward Nuss, Lawrence Hamilton, Harry Bates, Sam Linder, Earl McGee, Mr. Cahall (teacher), Robert Goldringer, Alfred Mohrfield, Unidentified, and Unidentified.

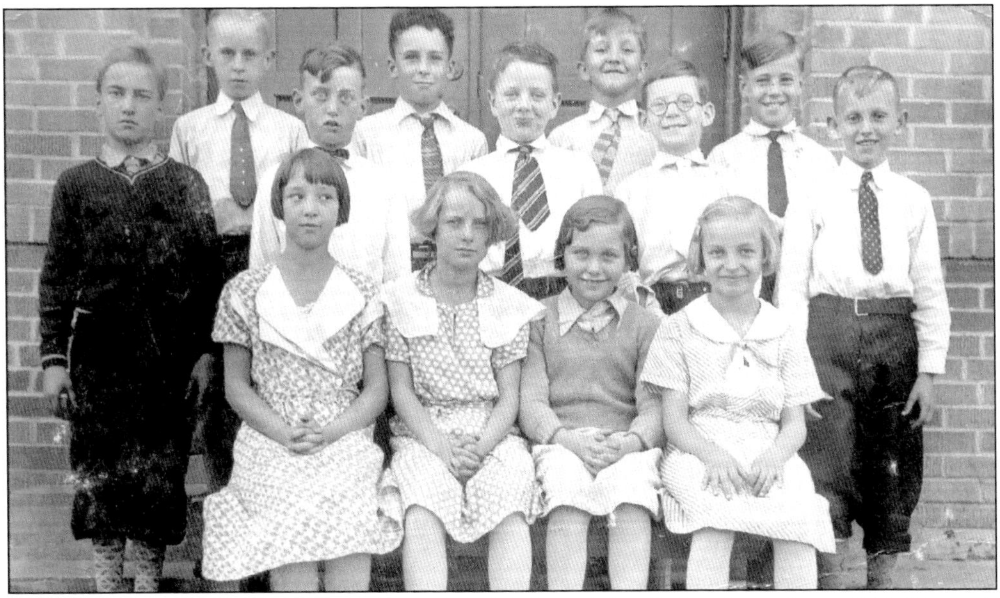

These smiling youngsters were members of St. Michael School's fourth grade in 1934. Pictured, from left to right, are (girls seated) Edna Deck (?), Rita Schmidt, Evelyn Hardesty, and Ellen Roth; (boys standing) Joe Browne (?), John Vogelsang, Elmer Wesseler, G. Richard Hagee, Bill Powers, Bill Huening, Paul Siebenbargen, Eugene Burwinkel, and Earl Bosken.

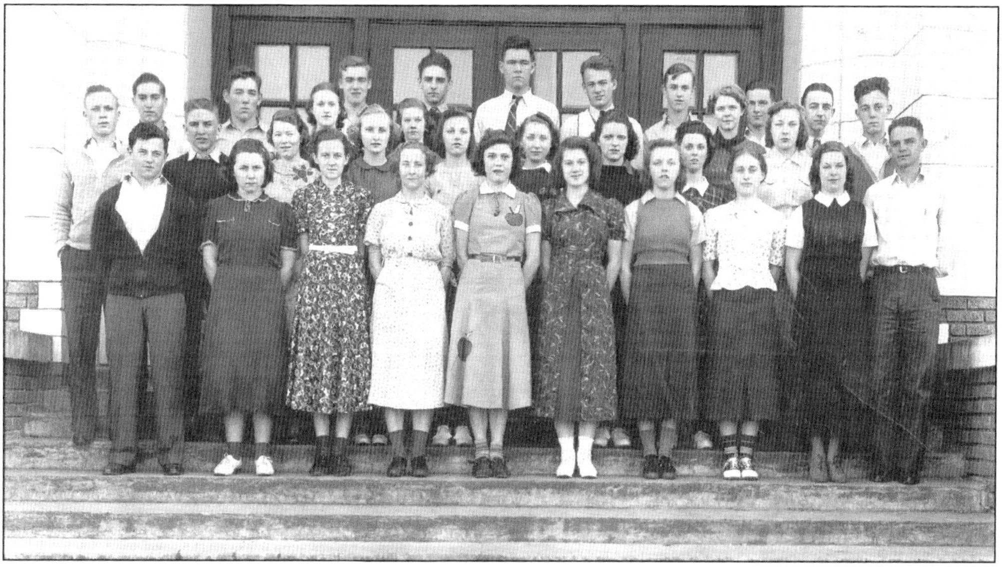

There was a new group of teenagers at Sharonville High School (also called Sharon High) in October of 1935. Many of these freshmen would go on to graduate in the class of 1939. Pictured, from left to right, are (first row) Lloyd DeSerisy, Virginia Price, Ruby Clark, Elva Mae Bartholomew, Norma Collins, June Kelley, Virginia Barkau, Mary Martha Deyhle, Ernestine Brown, and Walter Radford; (second row) Thomas Floyd "Bub" Mehaffie, Paul Kuhlman, Dorothy Sies, Mary Anne Hirschauer, Ruth Eickenhorst, Rosella Kolbinsky, Marjorie Donohoue, Evelyn Diesel, Jean Sears, and Dick Runyan; (third row) Harold "Tim" McClung, Bill Branigan, Melba Schewa, Jean Leary, Clayburne Revis, Frank Bixby, Lester Montanye, Mary Louise McWhorter, and Bob "Doc" Goldrainer; (back row) Elwood Rovekamp, Eugene Betscher, and Fred Davis.

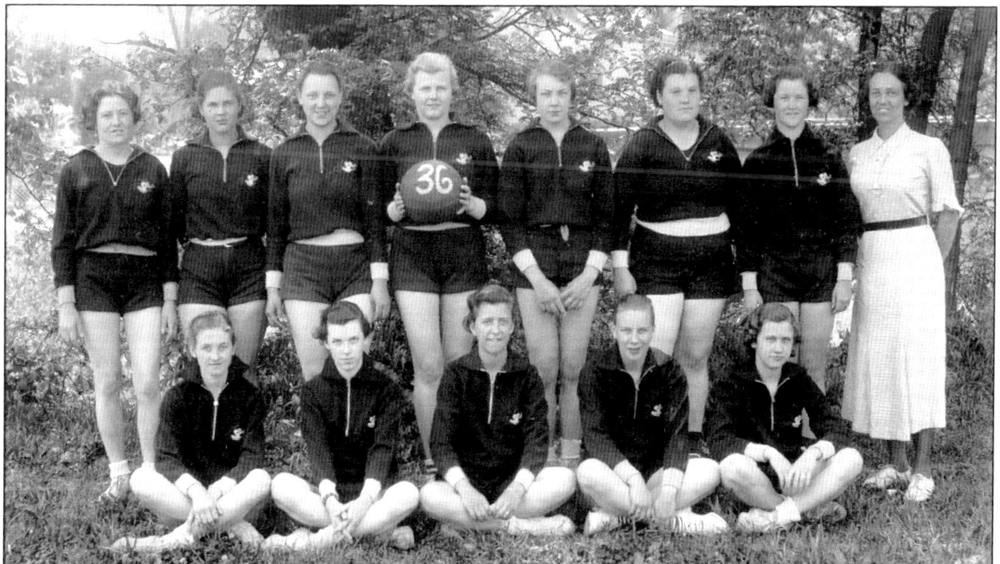

The girls at Sharonville High School were playing competitive basketball back in 1936. Pictured, from left to right, are (front row) Zella Morgan, Gail Williams, Margaret Byron, Florence Dillon, and Pauline Leary; (back row) Mary Frances Winters, Jean Fahrenbruck, Doris Shape, Jean Sears, Dorothy Rieck, Catharine Wright, and teacher Alyce Stephenson.

SECOND ANNUAL BASKET BALL GAME

ADDED ATTRACTIONS

Amos Jones and Ruby Taylor Wedding

ALUMNAE BASKET BALL GAME

QUARTET - SINGING,

PRESENTED BY

SHARONVILLE SCHOOLMEN'S CLUB

TUESDAY, FEBRUARY 11, 1936.

DOOR PRIZE, DONATION 25c & 15c

Fat Men, Skinny Men - Basket Ball Game.

Fat Men		Skinny Men	
Wesley Clark	180 lb	Leroy Smith	165 lb
C F Sanger	176	Carman Dozier	150
Ed Seilkop, Sr.	210	John Goldman	149
Maynard Gray	181	Jerry Six	90
Wm. Potthoff, Jr.	290	Ted Lautenslager	150
James Wright, Jr.	182	Bill Runyan	135
Charles Worley	175	Gay Clark	115
Charlie Ballback	181	A O Sears	160
Guy Gilbert	180	Claude Perkins	168
George Evans	177	Tom Wilcox	127
John Evans	190	Ed Eichenhorst	139
Bill Koviak	195	Roy Hawkins	169
C W Coleman	181	Kelsey McWhorter	166
E P Gorsuch	185	William Lewis	151
Bill Gorman	175	Homer Lantz	147

Quartet: Ed Hanna. Kenneth Morgan. Joe Roth. Jim Stadtlander.

WEDDING

AMOS JONES AND RUBY TAYLOR

Cast of Characters:

Amos	William Runyan
Andy	Leroy Smith
Ruby Taylor	Mr. Cross
Madam Queen	Ed Hanna
Aunt Lillian	Willard Mc Clung
Brother Crawford	H H Dunlap
King Fish	W E Clark
Battle Ax	D Muchmore
Lightning	Jim Benson
Prince Ali Bendo	Cliff Schneeman
Senorita Butterfly	Lloyd Barr
Mr. Van Porter	Curtis Whited
Mr. Weber	Kenneth Hanna
Preacher	Carl Gruber
Flower Girl	Delbert Little
Ring Bearer	A O Sears
Ruby's Father	C E Sears
Ruby's Mother	Roy Levesay
Mrs. Crawford	Joe Roth
Mrs. Lightning	Jim Stadtlander

Bridesmaids: Wooday Butler. Frank Gorman. John Goldman. Roscoe Mehaffie.

Pictured is a flyer from a February 11, 1936 Sharonville Schoolmen's Club Alumnae Basketball game and drama production.

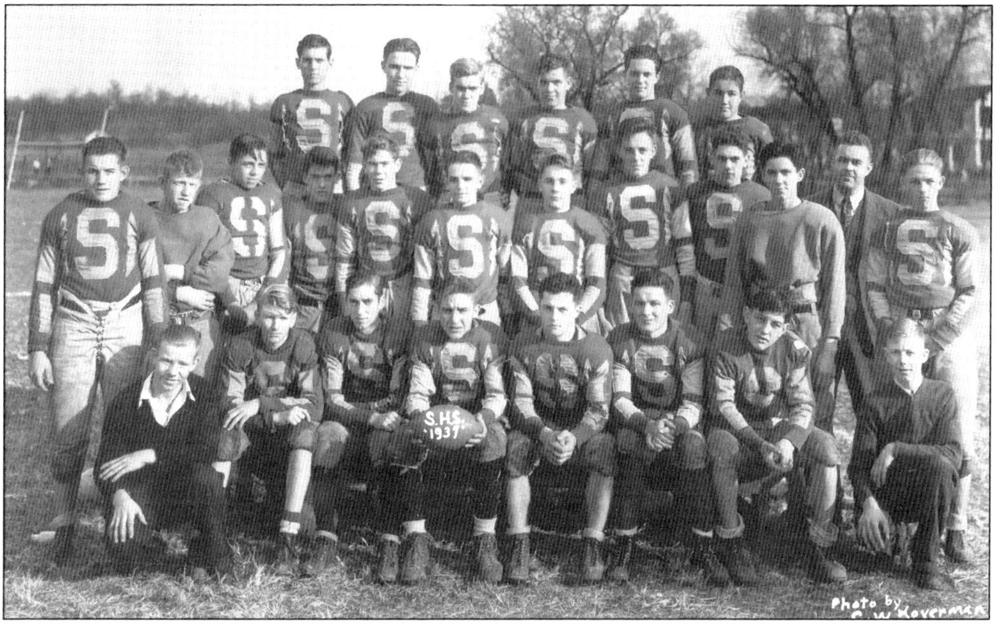

Football uniforms were a little bit different in 1937, when members of the Sharonville High School team posed for this photo. Pictured, from left to right, are team members (front row) Benny Brate, Unidentified, Harold McClung, Paul Kuhlman with the ball, Lloyd DeSerisy, Fred Davis, Bob Hassler, and Jim Even; (middle row) John Cavin, Unidentified, Unidentified, Gene Krick, Jack Wagner, Unidentified, Bud Kussman, Dick Runyan, Al Krick, Elwood McClung, Coach Dolf Forance, and Unidentified; (back row) Walter Radford, Bob Crockett, Elwood Rovekamp, Unidentified, and Bill Gandert.

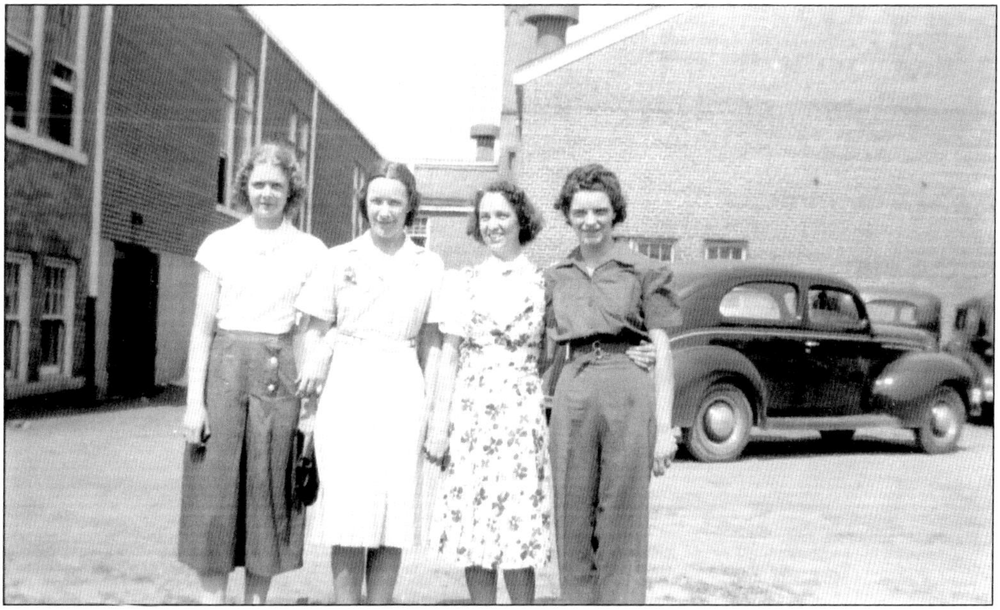

An afternoon in 1938 found these ladies posing for a picture outside Sharonville School. They are, from left to right, Mary Louise McWhorter (class of 1939), Miss Gunkel (teacher), Alyce Stephenson (teacher), and Margie Donohoue (class of 1939).

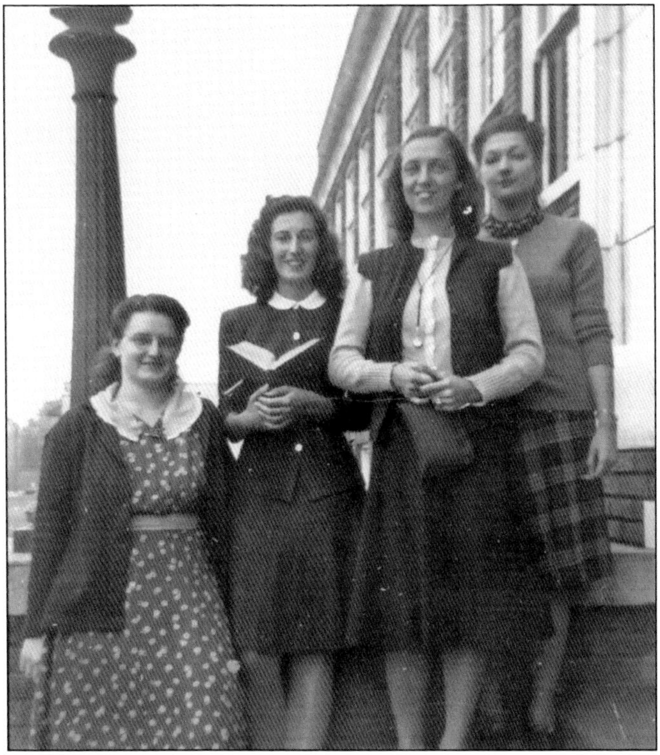

Four teachers from Sharonville High School gathered for this photo in the early 1940s. Pictured, from left to right, are Anna Graham, Virginia Shewalter, Alyce Stephenson, and Olivia Prosser. Back then, teachers were paid monthly, and not during the summer. They made about $2,000 per year. In later years, Virginia wrote a history of Union Township, Butler County. She was in the Woman's Army Corps (WACS) during World War II.

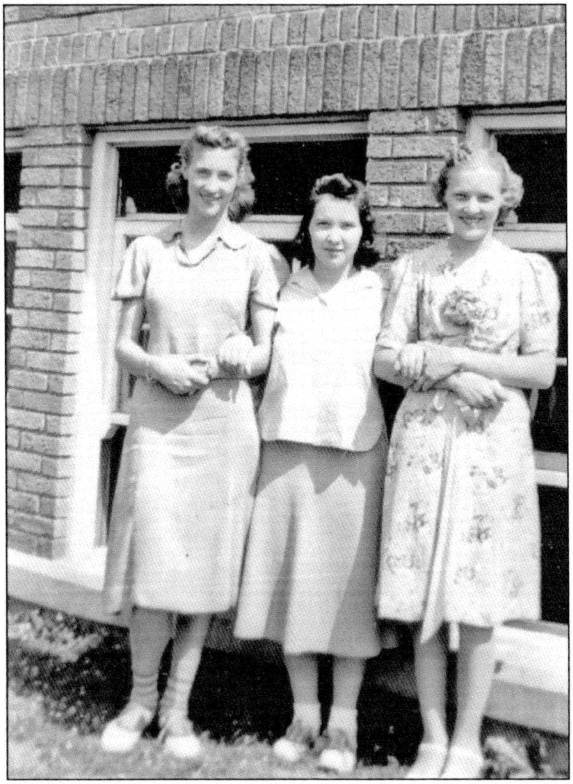

Three friends from the Sharonville High School class of 1940 stood in the sunshine next to the school for this memory maker. They are, from left to right, Mona Morgan, Vivian Revis, and Pearl Riouff.

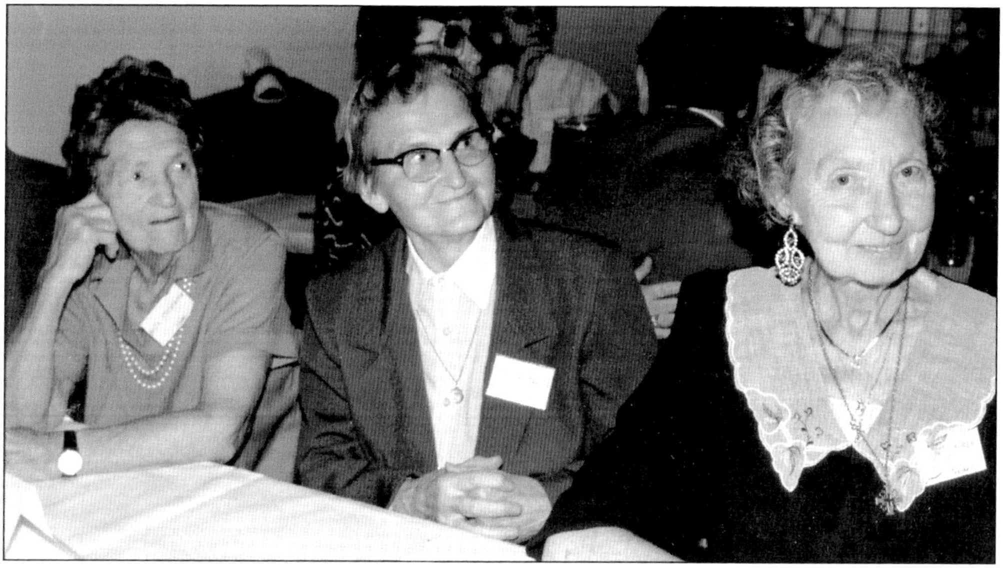

Many of the Sharonville School teachers were present at the all-class reunion on June 9, 1990. Pictured, from left to right, are Alyce Stephenson, Anna Graham, and Edna Prosser. Edna taught first grade starting in 1938 and later went into the Navy. She had 39 students her first year.

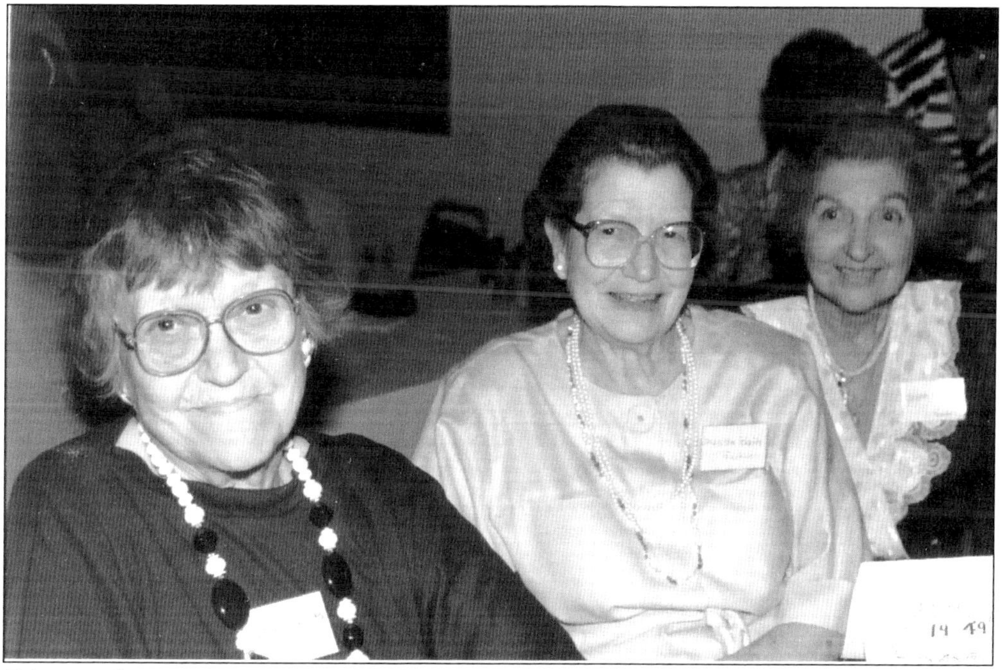

Other teachers were present at the Sharonville School reunion June 9, 1990. Pictured, from left to right, are Elenore Ayers, Drucilla Bain, and Olivia Prosser. Olivia taught high school for six years starting in 1939. Drucilla taught second grade from 1939 to 1950. She had to drive to school from Madeira, but the first year she didn't have her permanent license and was supposed to have a licensed driver with her. Since no one was going to ride with her and sit all day while she taught school, she drove her dad's Plymouth by herself, illegally, for a whole month.

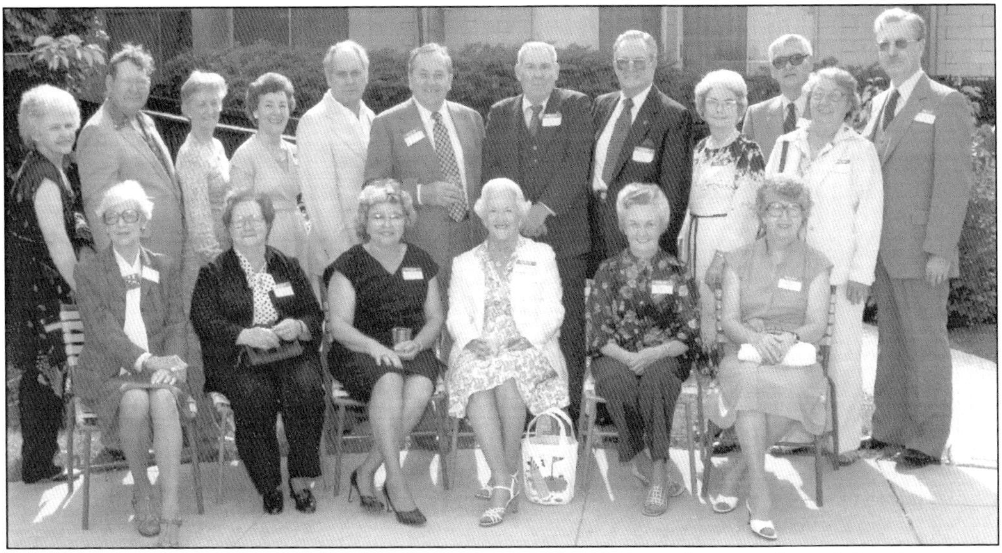

The Sharonville High School class of 1938, meeting 43 years later, gathered for this photo in May, 1981. Pictured, from left to right, are (front row sitting) Virginia Edmonds, Bette Dunlap Long, Dorothy Gilbert, Catherine Wright Elsbrock, Theda Clark, and Helen Gandert (Bill's wife, not in class); (middle row) Alma Hendrix, Ed Bland, Margaret Byron Keifer, Betty Kussman, Al Krick, Dick Elsbrock, Jack Wagner, Bill Gandert, Dorothy Yeager Birt, and Esther Roth Knueven; (back row) Unidentified, and Unidentified.

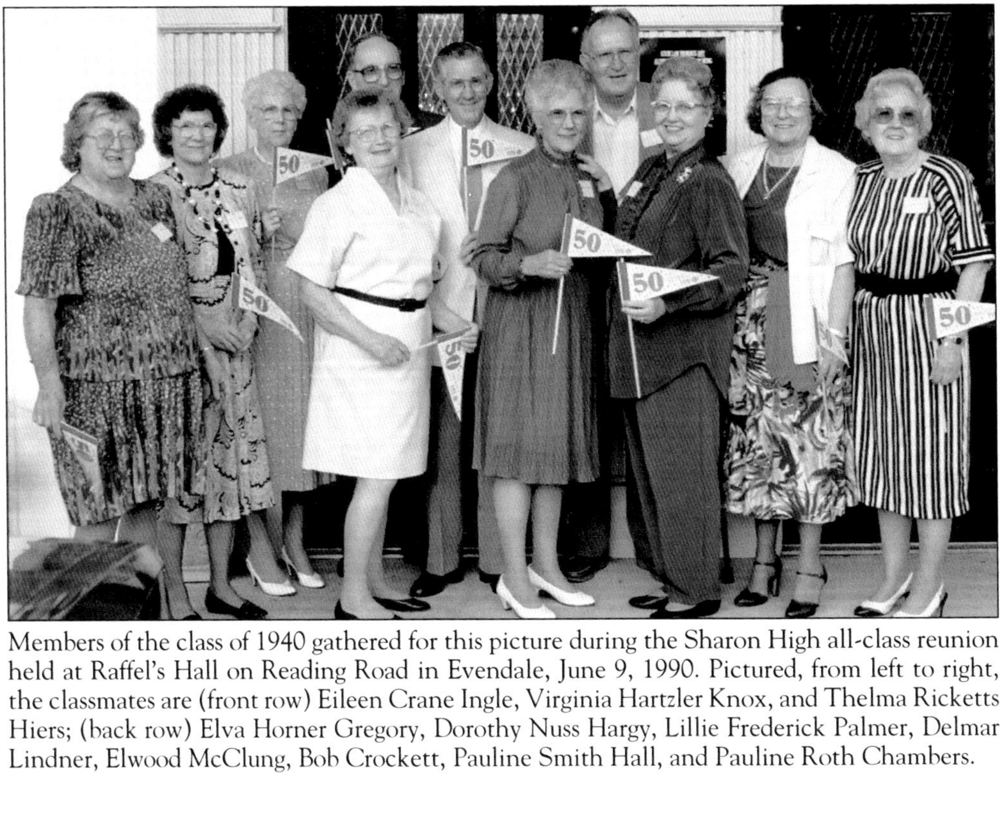

Members of the class of 1940 gathered for this picture during the Sharon High all-class reunion held at Raffel's Hall on Reading Road in Evendale, June 9, 1990. Pictured, from left to right, the classmates are (front row) Eileen Crane Ingle, Virginia Hartzler Knox, and Thelma Ricketts Hiers; (back row) Elva Horner Gregory, Dorothy Nuss Hargy, Lillie Frederick Palmer, Delmar Lindner, Elwood McClung, Bob Crockett, Pauline Smith Hall, and Pauline Roth Chambers.

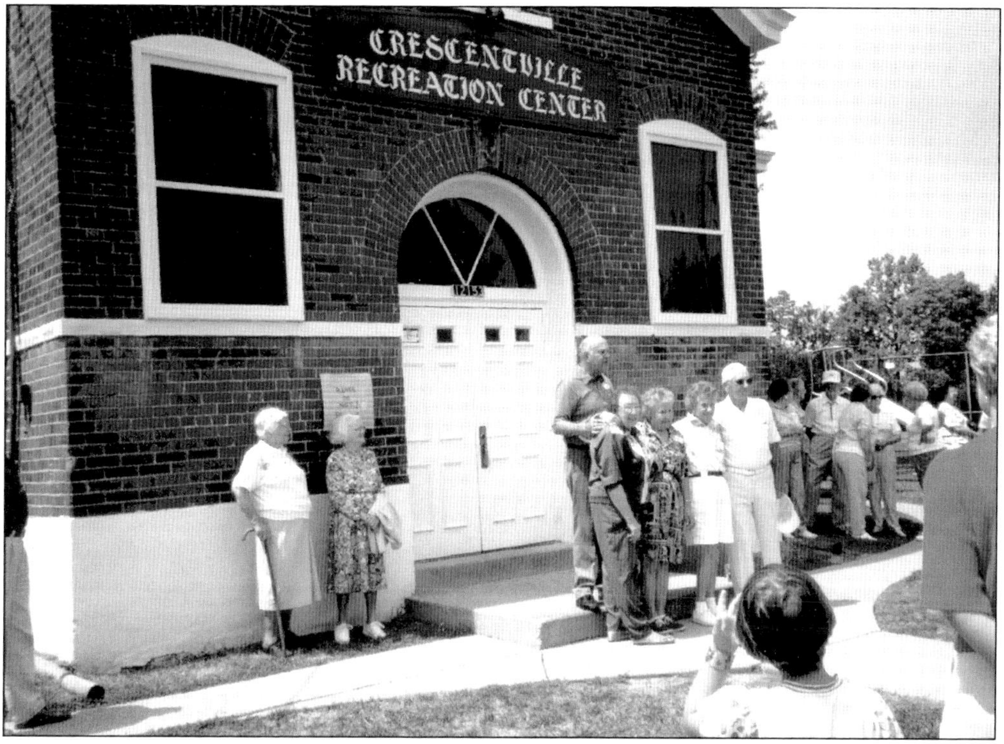

Each summer, former classmates from the old two-room Crescentville School, built in 1904 (and closed in the mid-1950s), gather at the school-turned-rec-center for a reunion picnic. Their reunion in August of 1994 had the added attraction of the unveiling of a historic plaque by the historical society.

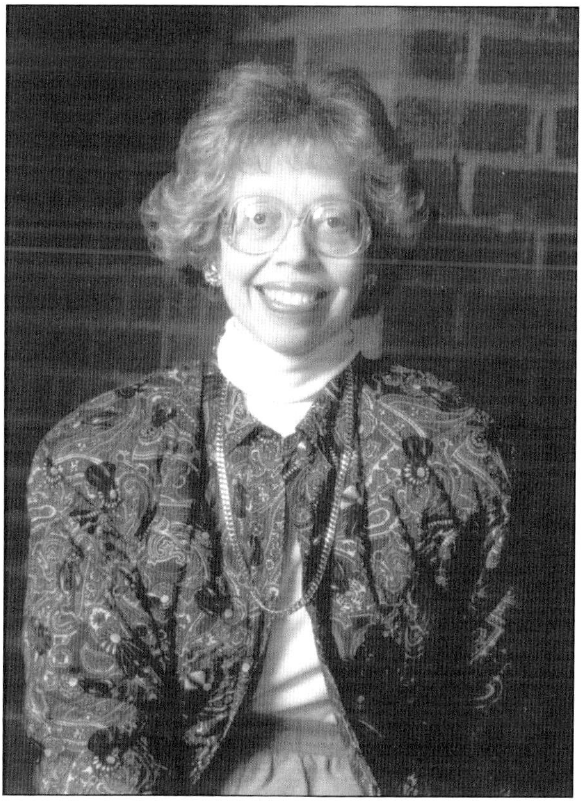

Sara Lou Teets taught for 30 years in the Princeton City School District, with 26 happy years at the Sharonville Elementary School (1962-1988). She enjoyed sharing a love of learning and history with her third grade students. Miss Teets felt it was her privilege to teach skills and values and to help her students set goals in life. Sara Lou was a charter member of the Society of Historic Sharonville and remains a member and supporter of the Society in 2002.

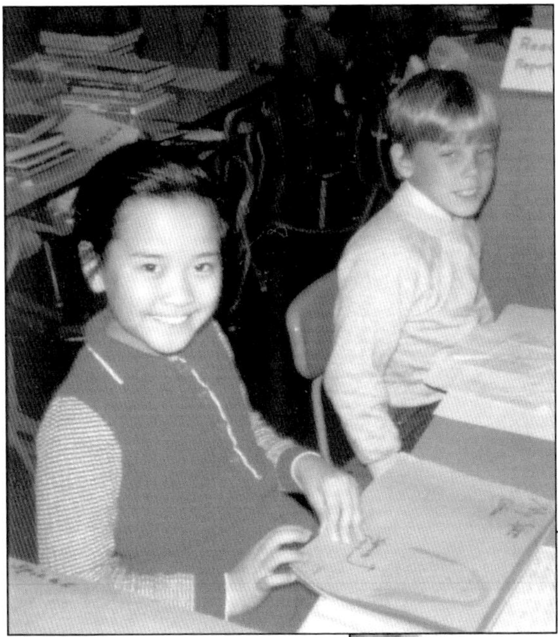

Miss Sara Lou Teets took photos of her third grade students during the 1983–1984 school year at Sharonville Elementary. Man-Ching Wong and Mark Keller enjoyed their classmates' Christopher Columbus' spice projects in 1983.

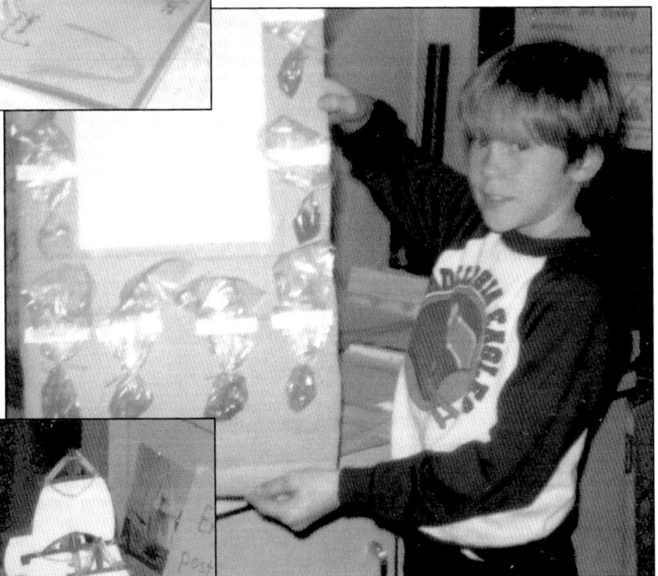

Kyle Kensley presented his spice project in October, 1983.

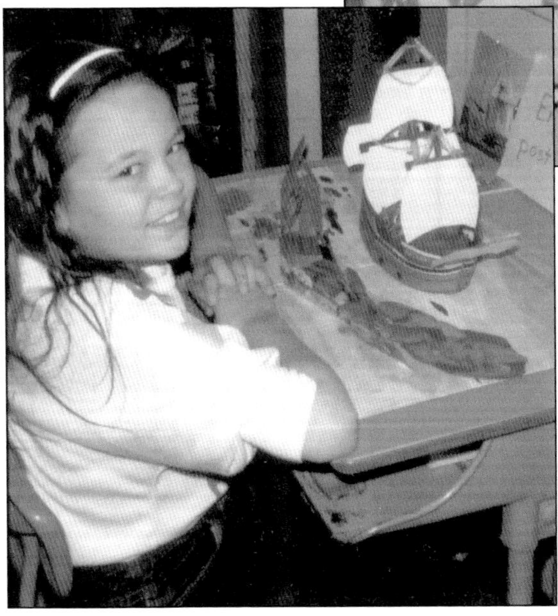

Tracy Musick enjoyed a Mayflower station in November, 1983.

Ashley Burke presented some autumn pictures and "good work" of autumn 1983.

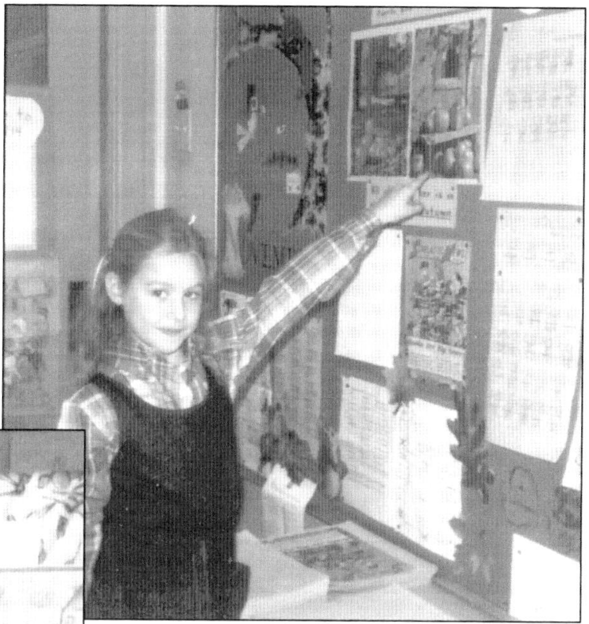

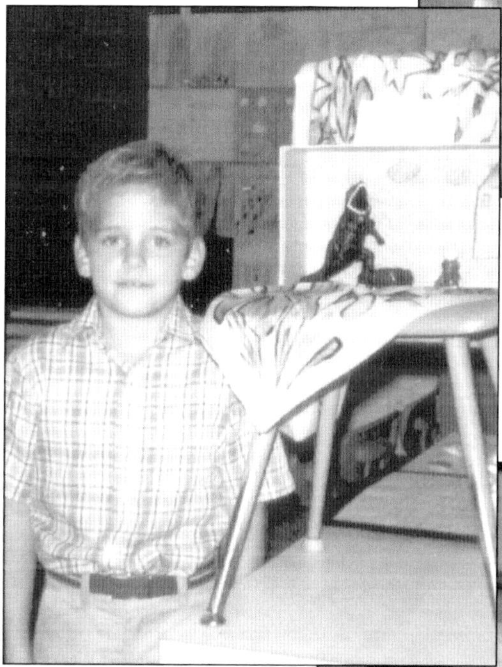

Dennis Miller gave a book talk with his diorama for Children's Book Week, November, 1983.

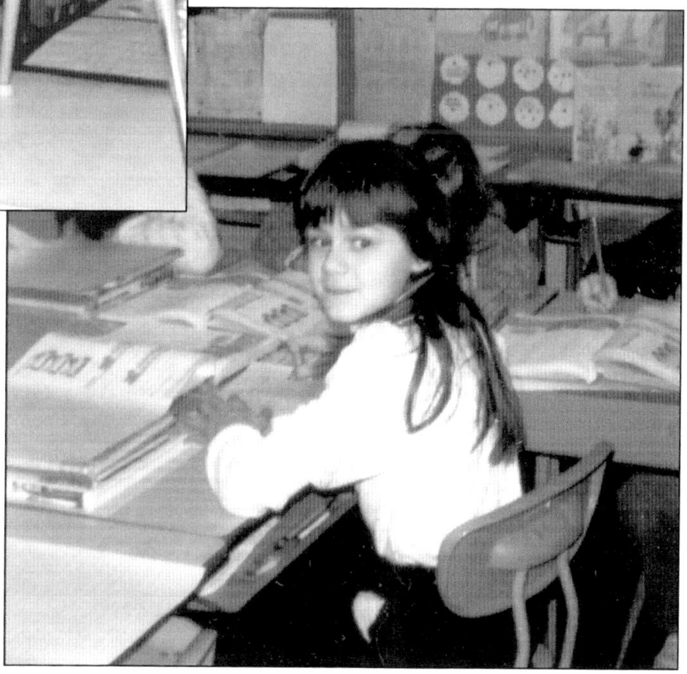

Kristi Long and some classmates studied in January, 1984.

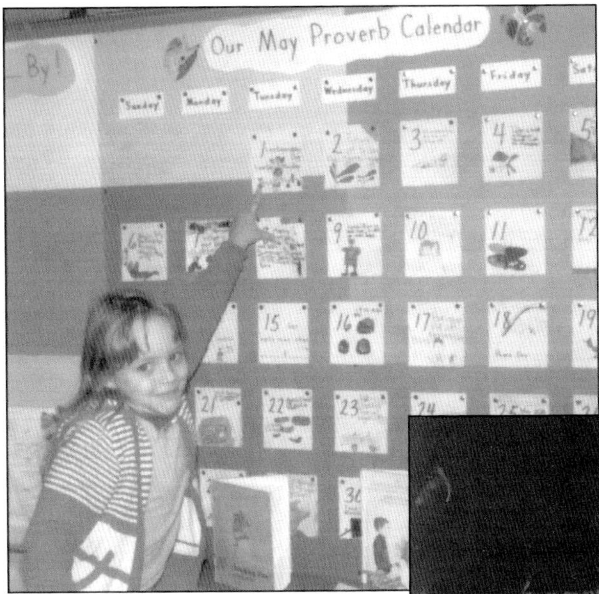

Sherry Arbaugh pointed out the 1984 Proverb Calendar made by the whole third grade class.

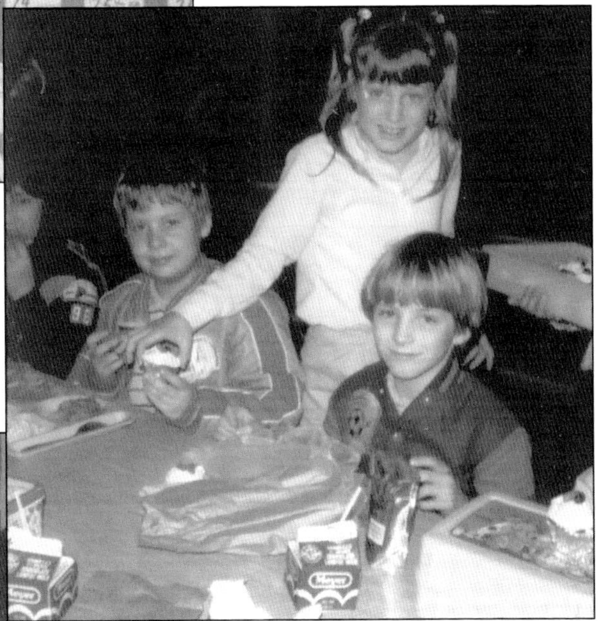

Lori Lucas shared her April, 1984 birthday cupcakes with classmates. Pictured, from left to right, Brendan Goodall, Joshua LeQuire, Lori Lucas, and Gregory Potts.

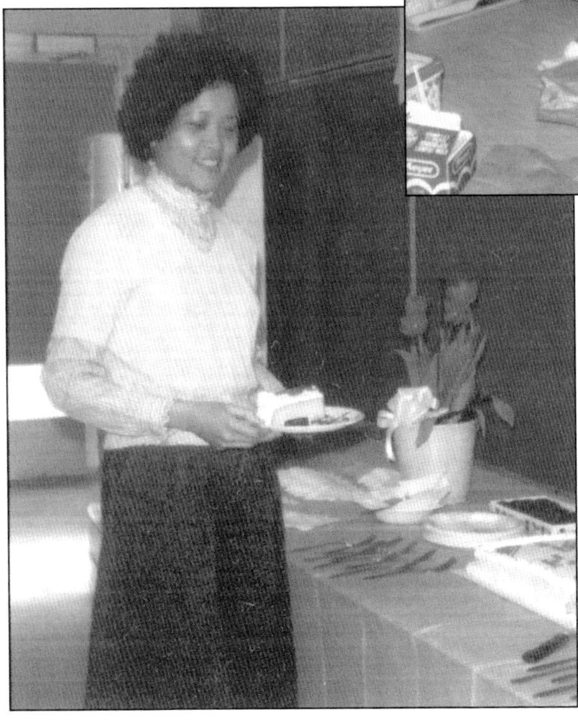

Miss Teresita Jose, second grade teacher at Sharonville Elementary, enjoyed a faculty/staff reception hosted by the 1983 Right to Read Committee. It honored Music in Our School Week, Physical Education Month, and Right to Read Week.

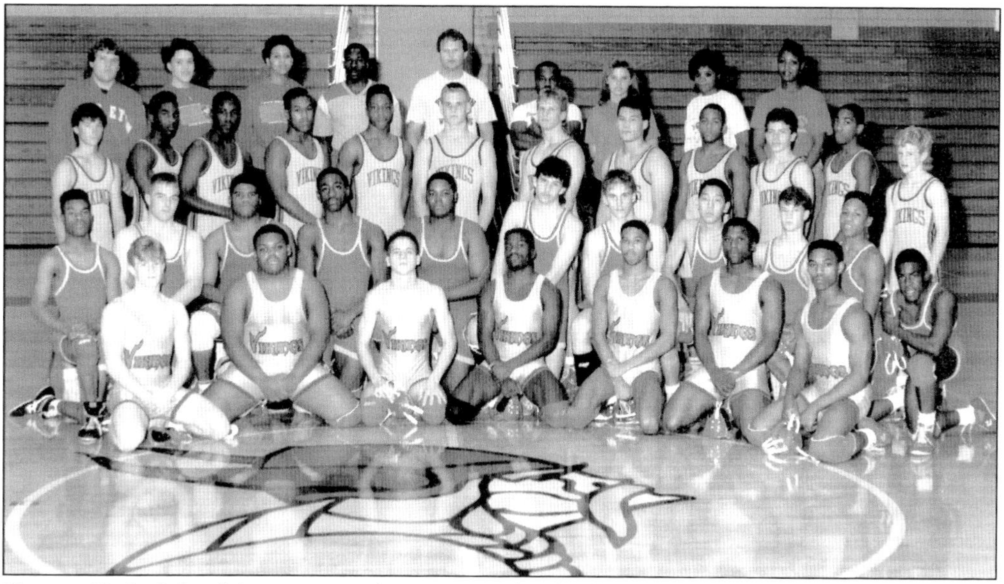

Sharon High School became an elementary school when Princeton High opened in 1959. Pictured are members the 1990 Princeton High School wrestling team, from left to right, (first row) David Pender, E. Allen, Darren Darling, A. Brookins, D. Davis, R. Shoemaker, and J. Austin; (second row) Quincy North, D. Allen, A. Thomas, Chris Miree, Marcus Vicars, Matt Siry, Casey Herring, Will Suyemoto, L. Shelton, M. Larkins, and B. Barner; (third row) Brian Colegrove, H. Nash, R. Grove, Jason Whitehead, Andre Braunskill, Brian Keeton, Aaron Boszan, Bruce Montgomery, Robert Kinsey, Tony Shaw, Duane Kinsey, and Jason Pender; (fourth row) team managers and coaches M. Birkemeyer, A. Williams, S. Seniors, D. Campbell, Dan Moody, Mike Hill, Melissa Vail, K. Woods, and L. Goodsmith.

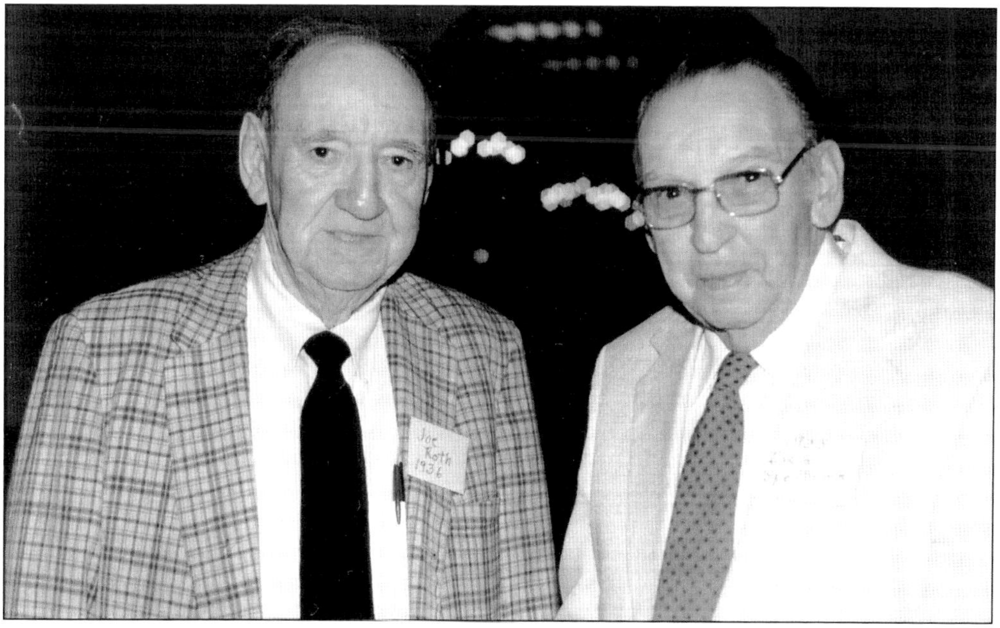

Long time buddies, Joe Roth (class of 1936) and Dick Spellmire (class of 1935) stopped chatting long enough to oblige the photographer at the June 1996 Sharon High Reunion.

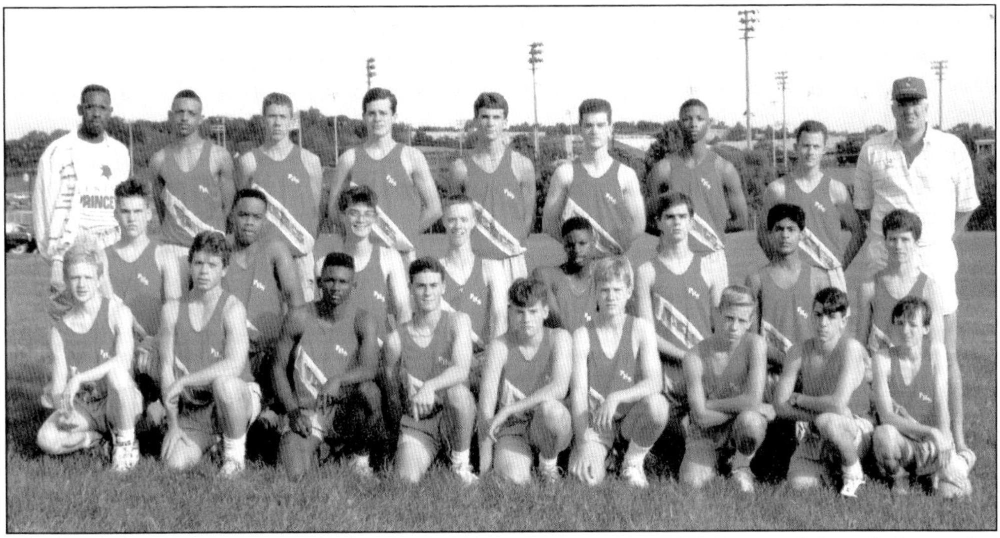

Princeton High School fielded a strong cross country team in 1992. Pictured, from left to right, are (front row) Jason Pender, Tony Shaw, L. Thompson, Sean Raboin, J. Isaacs, Scott Wallace, A. Austin, Kevin Antelo, and Randal Reece; (middle row) J. Surekamp, D. Hillard, Marty O'Connor, Brent Conley, M. Powell, M. Ostrander, Vijay Rajendran, and Mike Galvin; (back row) Coach Olverson, Simeon Holloway, Billy Robinson, Patrick Wentzel, Adam Burbules, Sean O'Connor, M. Murray, Tom Simpkins, and Coach Ken Meibers.

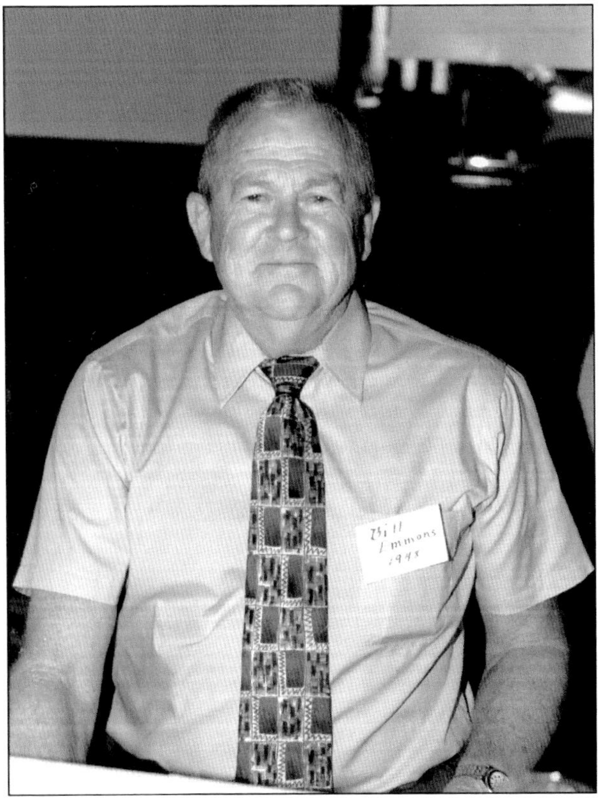

Former Sharonville Volunteer Fireman Bill Emmons (class of 1948) can usually be found manning the raffle table at the Sharon High reunions. He's pictured at the June, 1996 reunion.

Four

Honoring Our Veterans

Sharonville has had its share of veterans—from the farmers of the 83d Ohio Volunteer Infantry in the Civil War, to our reservists called up to protect us from 21st century terrorism. The following is an excerpt from an essay written for Veteran's Day 2001 by David Huynh, a fifth grader from Sharonville Elementary: "Without veterans none of us would be here. Veterans give us the future. Someone who will risk his/her life to protect us all should have great heart. Their heart must have kindness, love, and courage, and should be worthy of honor. Veterans have done what they could to extinguish the flames of war and hatred. What do they seek? Not glory, fame, or praise, but only the safety of all of us. They should be honored for what they have done for us…every one of them is a hero."

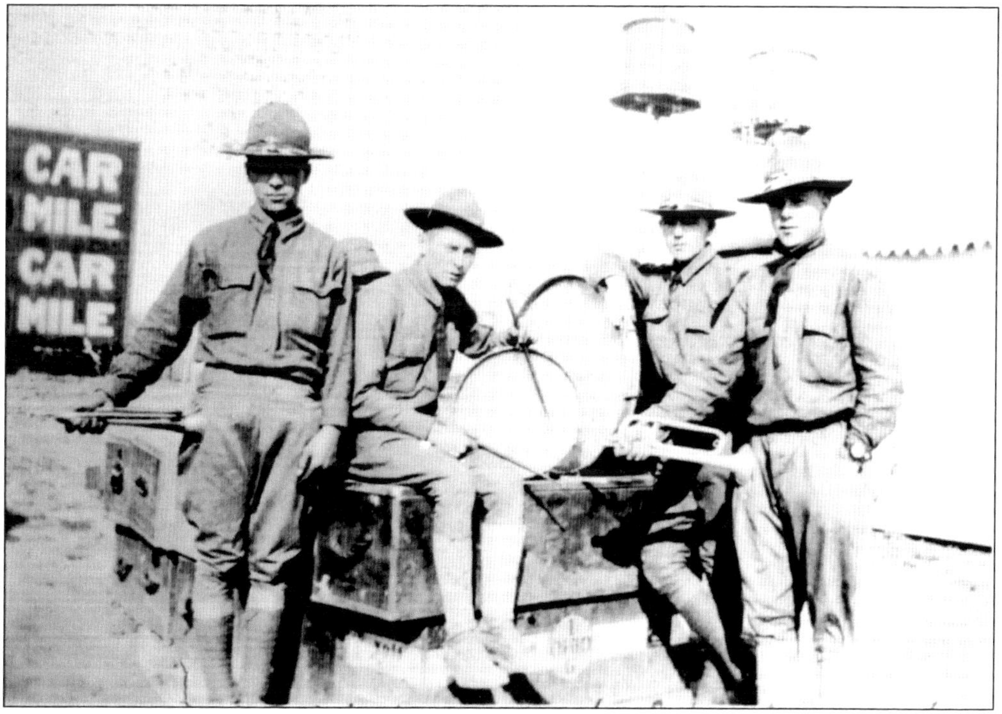

An Army field band assembled at the Sharonville military depot during the World War I era. Notice the old Speedway tote board displaying "Car mile, Car mile" in the background. It was used to indicate the number of the race car and the miles completed in a race. No one was thinking about racing now. Their minds were on the activities in Europe.

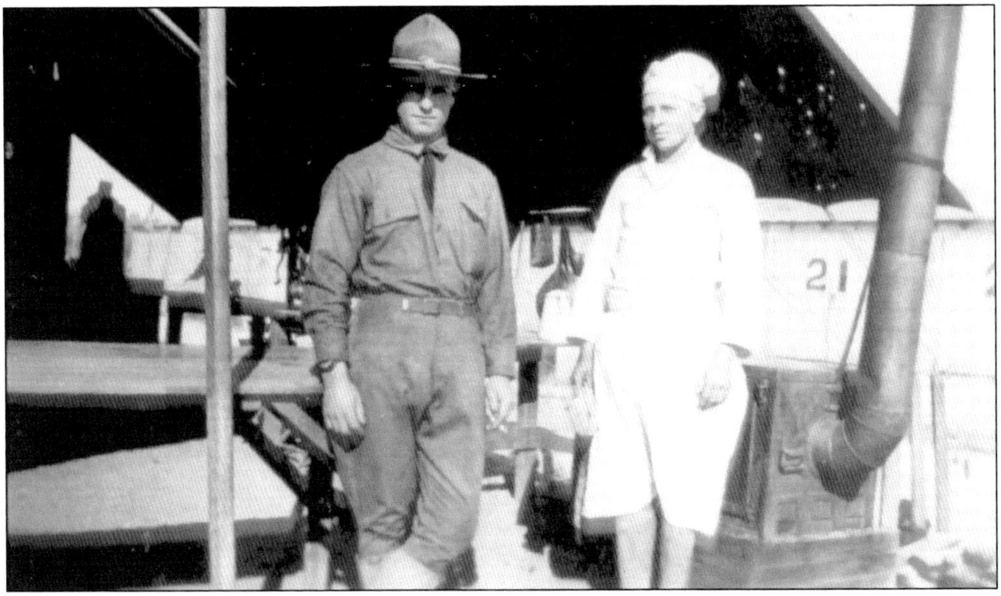

After its brief heyday, the old Cincinnati Speedway grounds were converted into a military depot for soldiers during World War I. Pictured are an unidentified soldier and cook at the camp kitchen.

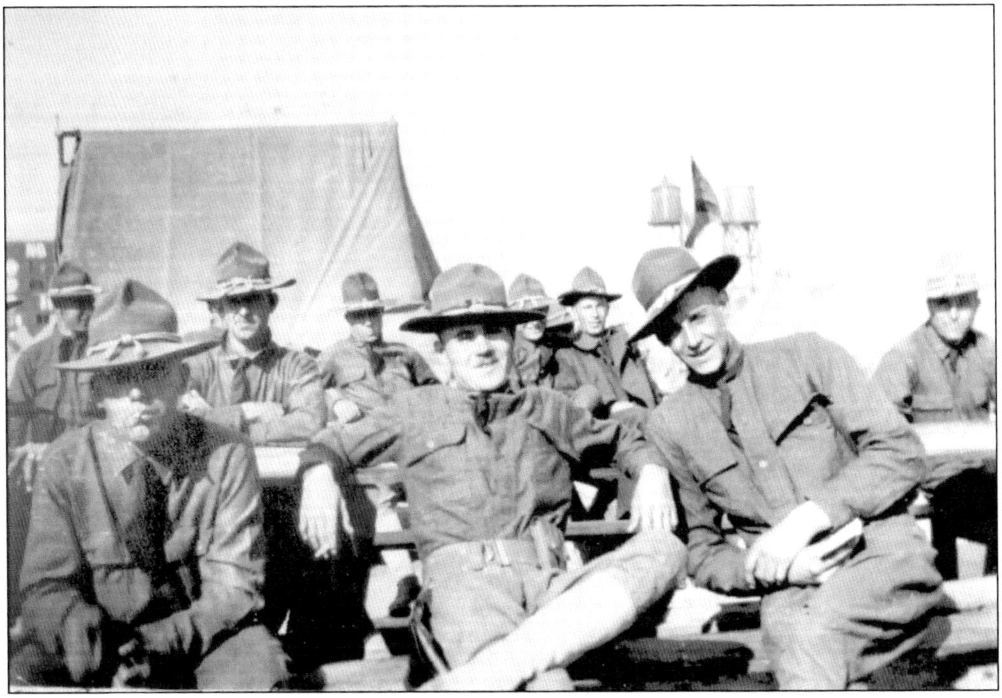

These World War I-era soldiers awaiting further orders relaxed and smiled for the photographer at the old "Speedway" military depot. The Speedway, and subsequently, the Depot, was located in the area presently bound by Kemper Road to the south, Mosteller Road to the west, Crescentville Road on the north, and Reading Road/Cincinnati-Dayton Pike on the east. The track was a two-mile board oval. You can read more about it in the book *Sharonville, Then and Now.*

Pictured is a fragment of a letter that Civil War Veteran Samuel F. Beeler wrote to his wife from a military hospital in Memphis, Tennessee, on March 24, 1863. It mentions their three children: Arealus, Leavonia E. "Etta," and Aranza (later Mrs. Edmund Gilbert). According to army records, Samuel was born in Warren County in 1832. He lived most of his adult life in the Sharonville area. He volunteered for three separate tours of duty: 72nd Regiment Ohio Volunteer Infantry (OVI), Company K; 83rd Regiment OVI, Company E; and 138th Regiment Ohio National Guard (ONG), Company I. The letter, from which only a fragment remains, was written while he recovered from a gunshot wound to his left hand, received at the Battle of Arkansas Post, January 11, 1863.

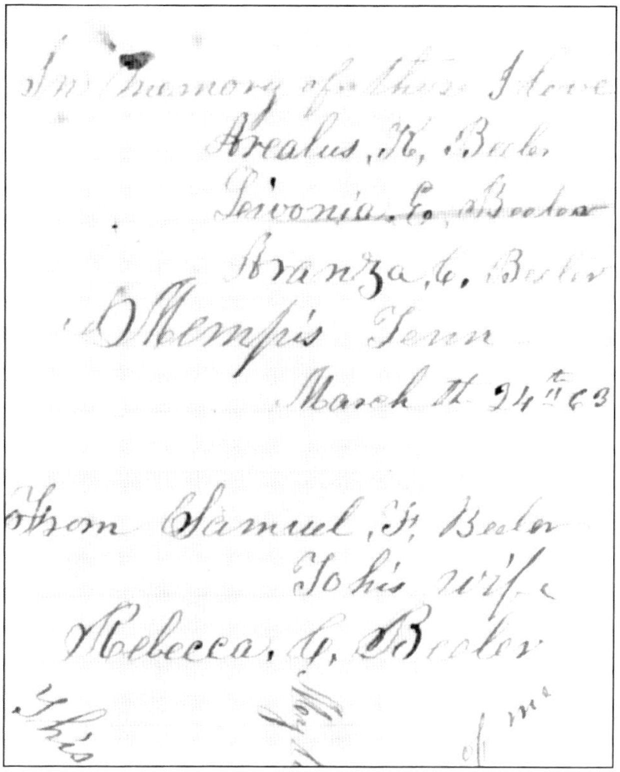
In memory of those I love
Arealus, K, Beeler
Leivonia E, Beeler
Aranza C, Beeler
Memphis Tenn
March the 24th 63
From Samuel, F, Beeler
To his wife
Rebecca, G, Beeler

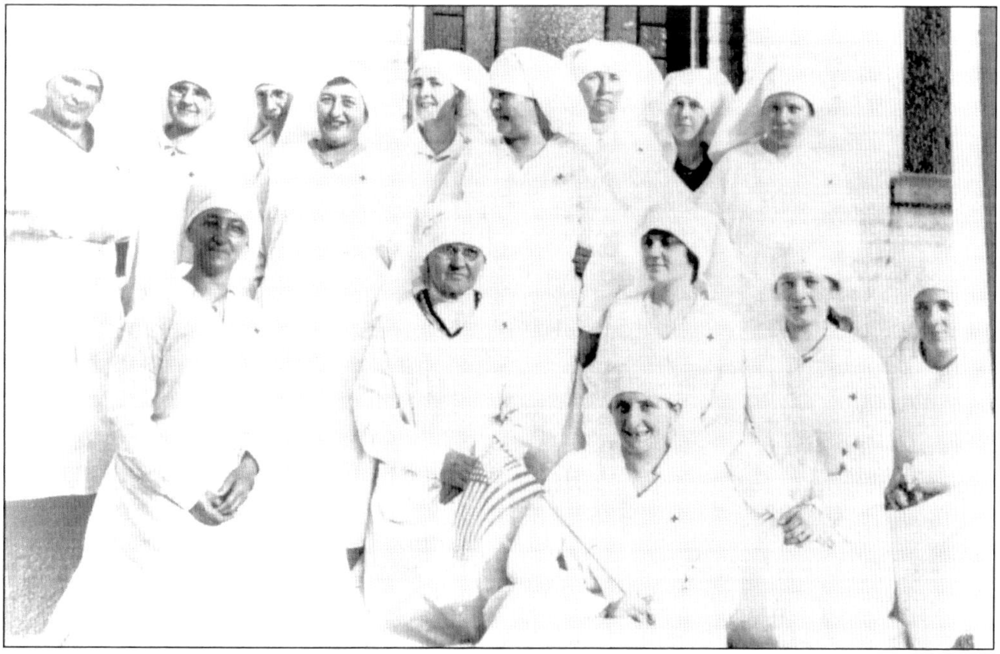

No, these ladies are not residents of a convent. They are Red Cross workers who lived in Sharonville during World War I. The women knitted mittens, socks, and sweaters for the servicemen. The only one who is identified is in the back row, third from the right. She is Elizabeth Prenatt, who was also a wife, mother, and midwife.

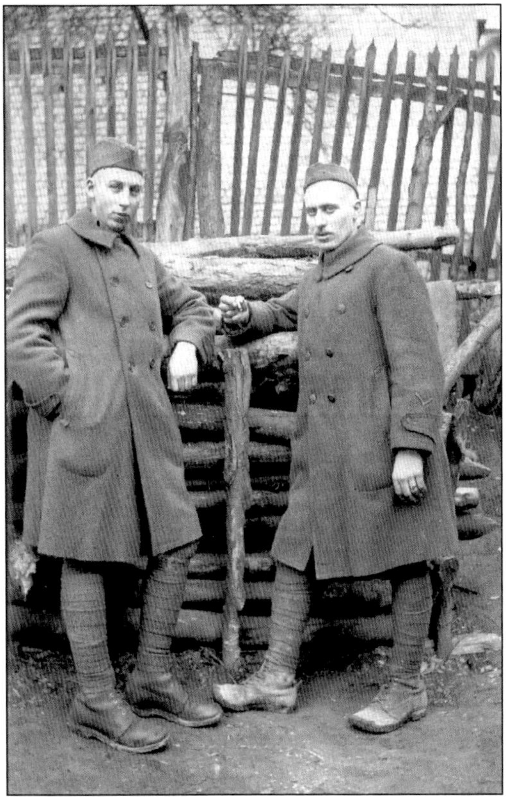

George J. Hagee served in the Army in World War I and was stationed in France and Germany in 1918 and 1919. George J., father of G. Richard and Robert J. Hagee, had this postcard photo taken with Corporal Rumery (on right) in Heinbach, Germany, in March, 1919. It was sent to Loretto E. O'Brien in Cincinnati, who would marry George in 1924.

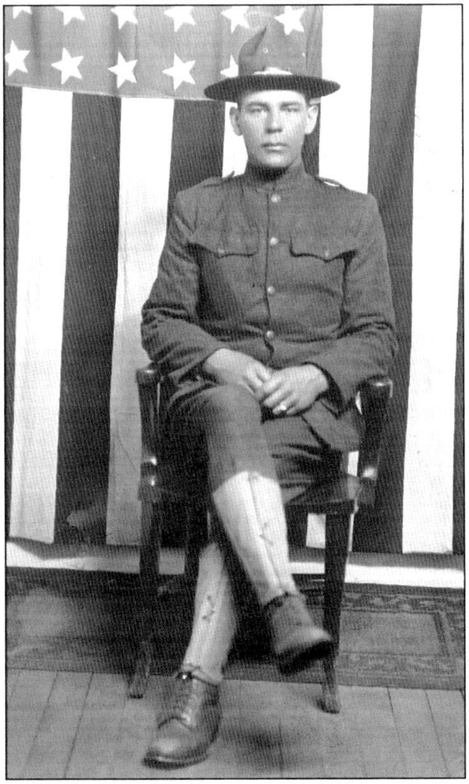

This blue-eyed World War I veteran is Edward Nuss. He was stationed at Camp Sherman in Chillicothe, and in France during the war. This photo could have been taken at Camp Sherman before the men shipped out. Edward's daughter, Dorothy Nuss Hargy, still cherishes the many letters that he wrote to her mom, Vivienne. They were married September 27, 1919.

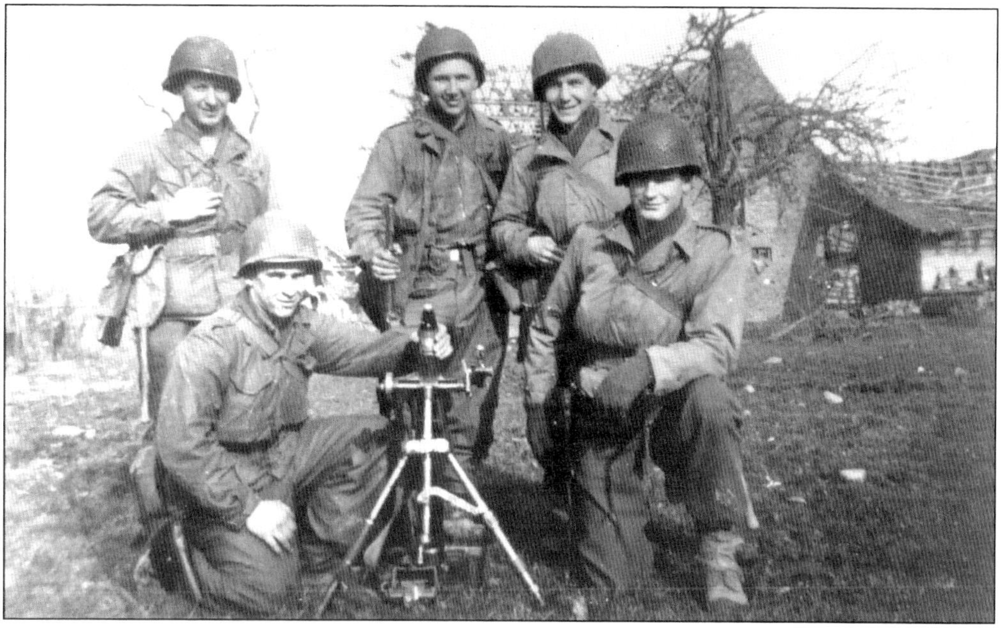

G. Richard Hagee graduated from St. Xavier High School in 1943 and entered the army shortly thereafter at age 18. He was shipped overseas in September of 1944. In February 1945, G. Richard Hagee was a member of a 60mm Mortar Squad in Geich, Germany, with the 104th (Timberwolf) Infantry Division. Pictured, from left to right, are (kneeling) G. Richard Hagee and Chuck Angel; (standing) Seymour Black, Robert Wayne, and Al Thorpe.

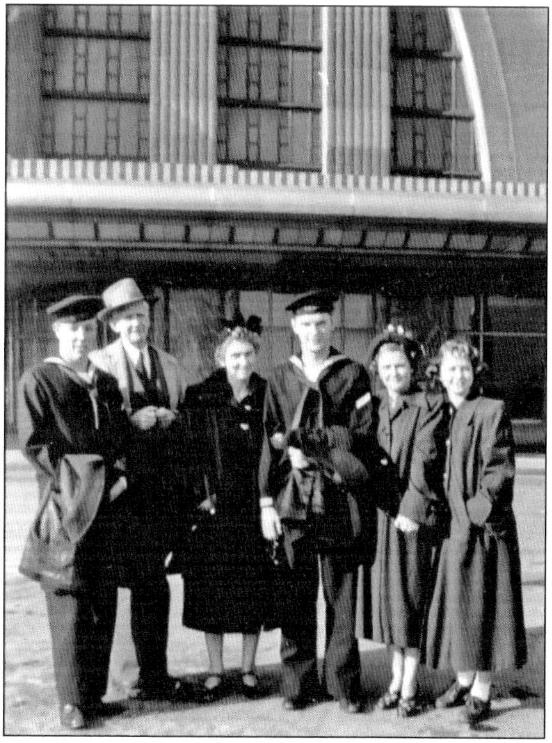

Cincinnati's Union Terminal saw many veterans pass through its doors during the era of World War II, and many families gathered to welcome returning vets or send them off with the wish of a speedy and safe return. The Lewis family was no exception as young Bill left to serve in the Navy. Pictured, from left to right, are George Cook (Bill's Navy buddy), Bill's grandparents G.H. and Gladys McWhorter, Bill Lewis, Bill's mom Kathryn Lewis, and Shirley Lewis.

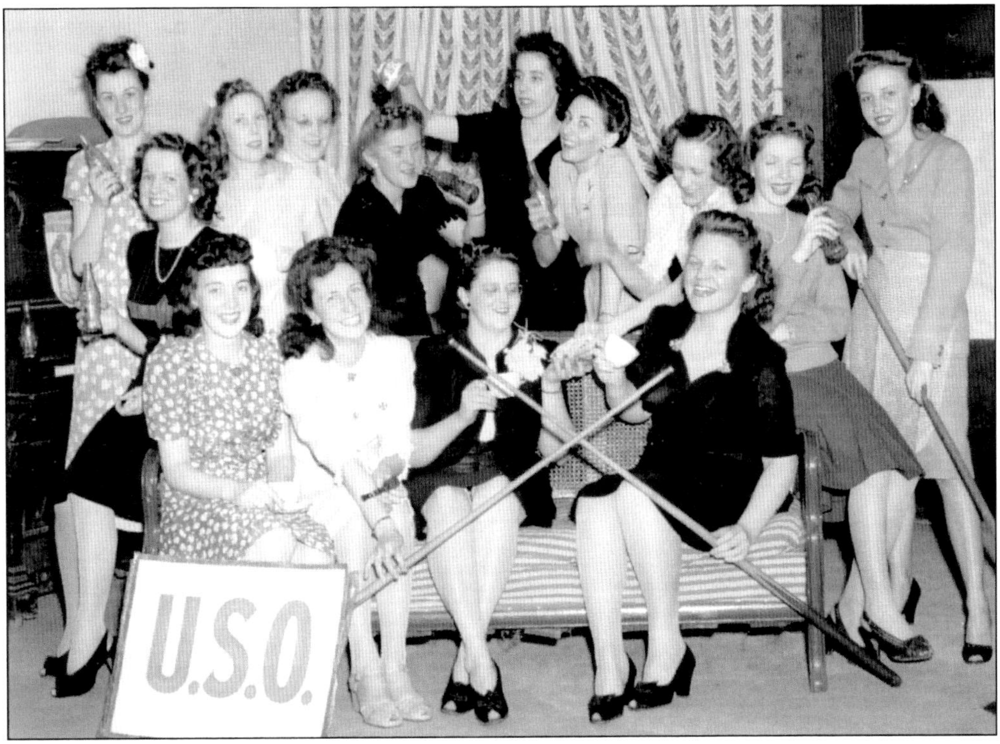

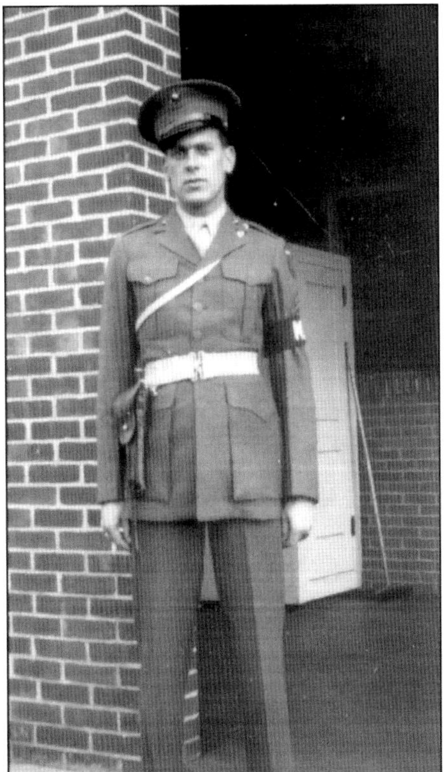

The USO was active in Sharonville in the 1940s. They did their part locally to entertain troops stationed at the army depot (formerly the Cincinnati Speedway grounds). Pictured c. 1944, from left to right, are (seated) Jeannette Haubner (on arm), Jeanne Lehrter, Audrey Fenstermacher, Mildred Sheldon, Ruth Potthoff, and Erma Dunlap (on arm); (standing) Ione Glaser, Frances Even, Abigail Mehaffie, Elaine Duermit, Kathleen Jesse, Pauline Lehrter, Ruth Mehaffie, and Florence Barkau.

Al Krick (Sharonville High class of 1938) stopped for this Marine Corps photo at the Quanset Point Air Station gate, c. 1945.

In 1943, Vernon Lovins was drafted into the Army for World War II. He and his wife, Helen Hubbard Lovins, had two little boys at that time. Since they had no telephone and Helen didn't drive, she and the boys moved in with her husband's family, William and Rebecca Lovins, on Main Street in Sharonville for the 28 months Vernon was in the service. Vernon is pictured in front of the Main Street home while on leave in 1944.

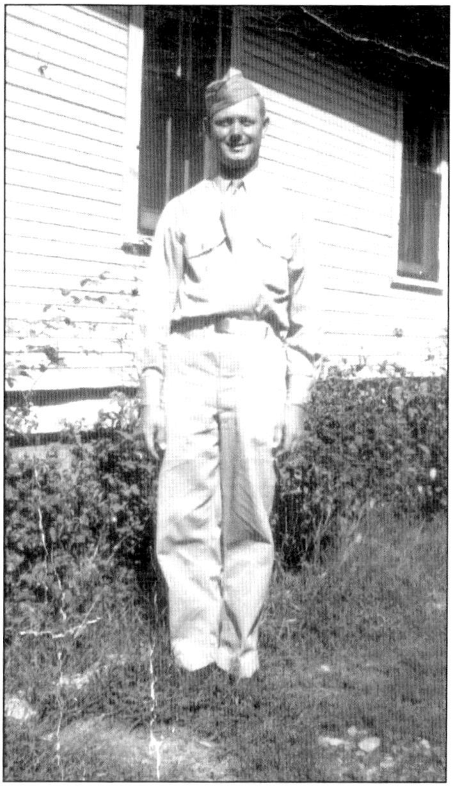

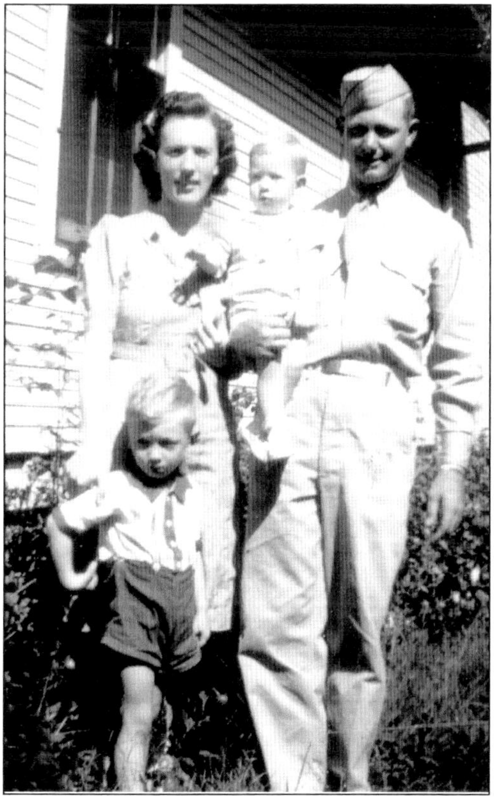

The Lovins family posed for this photo in front of William and Rebecca Lovins' home on Main Street in Sharonville while Vernon was home on leave in 1944. They are, from left to right: Wilbur, Helen, Robert, and Vernon Lovins.

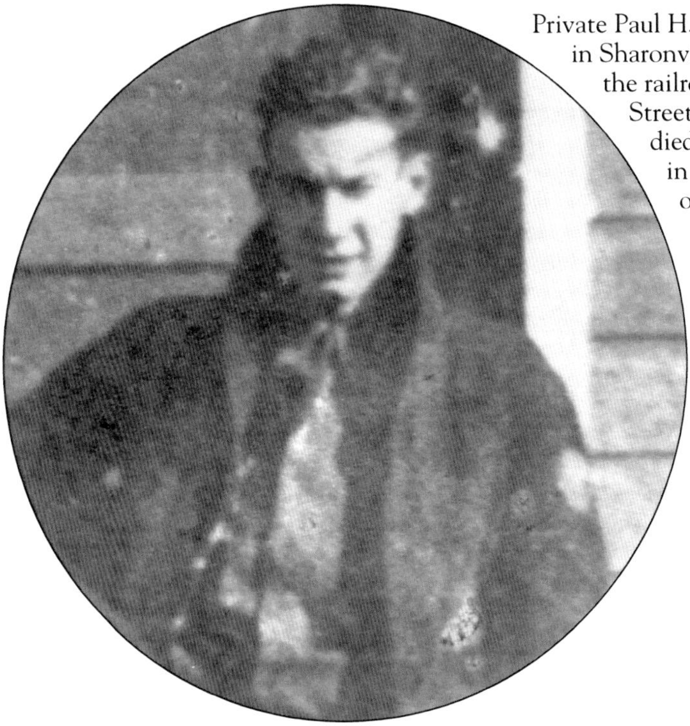

Private Paul H. Vail was born and raised in Sharonville. His family lived near the railroad tracks around Pine Street and Maple Avenue. He died in action on Batan Island in either January or February of 1942. This photo was taken in 3Cs and is one of the few pictures of Paul in existence. Today, Sharonville's Veterans of Foreign Wars (VFW) Post on Sharon Avenue is named after Paul.

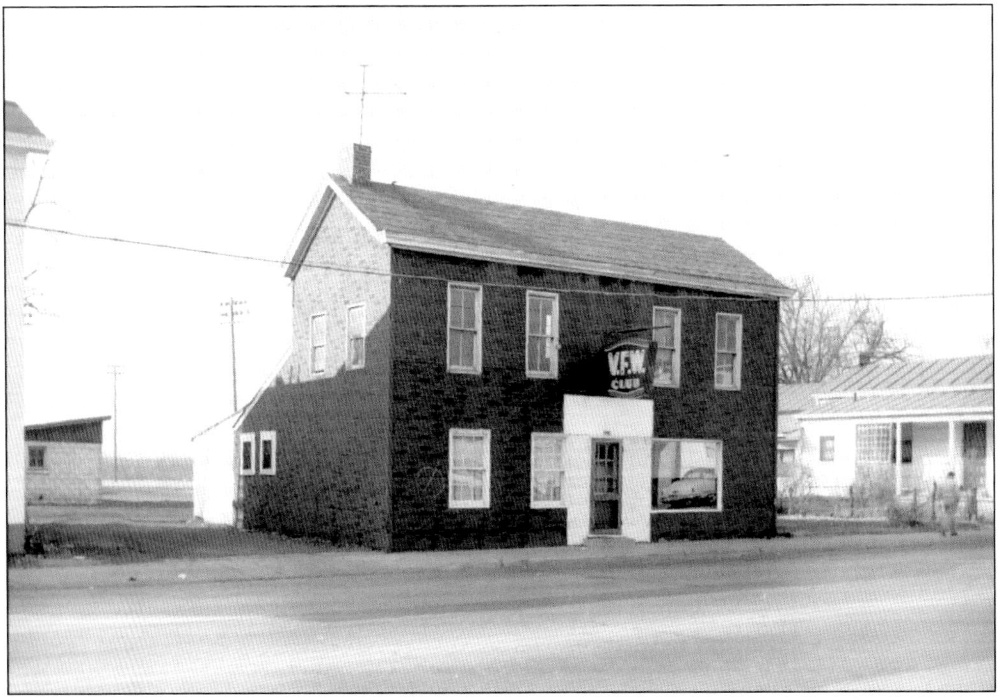

The old VFW Post was four buildings north of Sharon Avenue on the west side of Reading Road. It was just north of the Denman House. The smaller white house to the right belonged to the Cook family. Behind the building was a field used for Sharon High School baseball and football games.

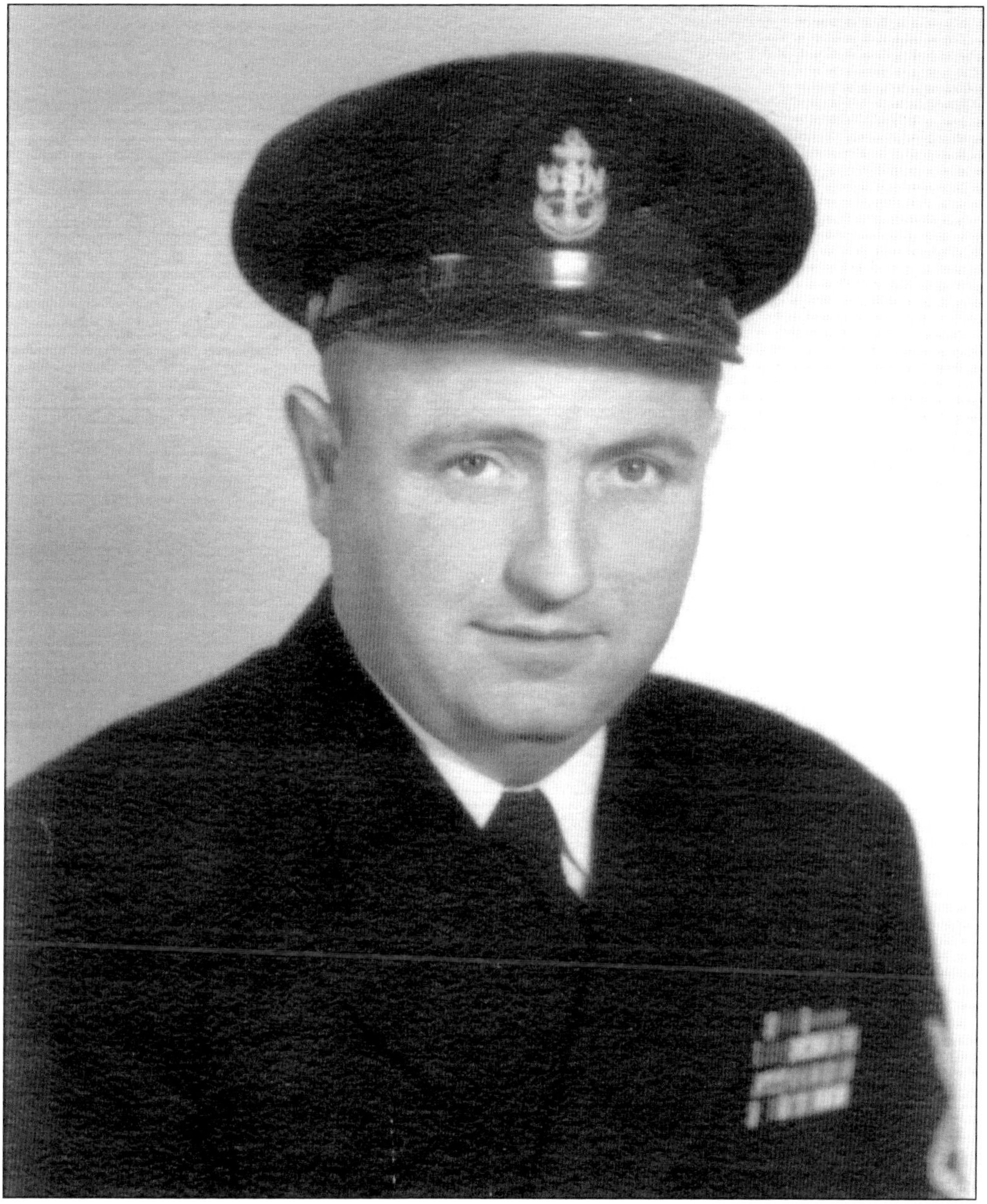

Thirteen is a lucky number for Samuel Hicks. He was the "13th man of a crew alongside gun No. 13 on the U.S. cruiser Atlanta which sunk Friday, the 13th day of November, 1942, near the Solomons"—and he was the only one of the 13 crew members to live to tell the story. At the time, Boatswain's Mate Hicks was a gun-pointer. A Japanese shell exploded in his battle station leaving him with "the loss of his left ear but for the miracle of plastic surgery, burns on his hands, 26 pieces of shrapnel in his back, legs, and head." He survived because one shell had already put a hole in the gun turret. After exiting through that hole, Hicks dove straight into the ocean, protected from sharks only by the oil leaking from the stricken ship. Following his rescue over 6 hours later, he received medical attention in a Guadalcanal foxhole from the Chief Machinist's Mate who had escaped the Atlanta's engine room without a scratch—his brother Benjamin F. Hicks.

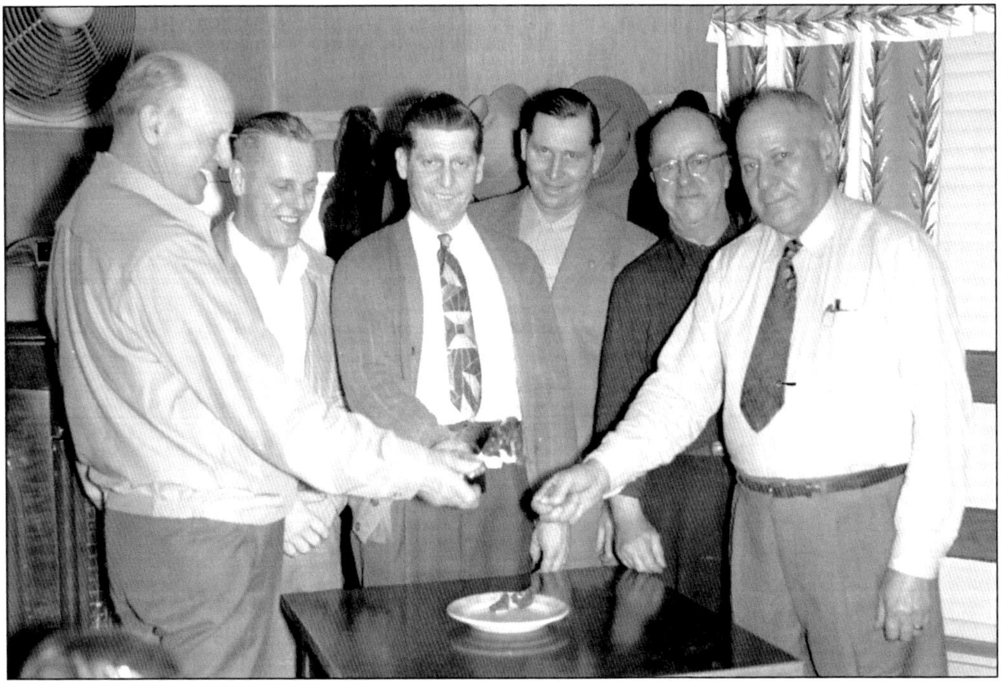

These men had the honor of burning the mortgage and celebrating the ownership of the Paul Vail VFW Post in Sharonville. Pictured on Saturday, January 26, 1952, from left to right, are Bob Hirschauer, Ed "Pete" Derrenkamp, Leroy "Red" Levesay, Albin "Al" Honerlaw, Charles "Hap" Grismere, and Harry M. Vaughn.

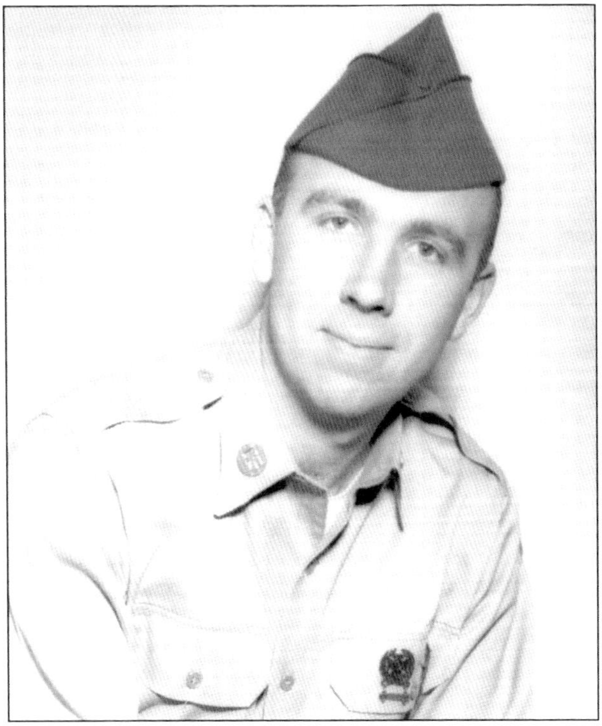

Robert W. Houston served in the U.S. Army at Fort Eustis, Virginia. This photo was taken in April 1958. It was while stationed in Virginia that Bob met his future wife, Ernestine. They were married in 1959 in her home town of Great Bridge, Virginia.

Married July 6, 1968, at St. Michael Church, Lloyd Shaw and Karen Seibert had been engaged since early 1966, but the wedding was postponed when Lloyd was drafted into the Marines in March of that year. He met best man Bruce Mazur in boot camp, while Karen's maid of honor, Betty Stacko, was a childhood friend from Pittsburgh. Ironically, Betty and Bruce met a few days before the Shaw wedding, fell in love, and were married a year later, July 5, 1969. Pictured, from left to right, are Betty Stacko, Karen Seibert Shaw, Lloyd Shaw, and Bruce Mazur.

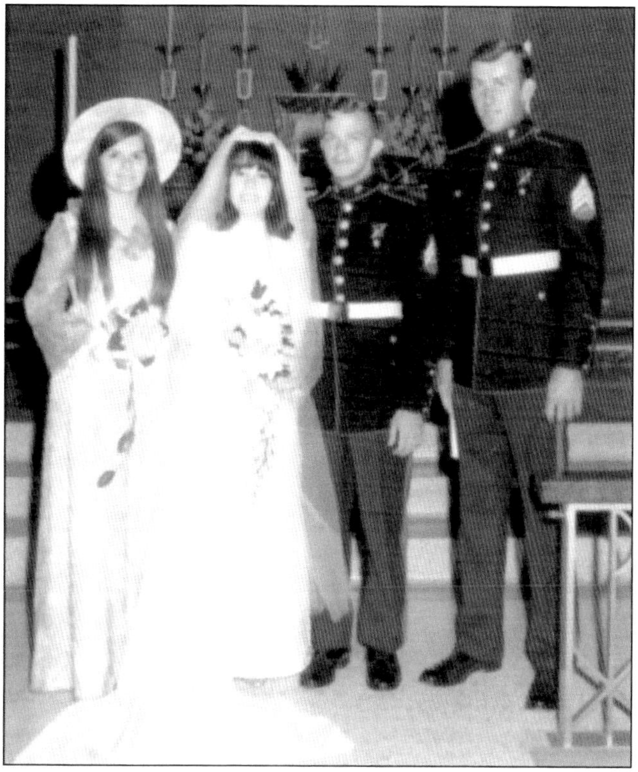

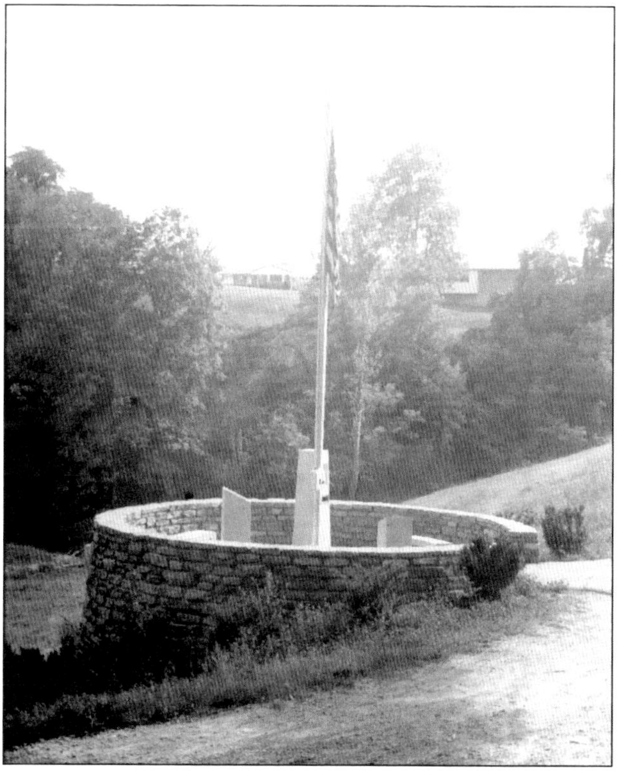

A small veterans' memorial was dedicated near the Creek Road dam on September 15, 1968. While it no longer exists, all of the names that were engraved on that memorial are receiving new memorial bricks in the Patriot Pointe memorial on Thornview Drive.

Dedication Ceremony

★Ohio National Guard	*Huey Helicopter Landing*
★Princeton HS Band & Choir	*Prelude*
★Ohio National Guard	*F16 Flyover*
★Hamilton County Bagpipe Corps	
★Sharonville Police Dept. Color Guard	*(all military veterans)*
★Jonathon Monroe, Bugler	*'Colors'*
★Princeton HS Band & Choir	*'Star Spangled Banner'*
★Nick Clooney, Master of Ceremony	
★John Marx, VFW Chaplain	*Prayer*
★Councilman William Lewis *(veteran)*	*Pledge of Allegiance*
★Major General John H. Smith	
★Mayor Virgil G. Lovitt, II	
★George Durinka, State Sr. Vice VFW	*"What is a Vet?"*
★Unveiling, narrated by Mayor Lovitt	*Symbolism of Patriot Pointe*
★Princeton HS Band & Choir	*'America the Beautiful'*
★Essay winner, David Huynh	*Placing of the Wreath*
★Hamilton County Bagpipe Corps	*'Amazing Grace'*
★Ohio National Guard	*21 Gun Salute*
★"The Perfect Blend", vocalists	*'God Bless America'*
★Daniel Moonitz, Bugler	*'Taps'*
★Mayor Virgil G. Lovitt, II	

Pictured is the program from the new Patriot Pointe Veterans Memorial dedication, Sunday, November 11, 2001.

The Sharonville Police Honor Guard checked their notes prior to presenting the colors at the Patriot Pointe Veterans Memorial dedication, on November 11, 2001. Pictured, from left to right, are Officer Ray Hugentobler, Sgt. Paul Healey, Sgt. Bobby Fisher, and Officer Aaron Hayes.

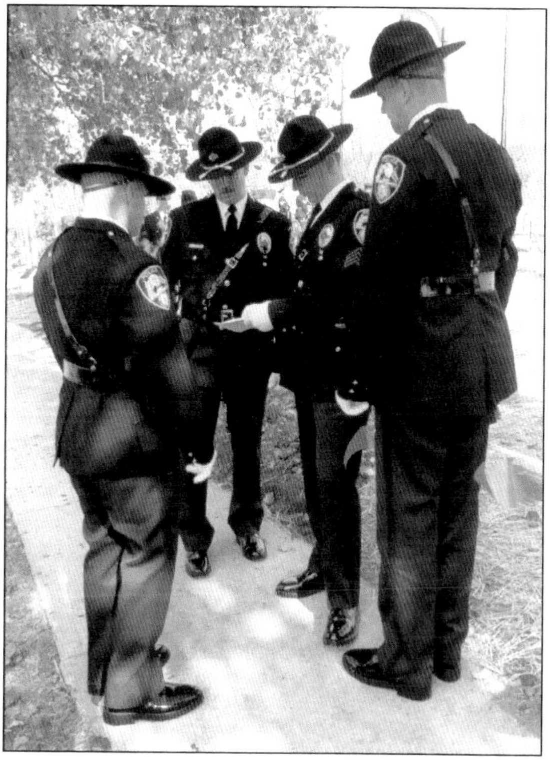

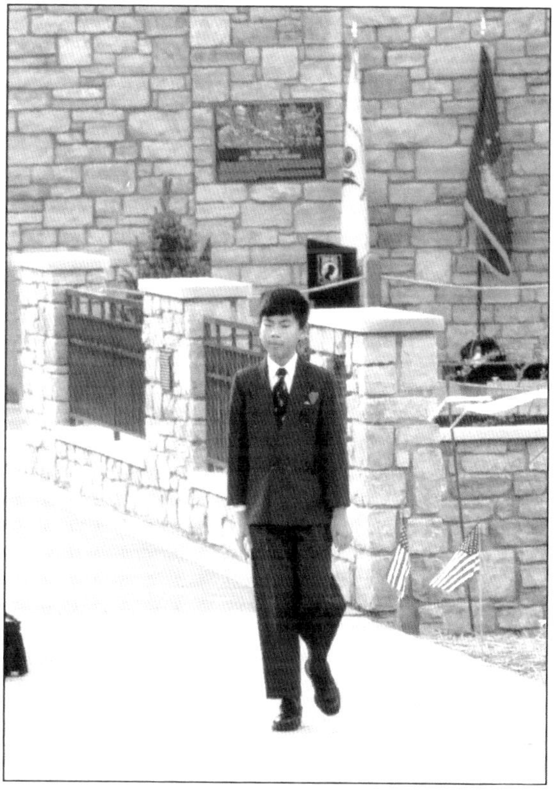

David Huynh, a ten-year-old fifth grade student at Sharonville Elementary School, wrote a winning essay called "What is in the Heart of a Veteran" and was given the honor of placing a memorial wreath during the dedication ceremonies at Patriot Pointe, November 11, 2001.

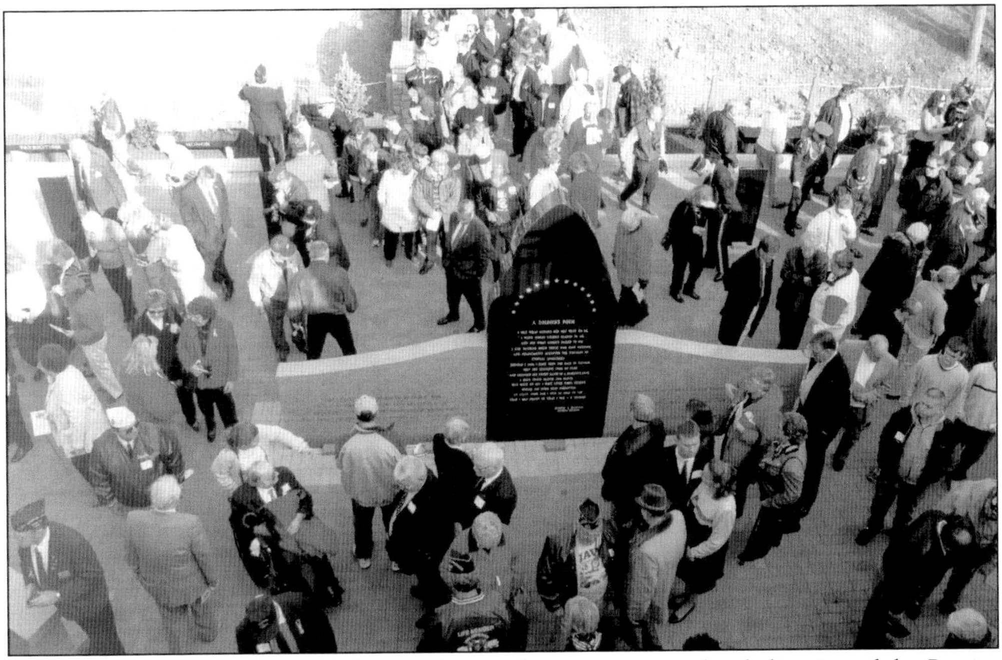

The people of Sharonville turned out to honor their veterans at the dedication of the Patriot Pointe Veterans Memorial, across from the Sharonville Regional Branch Public Library on Thornview Drive, November 11, 2001.

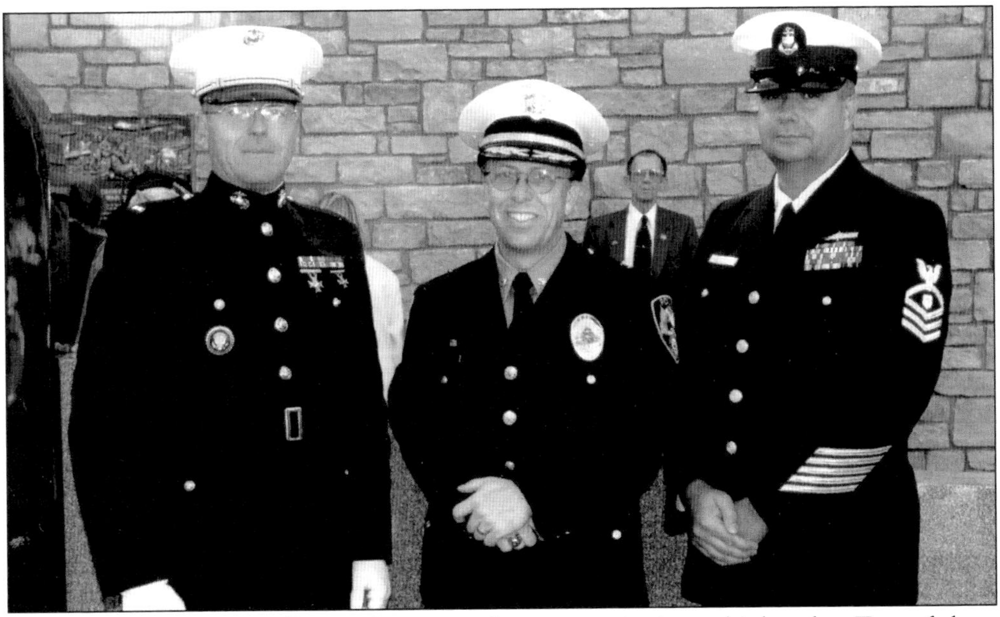

Our Sharonville Police Officers often serve the community in multiple roles. Two of these officers were dressed in their military uniforms for the dedication of Patriot Pointe, November 11, 2001. Pictured, from left to right, are Detective John Wallace, Warrant Officer, Marine Corps; Chief Mike Schappa; and Lt. Alan Hayes, Chief, Coast Guard. Officers Wallace and Hayes recently retired from the Sharonville Police Department after many years of exemplary service to our town.

Five

Our Police Officers

What picture comes to mind when you hear the words "police officer?" They don't stretch their arms out and fly or morph into superfast, high-tech, semi-human crime fighters, but they are heroes just the same. How many of us could handle a job that required teaching children about the dangers of drug use one minute and arresting folks who think they don't have to follow the rules the next? They have to learn to operate firearms but hope they don't have to use that knowledge. They investigate horrible crimes but would prefer to keep them from happening. They are social workers, administrators, highly trained negotiators, authority figures, and inside whatever uniform they wear, they are human beings. Sharonville is fortunate to have some really special people serve as police officers, as far back as 1911, and as recently as today.

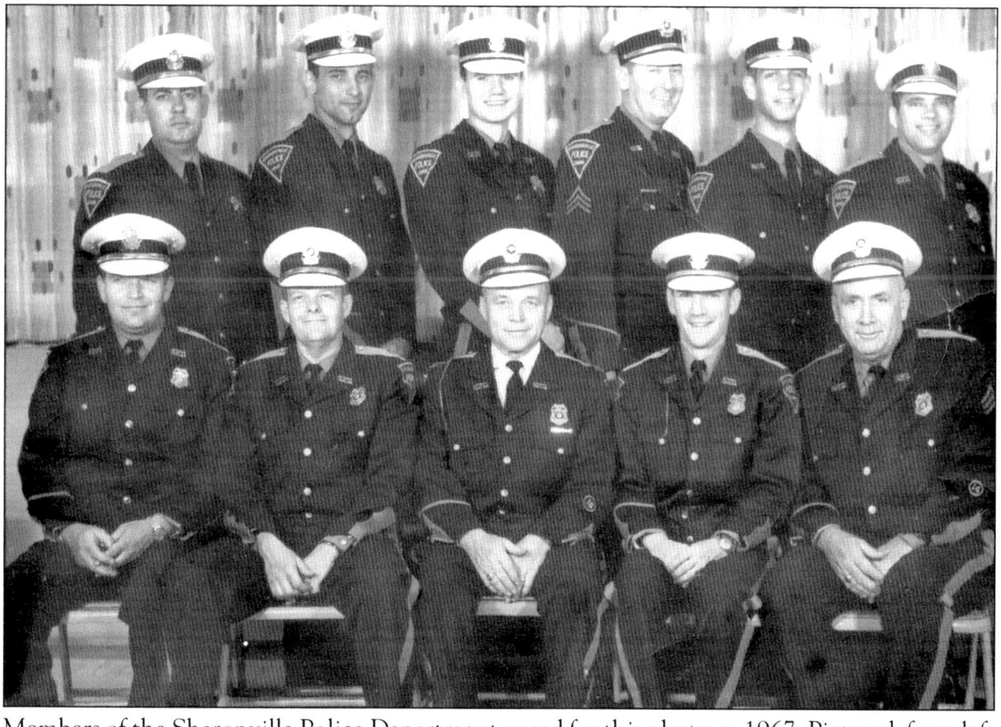

Members of the Sharonville Police Department posed for this photo, c. 1967. Pictured, from left to right, are (seated) Officer Pete Self, Lt. Bill Nuss, Chief Virgil Price, Officer Charlie Bell, and Sgt. Roy Miller; (standing) Officer Jim Holley, Officer Jerry Hehn, Officer Steve Mallon, Sgt. Harold Brockman, Cadet Jim Cramer, and Officer Bill Carlson.

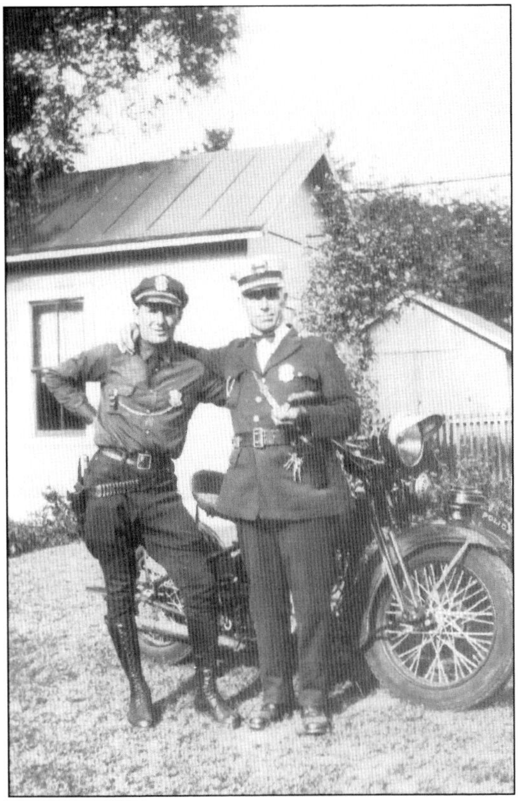

Motorcycle Officer Lloyd "Bud" Lape posed with Marshal Bill Koviak and their Harley-Davidson cycle in Mayor Harry McGrew's back yard off Main Street in November of 1934. Stories indicate that Officer Lape could be a bit of an acrobat while riding the motorcycle through the streets of Sharonville.

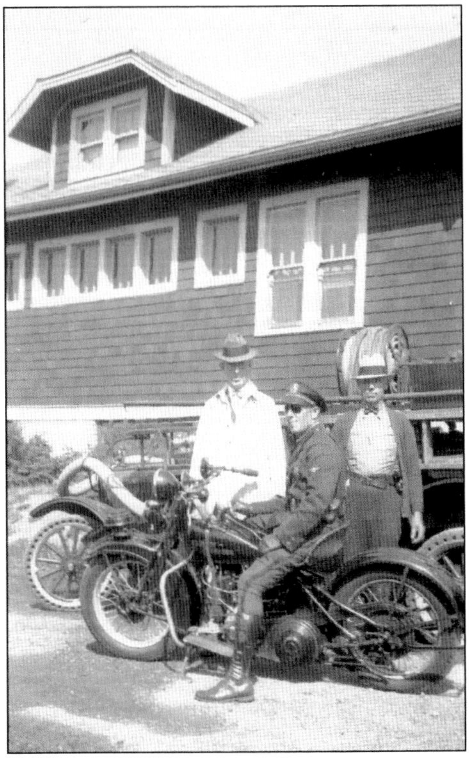

In November, 1934, Sharonville was a small town. Crime wasn't rampant. Long-time residents compare that era to television's "Mayberry." The town marshal handled complaints and the pace of life just wasn't that fast. Pictured, from left to right, are Mayor Harry McGrew, Town Marshal Bill Koviak, and Motorcycle Officer Lloyd "Bud" Lape.

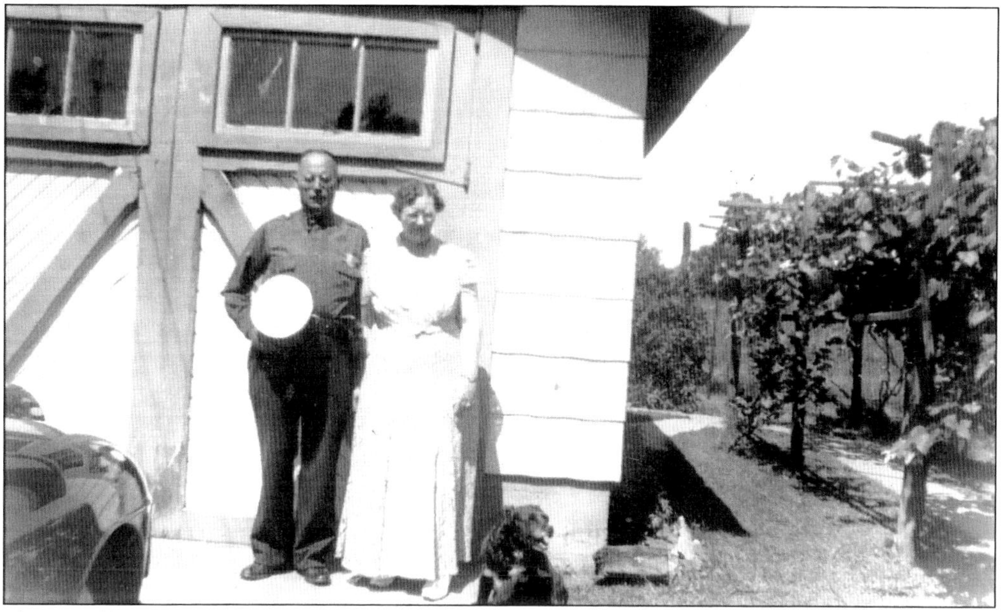

Sharonville Marshal William Koviak and his wife, Marie, posed for this photo near their garage, c. 1930s. Notice the garden arbor to the right of the photo.

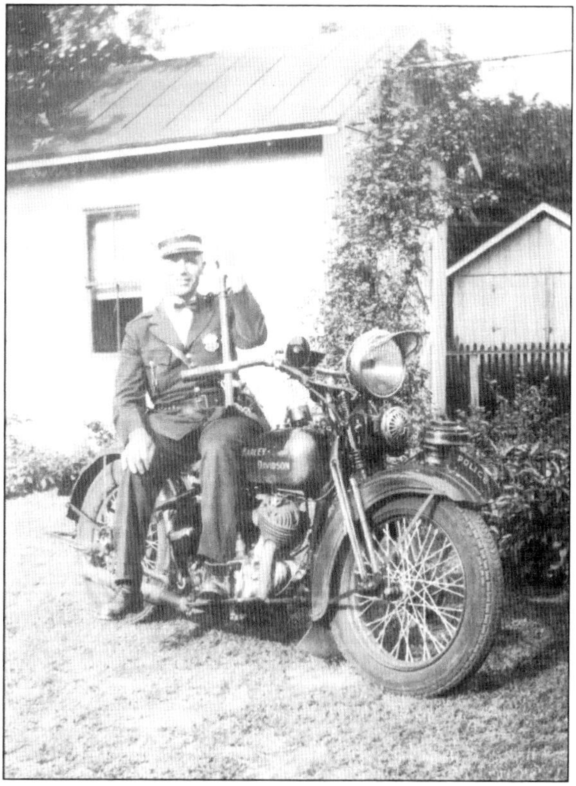

Town Marshal Bill Koviak posed on a Harley-Davidson motorcycle in mayor Harry McGrew's back yard off Main Street in November, 1934.

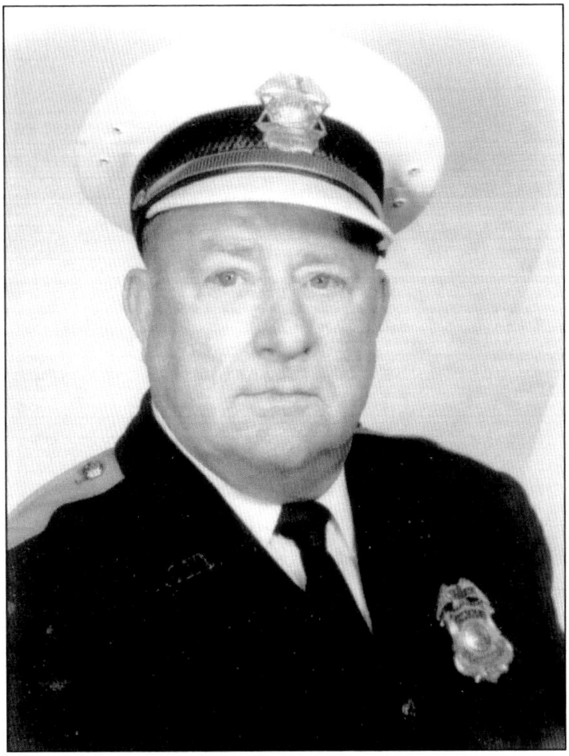

Chief Roy E. "Smitty" Smith worked for the department from 1946 to 1952. He patrolled the streets on foot until mayor Frank Pence decided to lend the village some money to buy a new police cruiser. Smitty was one of the original members of the Sharonville Fire Department. He was an original member of the Sharonville VFW and Village Life Squad. Later, he served as a park ranger in Sharon Woods, and at the time of his death in 1980, he had been employed as a Hamilton County Deputy Sheriff for 18 years.

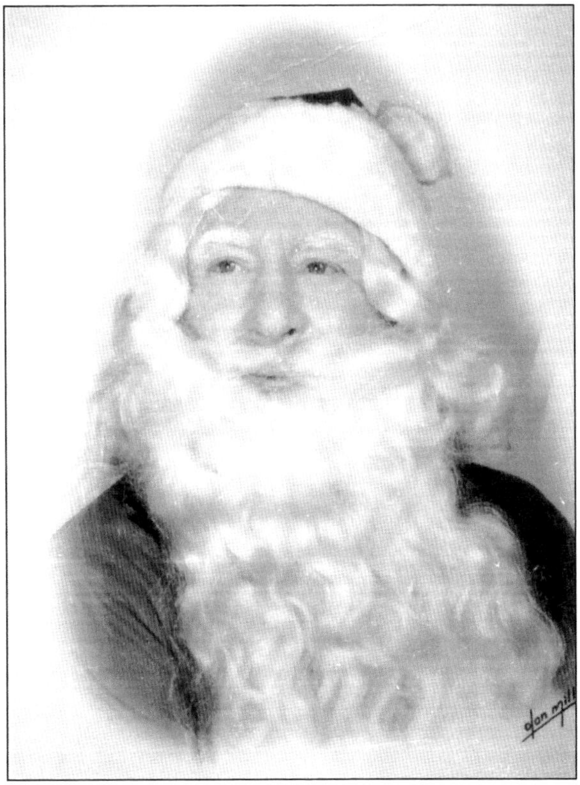

Roy Smith was also Sharonville's "official" Santa Claus for over 30 years, and made toys in his workshop for many of the children he visited. His payment was the happiness he shared with young and old alike as he visited schools, churches, organizations, and even private homes, at Christmas. He truly cared about the town and the people living here, and was inducted into the Society of Honored Sharonville Citizens in 1988.

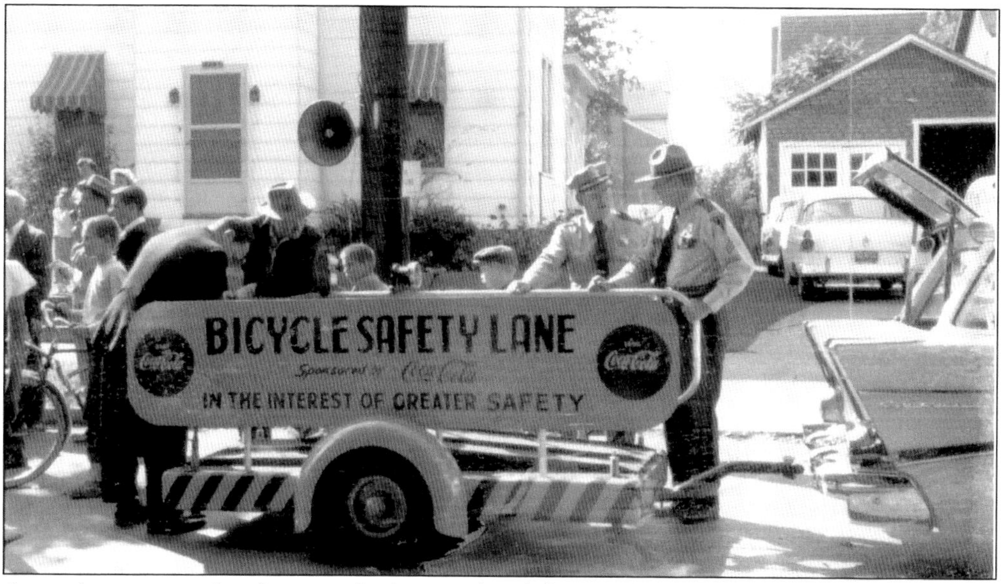

As roads were paved and more vehicles populated them, it became more important to educate the many citizens, young and old, who used bicycles as a form of transportation. In 1958, the Sharonville Police had a Bicycle Safety Lane that also helped riders make sure their bikes were in good working order.

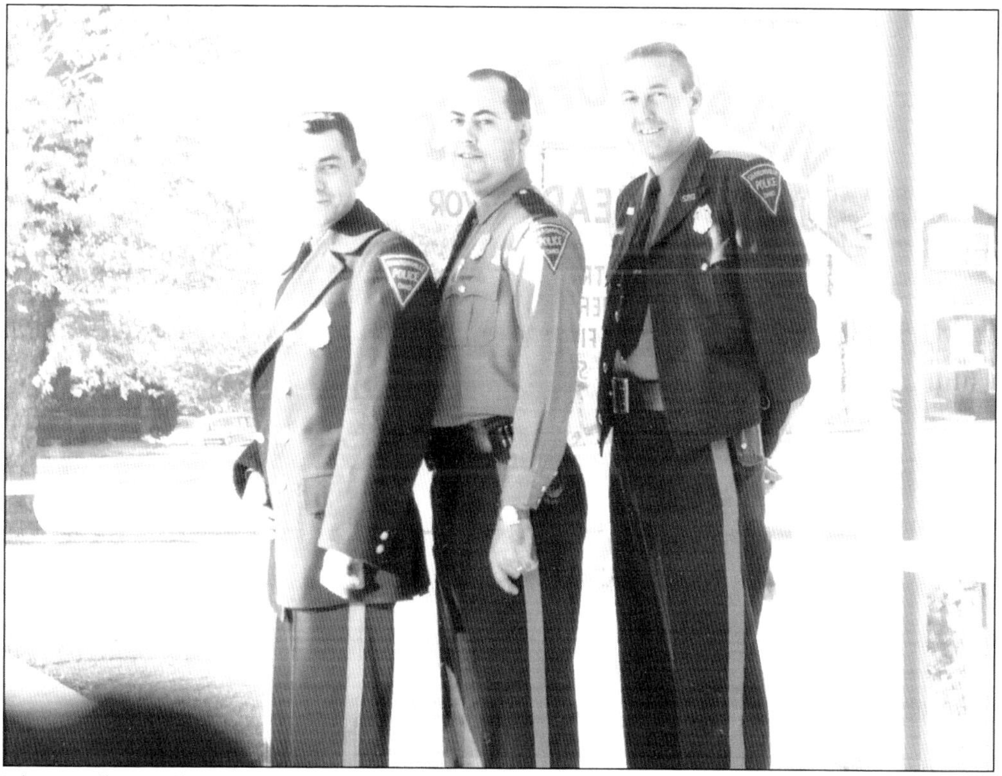
Three village officers posed for this picture at the door to the Village offices, c. late 1950s. Pictured, from left to right, are Officers Charlie Bell, Jim Holley, and Harold "Tip" Brockman.

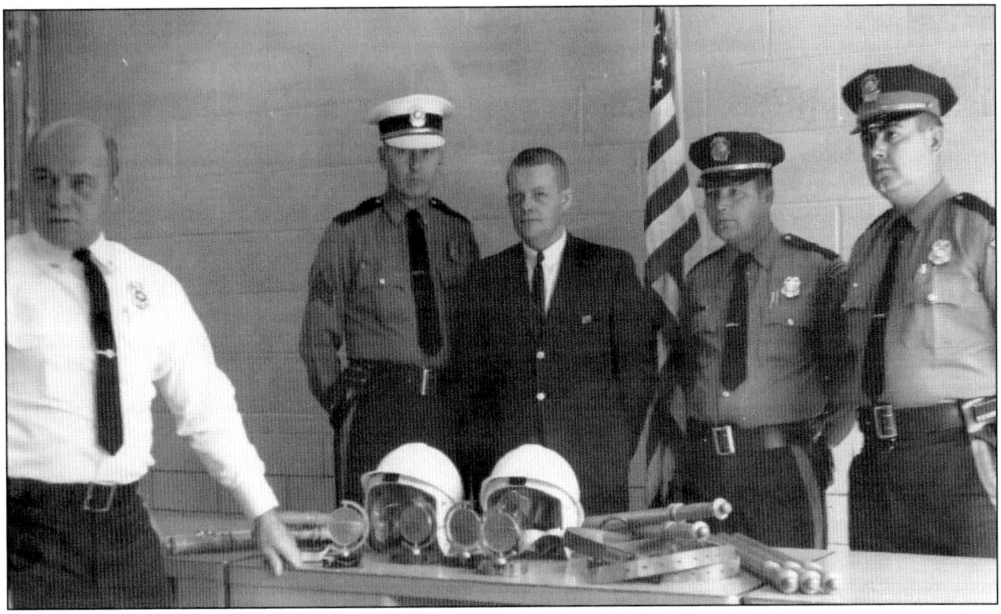

Chief Virgil Price spoke to unknown spectators as four of his men looked on, c. 1960s. They are, from left to right, Chief Virgil Price, Officers Harold Brockman, Bill Nuss, Pete Self, and Jim Holley.

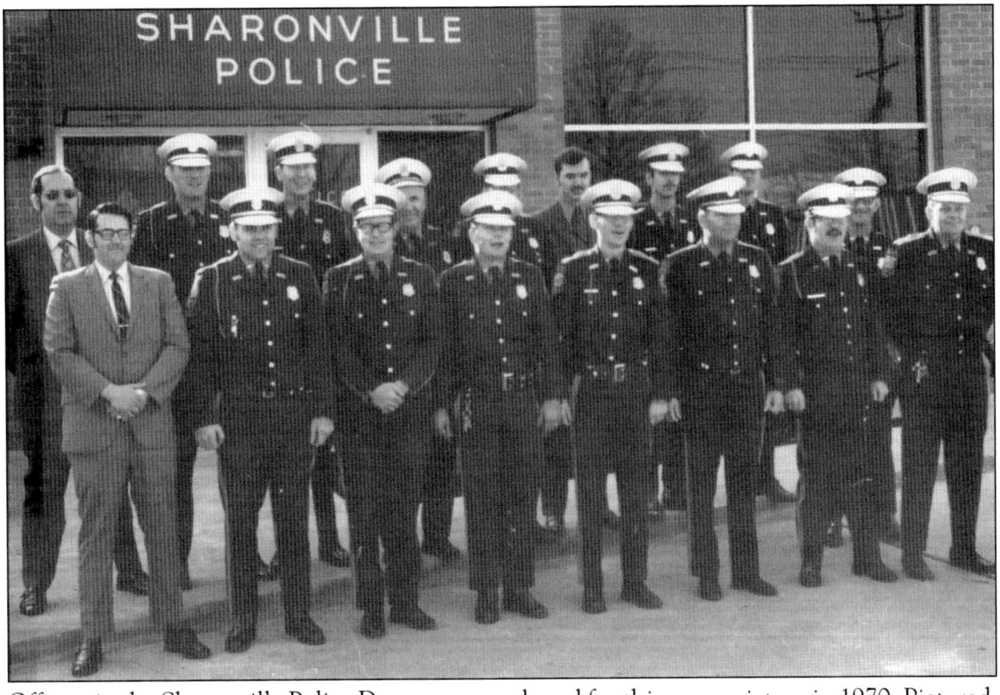

Officers in the Sharonville Police Department gathered for this group picture in 1970. Pictured, from left to right, are (front row) Jerry "Rocky" Reynolds, Robert Merkle, Richard Swick, Skip Rolfes, Charlie Bell, Pete Self, Clarence "Butch" Hodge, and Chief William "Bill" Nuss; (back row) Jim Holley, Earl McCoy, Harold "Tip" Brockman, Roy Miller, Bill Carlson, Steve Mallon, Jim Cramer, Ray Wallin, and Terry Jones.

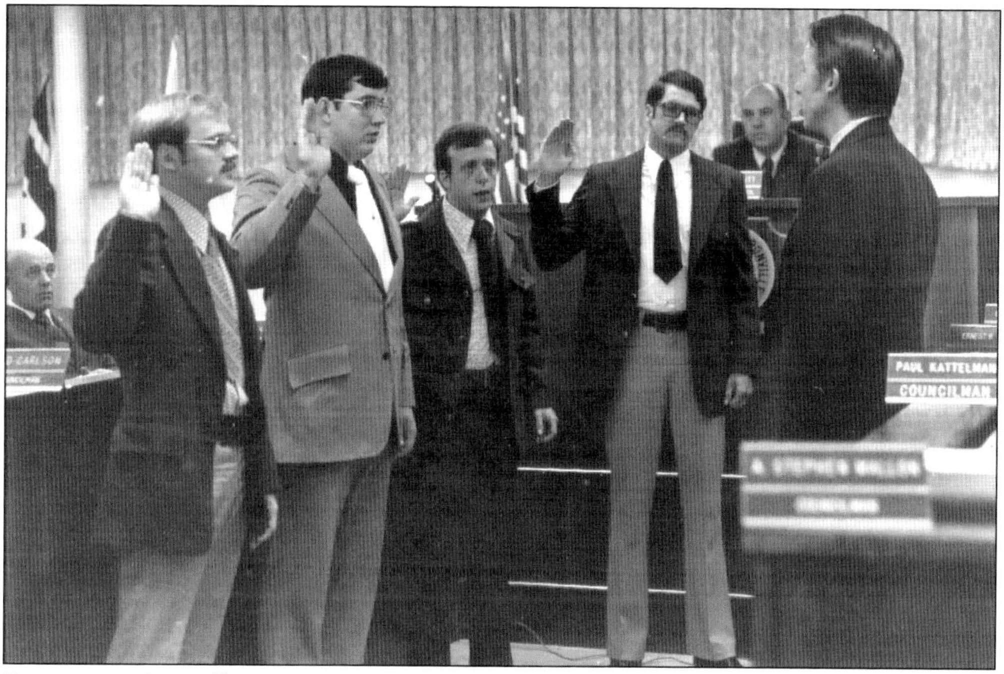

Four new police officers were sworn in during the Sharonville City Council meeting in September, 1973. Pictured, from left to right, are Greg Homer, Rodney Martin, Mike Schappa, Al Ledbetter, and Mayor John Dowlin. Observing the proceedings in the background are councilmen David Carlson (left) and Virgil Lovitt, Sr.

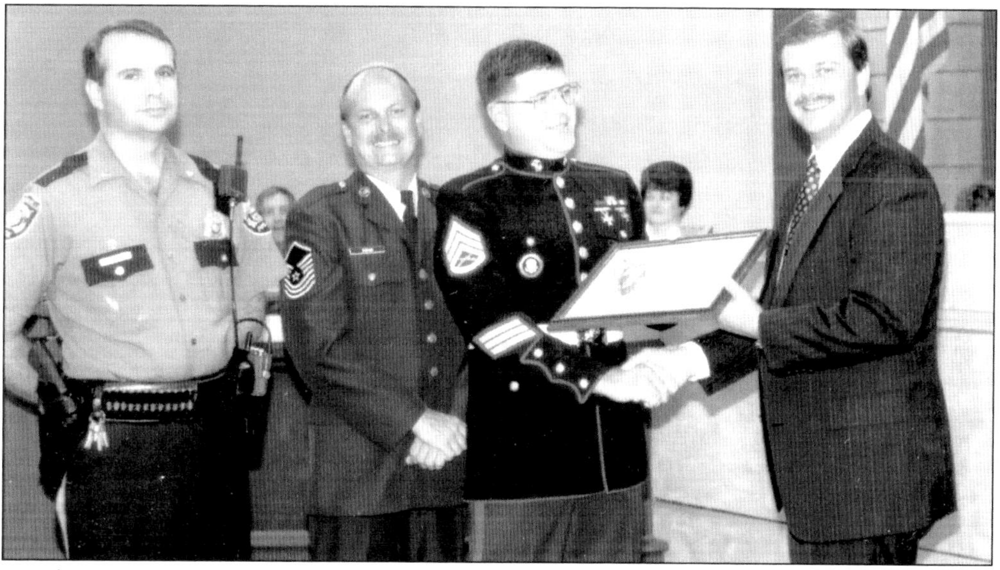

Members of the Sharonville Police Department were called to active military duty during Operation Desert Storm in the early 1990s. At a 1991 City Council meeting, three men were recognized for their service to their country. They are, from left to right, Officer Alan Hayes, Coast Guard; Al Morris, Service Department, Ohio Air National Guard; Officer John Wallace, Marine Corps; along side Mayor Virgil Lovitt, II. Council members in the background are Dewey Angel and Janet Barger.

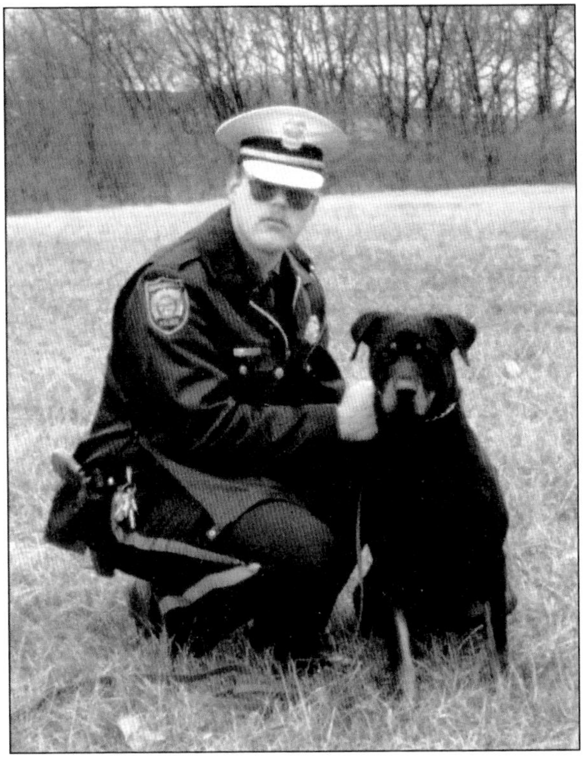

Caesar, a 95-pound black Rottweiller, was the first canine officer to serve the Sharonville police. From 1987 until mid-1993, Caesar went on 600 to 700 runs, mostly false alarms; but according to his "partner" Joe Witzman, "on the ones that weren't false alarms, everybody surrendered." He never had to bite anyone—intimidation was usually enough. In his free time, Caesar liked to play with the Witzman kids, Katie and Kenny, and wrestle with their Boston Terrier.

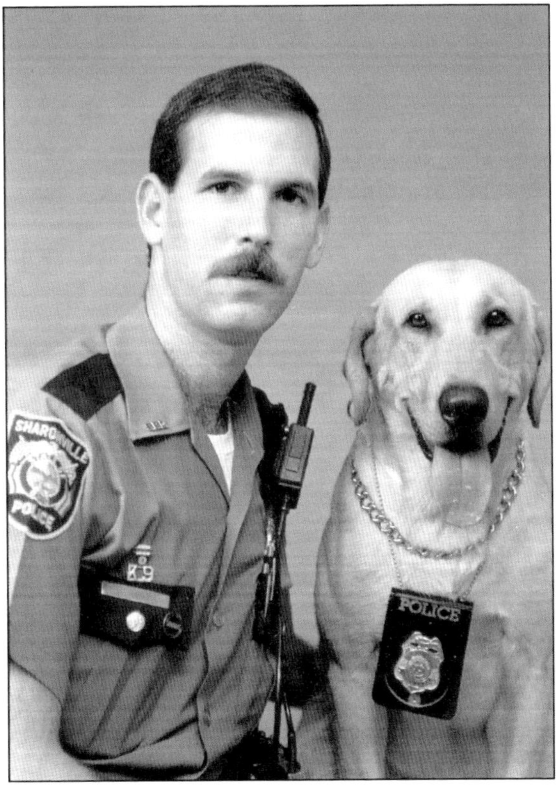

Billy, a Labrador Retriever, joined the Sharonville department in the 1990s. Billy was trained to sniff out drugs and could find them in a matter of minutes. Billy and his human partner, Paul Healey, would usually work third shift in Sharonville and were often on call to assist other departments with drug searches.

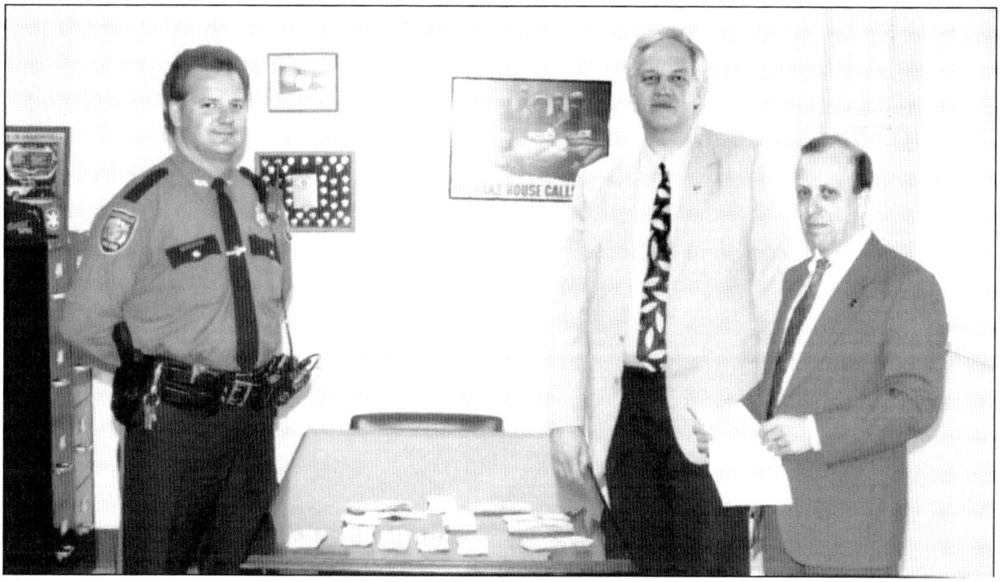

Thousands of dollars in cash and about 14 pounds of marijuana were seized from a Sharonville home from a drug search warrant. This photo was taken after the large drug bust in March, 1993. Pictured, from left to right, are Officer John Cook, Mayor Paul Kattelman, and Chief Mike Schappa.

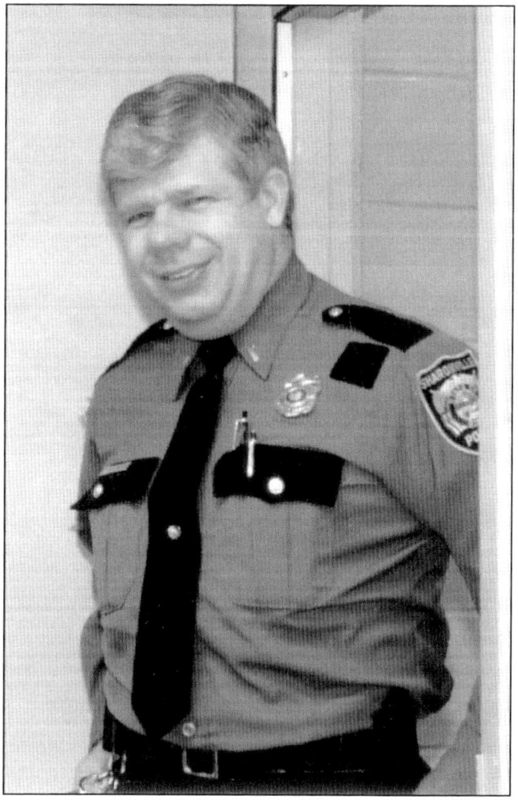

Sharonville Police Lieutenant Ben Dunaway was caught by the camera in the 1990s. The former Community Service Officer also worked for the Hamilton County Park District as a Ranger in Sharon Woods, following his retirement from the Sharonville Department.

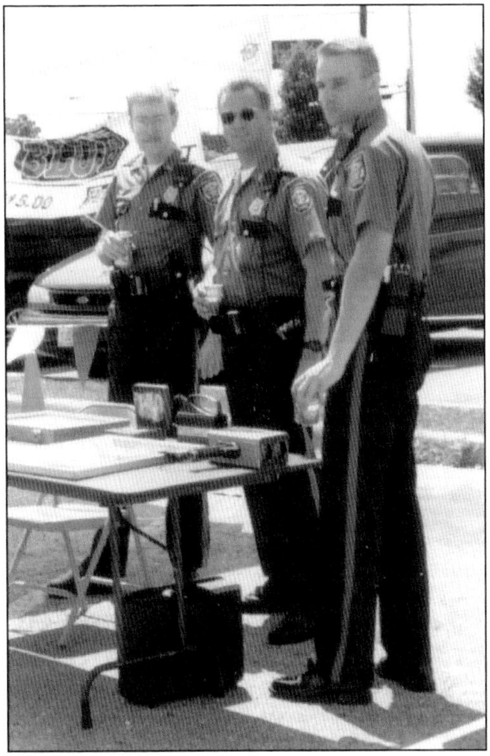

Local FM radio station WKRQ (Q102) sponsored a summertime "Back the Blue" event in Sharonville in 1996. Pictured, from left to right, are Sharonville Police Officers Mark Preuss, John Cook, and Aaron Hayes.

Sharonville Police officers gathered to congratulate Mark Preuss upon his promotion to Sergeant, March 16, 1997. Pictured, from left to right, are Sgt. John Cook, Officer Jim Levo, Sgt. Mark Preuss, Officer Brian Phillips, Lt. Greg Homer, Officer Jill Bechtel, Officer Kendall Trulock, and Clerk/ Dispatcher Amanda Chisman.

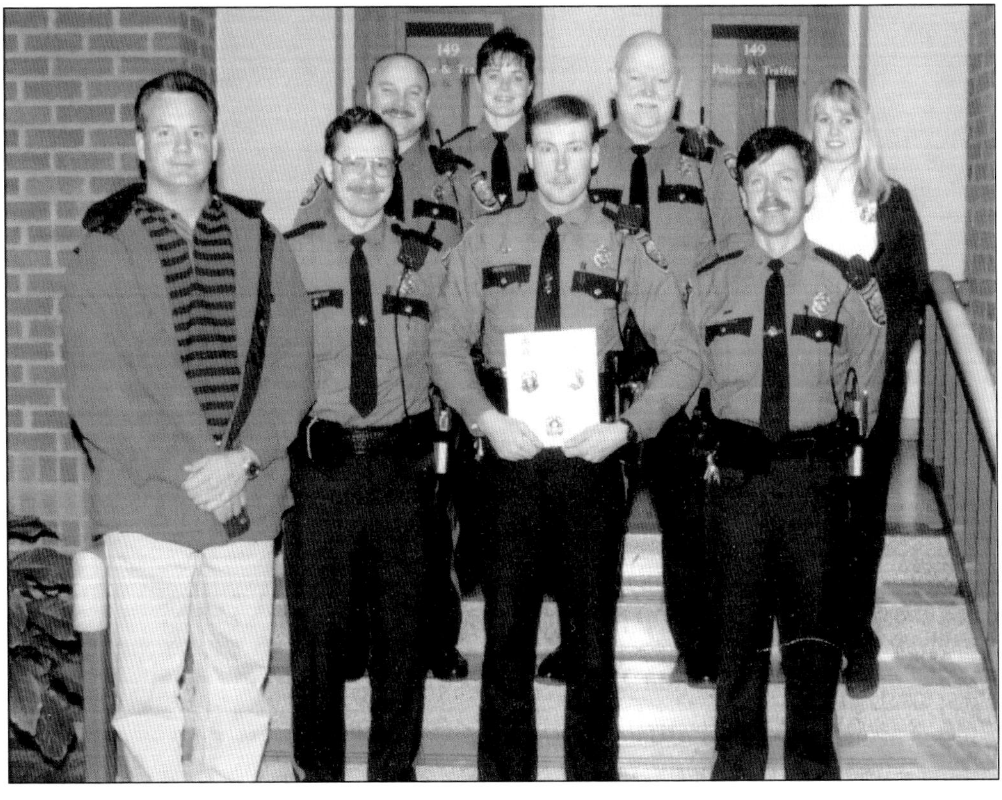

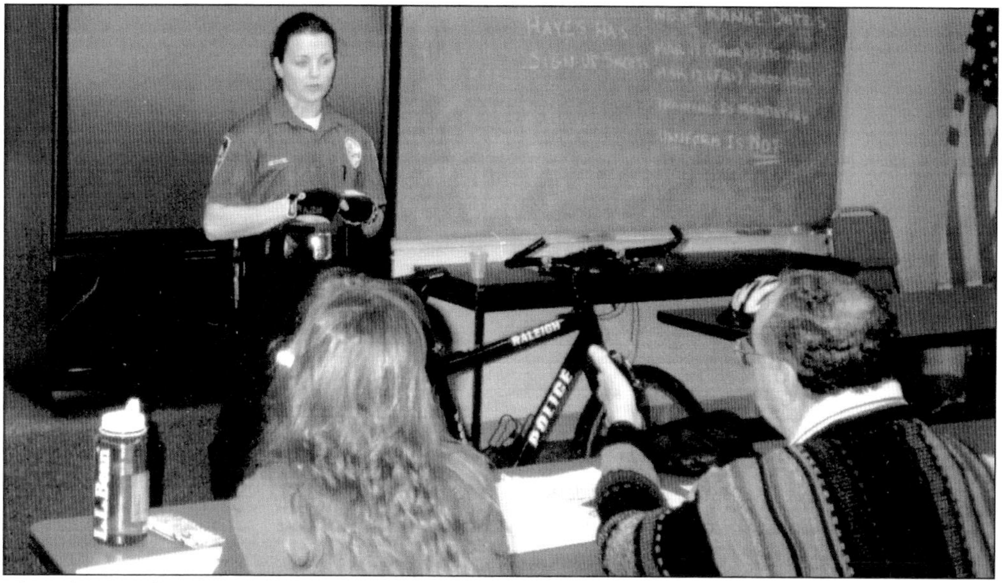

The Sharonville Police Department held its first Citizen Police Academy class in early 1998. During the ten-week course, local citizens were introduced to various components of police work as well as to many officers who serve as "teachers" each week. Officer Jill Bechtel talked to the second Citizen Academy class about her experiences with the police bicycle patrol in March, 1999.

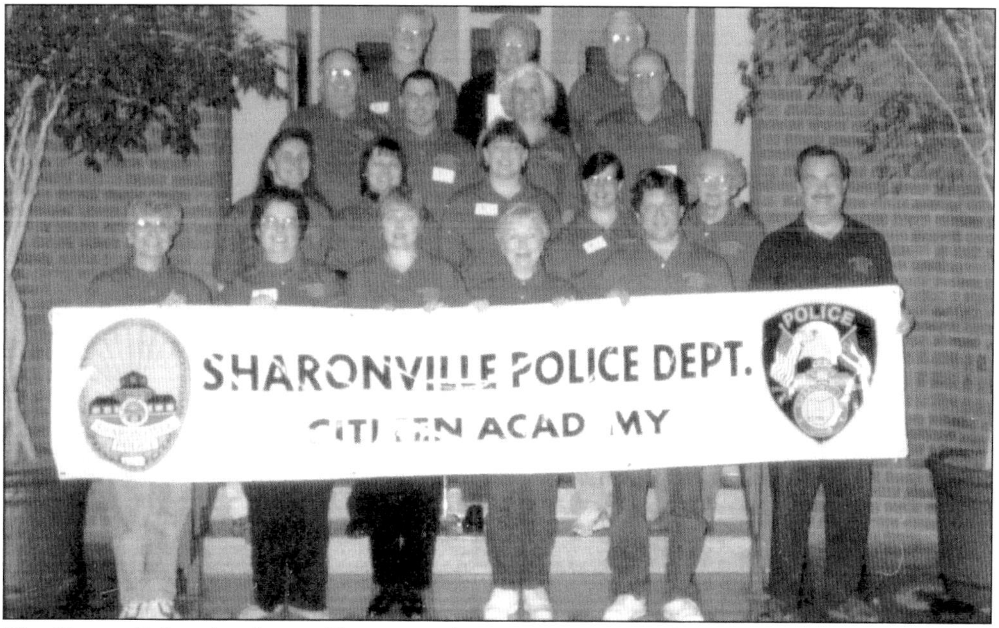

The Citizen Police Academy offers a great learning experience for citizens as well as the police department. Officer Bob Menth coordinated the classes from 1998 to 2000. Pictured in February, 1999, from left to right, are (first row) Irene Johnson, Barb Trulock, Christine Doverspike, Honeylou Bortz, Dan Stein, and Bob Menth; (second row) Maria Eckhoff, Susan Ernst, Pat Maciag (?), Judi Johnson (?), and Dorothy Magella; (third row) Milton Bortz, Rick Johnson, Renmarie Aylward, and Don Johnson; (fourth row) Bill Lewis, Ann Heath, and Bill Preuss.

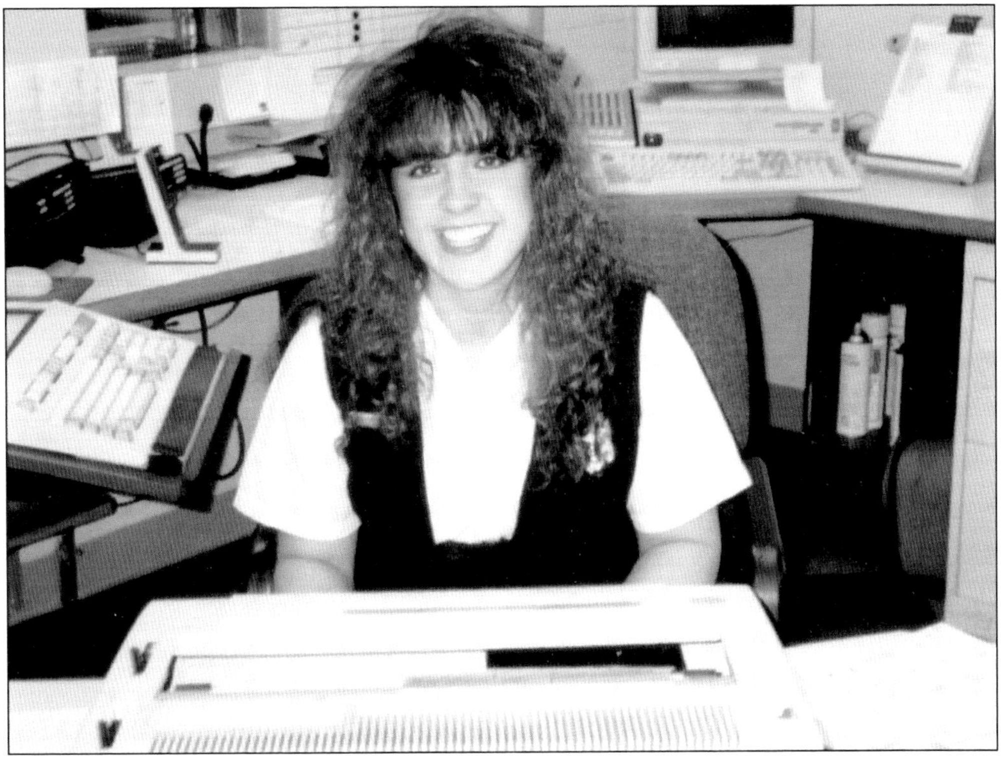

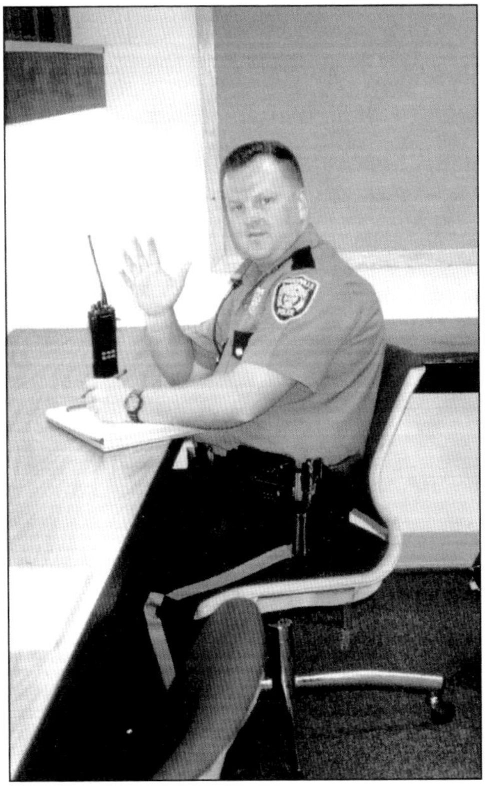

The Sharonville Police Department includes a group of people that often go unrecognized. Among their many duties, Clerk/Dispatchers accept payment of fines, enter warrants, auto accident, and case reports into computers, run computer checks for officers on the beat, dispatch radio runs, and greet visitors to the police department. Pictured is Clerk/Dispatcher Pam Hayes, c. late 1990s.

A police officer's shift requires more than riding around in a vehicle for hours on end. There is also paperwork, and how much paperwork can depend on just how eventful the daily tour of duty is for the officer. Officer Chris Wilson took time to look up from his paperwork long enough to wave and smile for the camera, c. late 1990s.

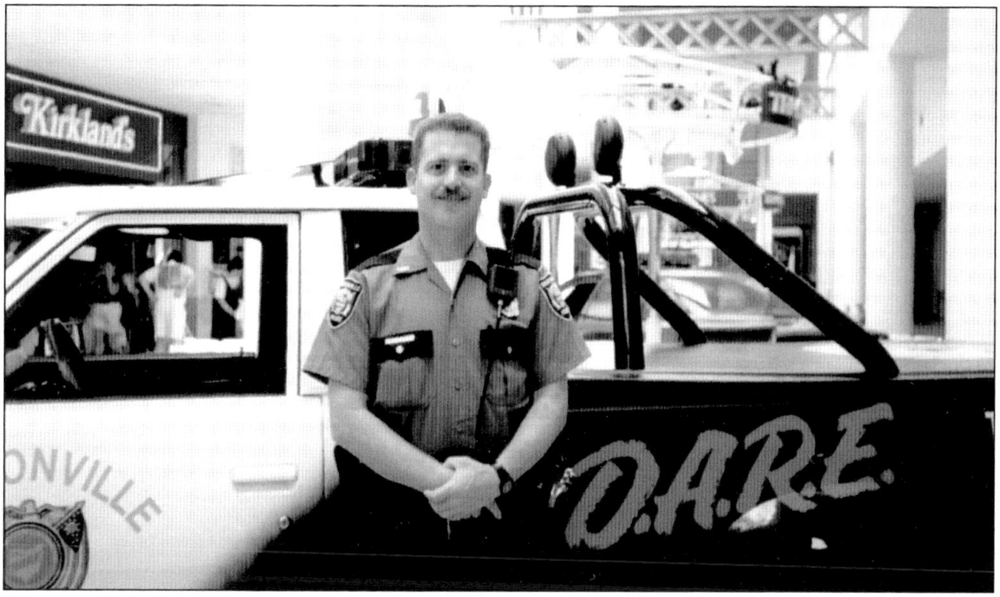

Sharonville Police officers share their time and expertise with the community for many events. Rob Tankersley represented the department at the Tri-County Mall Law Enforcement Expo in the late 1990s. Sharonville officers participate in the Drug Abuse Resistance Education program (D.A.R.E.), which helps elementary school kids learn to say "no" to drugs and resist peer pressure.

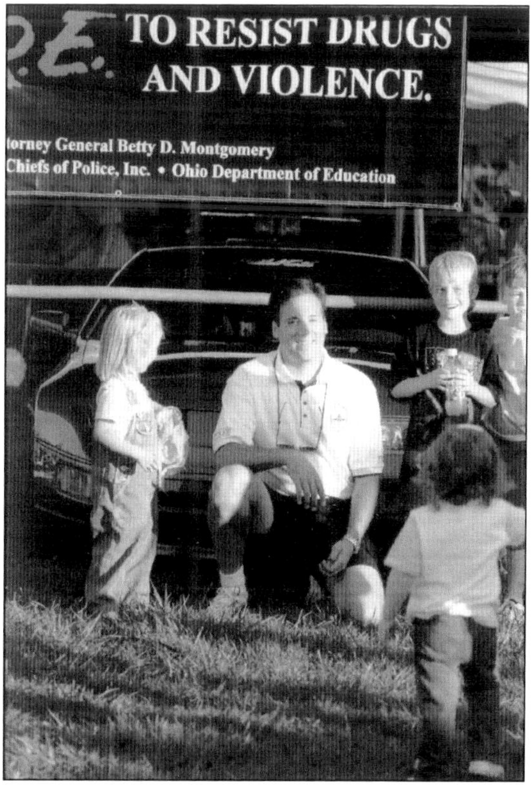

The annual Sharonville Fire Department Festival is yet another example of the people of Sharonville coming together for a common cause. Current and former police officers and firefighters work side-by-side, making it a fun and profitable event. Pictured on July 21, 2000, is police officer Billy Hensley, who participated in the D.A.R.E. program with the Sharonville Schools for many years.

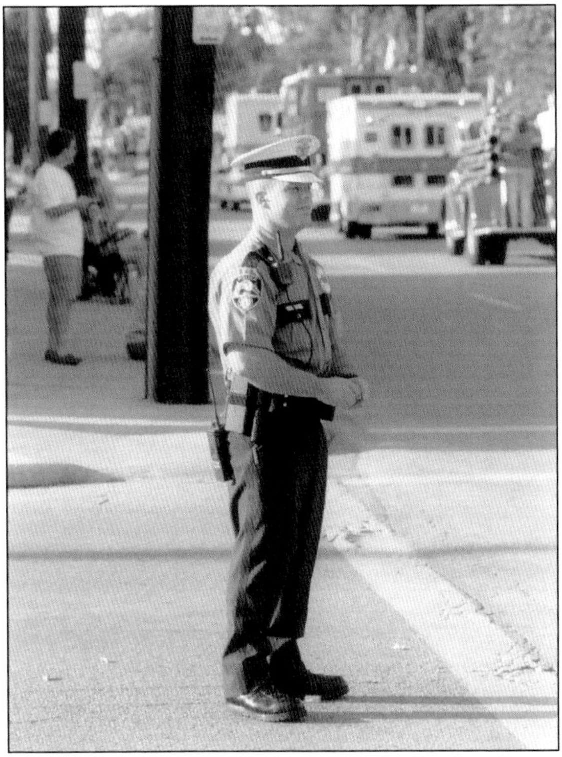

Sharonville police officer Ryan Shaw had a great view of the many trucks in the Fire Department Festival parade as he blocked traffic at Main and Walnut Streets, July 27, 2001. Officer Shaw grew up in Sharonville and graduated from Princeton High School.

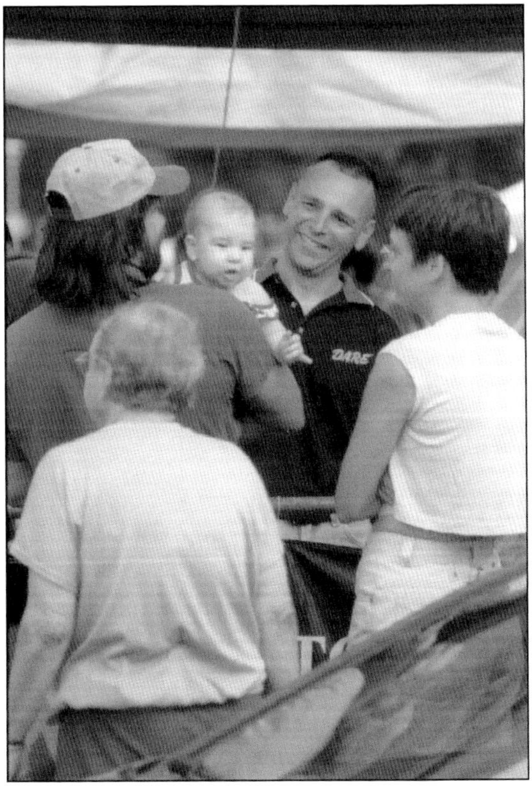

Police Sgt. Bobby Fisher met one of the newer members of the community as he manned the D.A.R.E. booth at the July 27, 2001 Fire Department Festival. Pictured, from left to right, are Doug Schneider, his mother-in-law Mary Haimerl, Robert Schneider (the newest addition to the family), Officer Bobby Fisher, and Susan Schneider.

Six

OUR FIREFIGHTERS

The firefighting profession was given extreme recognition when hundreds of men and women "just doing their jobs" lost their lives trying to save people inside New York's two World Trade Center buildings after the terrorist attack on September 11, 2001. We have no skyscrapers in Sharonville, but that doesn't make the work any less dangerous. Today's firefighters are male and female, and are trained as emergency medical technicians as well as in fighting fires, dealing with hazardous materials, establishing home and business safety, and even rescuing the occasional cat up a tree. For all of its history, Sharonville's firefighters have also been mostly volunteers. Thanks to a small increase in the city income tax, Sharonville is working to achieve a full-time, fully-trained paid department within the next couple of years.

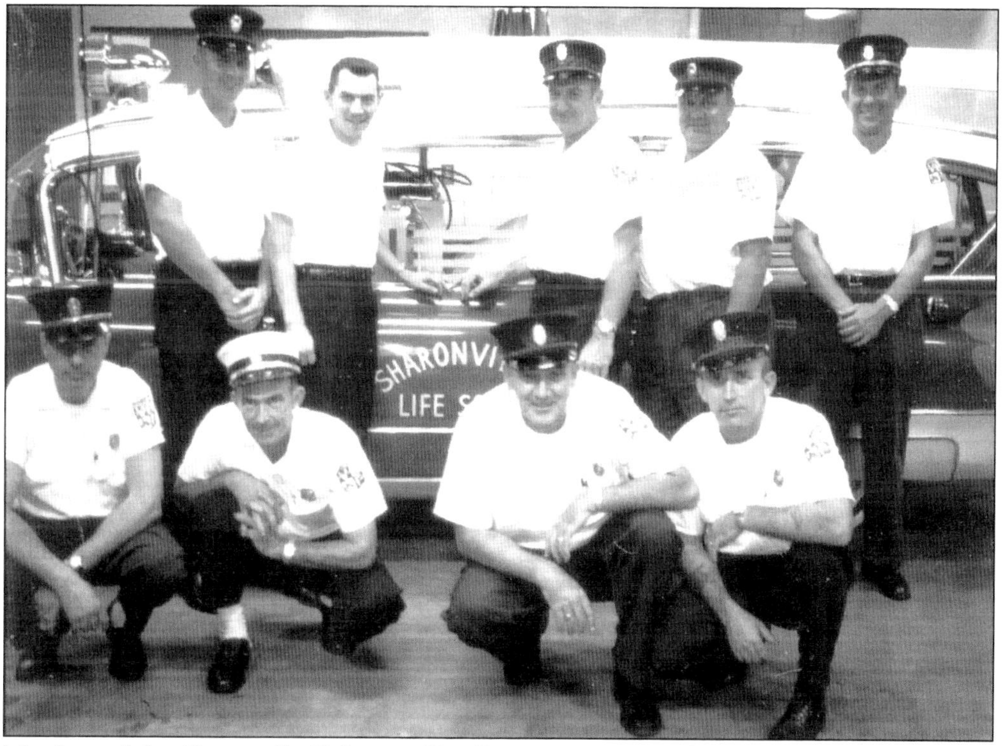

Members of the Sharonville Volunteer Fire Department stopped to share their smiles, c. late 1960s. Pictured, from left to right, are (front row) Doug Mullins, Chief Robert "Bob" Yeager, Frank Gorman, and Harold Beasley (?); (back row) Ken Eickenhorst, Charlie Bell, Jim Morrison, Mike Suher, and Walt Duermit.

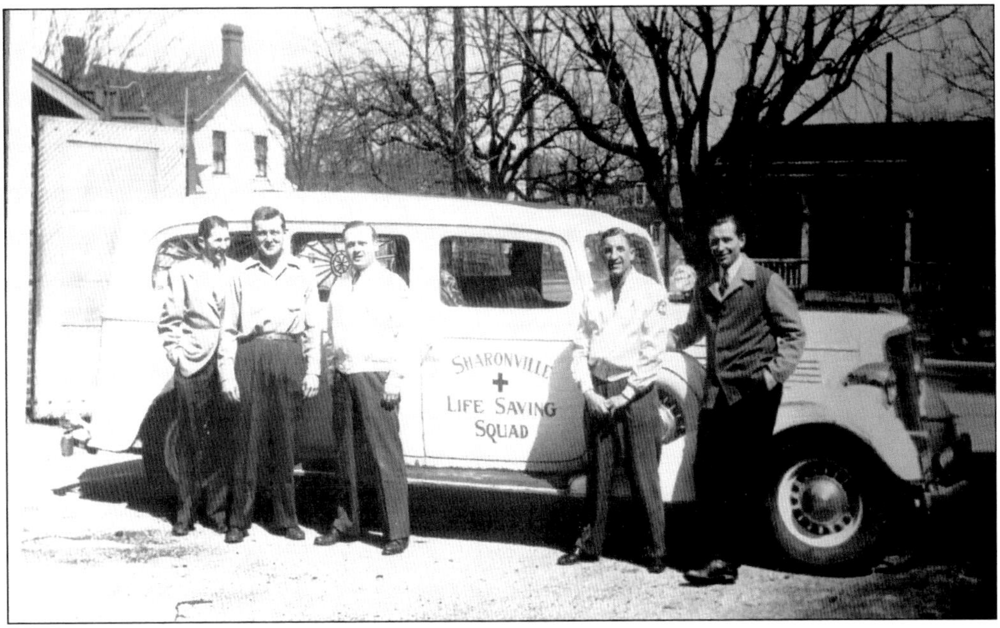

Members of the Sharonville Life Saving Squad posed with their emergency vehicle, c.1940s. Pictured, from left to right, are Porter Painter, Charles Haverty, Bub Mehaffie, Fritz Grau, and Albin Honerlaw.

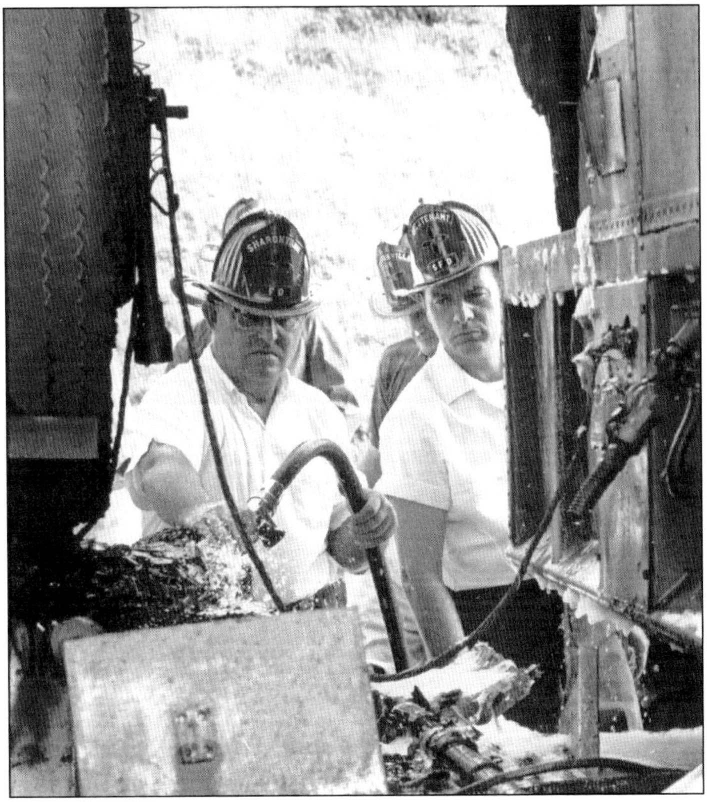

On Saturday, July 27, 1968, a parked tractor-trailer went up in flames near the intersection of Interstate 275 and Route 42. The trailer was full of military rockets and explosives. Not only was traffic in the area stopped, but people were evacuated from everywhere within three miles. In less than an hour, the Volunteer Firefighters of Sharonville had a potentially deadly situation under control. Pictured are Firefighters Jack Fogel (left) and Doug Mullins.

Sharonville firefighters literally had their hands full with this emergency. Pictured are volunteer firefighters Charlie Sanders (left) and Dale Duermit carefully unloading cases of rockets from the damaged semi-truck. The man wearing number 3 on his helmet with his back to the photo could not be positively identified.

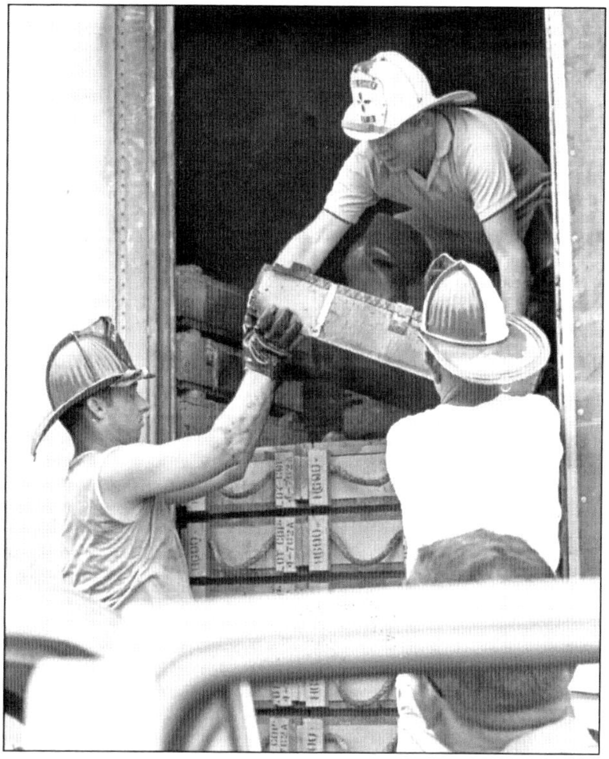

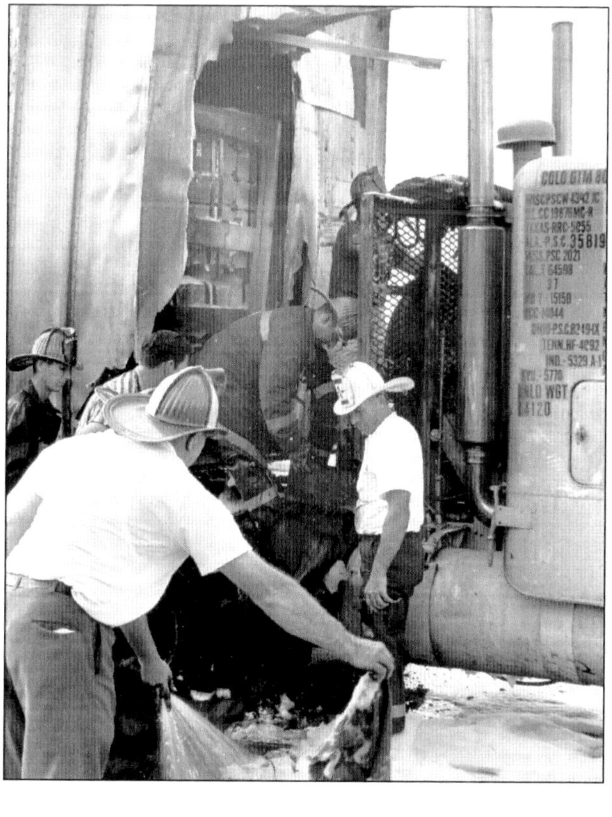

With the tractor-trailer looking like it had been opened with a giant can opener, the Sharonville firefighters flushed the foam that was used to fight the fire. Pictured here, from left to right, are Lee Brown (?), Unidentified, Don Murphy (#25), Unidentified, and Chief Robert "Bob" Yeager.

PROGRESS Taft PUBLIC TRUST

A WKRC EDITORIAL

TAFT BROADCASTING COMPANY

1906 HIGHLAND AVENUE, CINCINNATI, OHIO 45219 • 421-1750

Tuesday - August 6, 1968

SHARONVILLE EMERGENCY

Saturday, July 27th, in Sharonville was a normal one in most respects, until late in the afternoon when all kinds of activity broke loose in the area of Interstate 275 and Route 42.

A tractor-trailer was parked, in flames, near this busy intersection, loaded with military rockets and explosives. Sharonville firemen, who arrived quickly on the scene, sized up the situation and, with professional dispatch, ordered all traffic stopped and the area evacuated.

Then, under the guidance of Sharonville Fire Chief, Robert Yeager, the firemen moved into the deadly inferno to put out a potential sitting bomb. In just over an hour's time, the state of emergency was lifted.

The quick action of the Sharonville Volunteer Firemen not only saved the day, but was also responsible for saving many lives.

We're relating this incident to you because we think that perhaps we have a tendency to take this kind of dedication for granted. We're fortunate to have men like the Sharonville Volunteers who do NOT take our safety for granted.

Local television and radio station WKRC (Channel 12 and AM 550) broadcast this editorial after the Sharonville Volunteer Fire Department safely extinguished a potentially deadly truck fire in 1968.

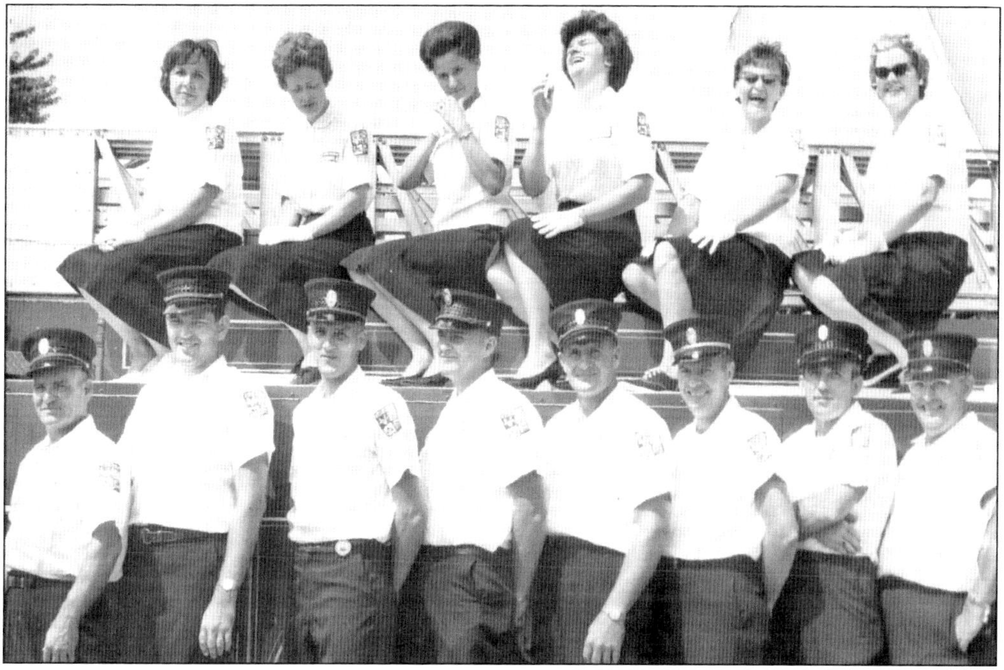

Members of the Sharonville Volunteer Fire Department and Auxiliary gathered for a group photo, c. mid 1960s. Pictured, from left to right, are (front row) Bill Gosney, Bob Davidson, Ken Eickenhorst, Richard Perkins, Brandon Roseth, Doug Mullins, Harold Beasley, and John Fogle; (back row) Irene Beasley, Ruth Baysore, Gerri Beatty, Mary Howard, Janet "Tex" Eickenhorst, and Ruth Gorman.

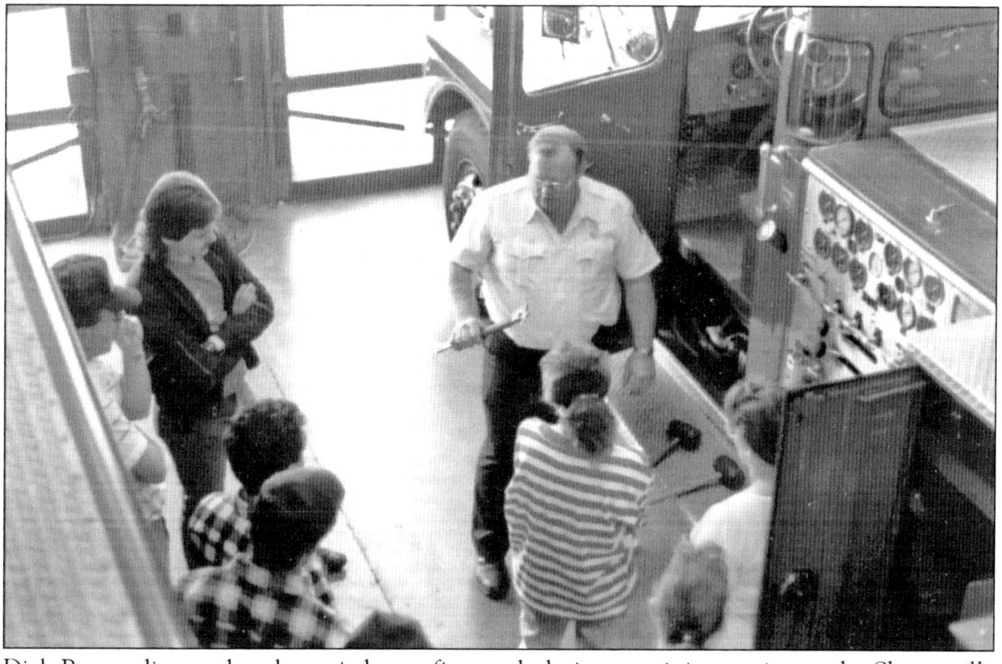

Dick Beatty discussed tools carried on a fire truck during a training session at the Sharonville Fire Department, c. 1984.

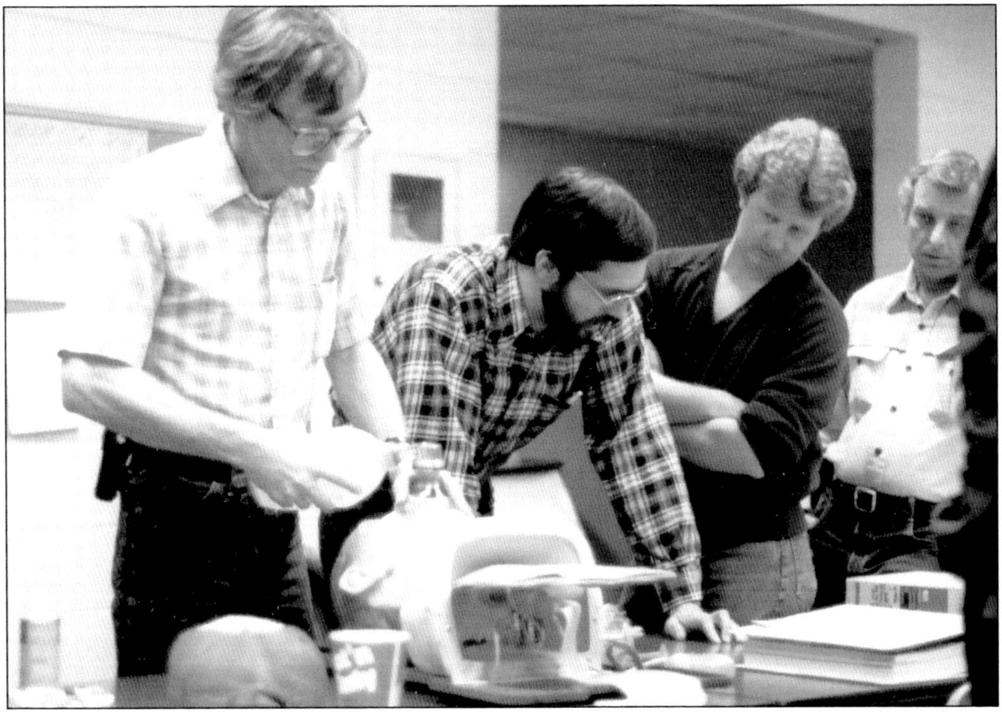

Sharonville Volunteer Fire Department members participated in resuscitation training in April, 1984. They are, from left to right: Rick Wickemyer, Paul Asbrock, John Mackey, and Charlie Sanders.

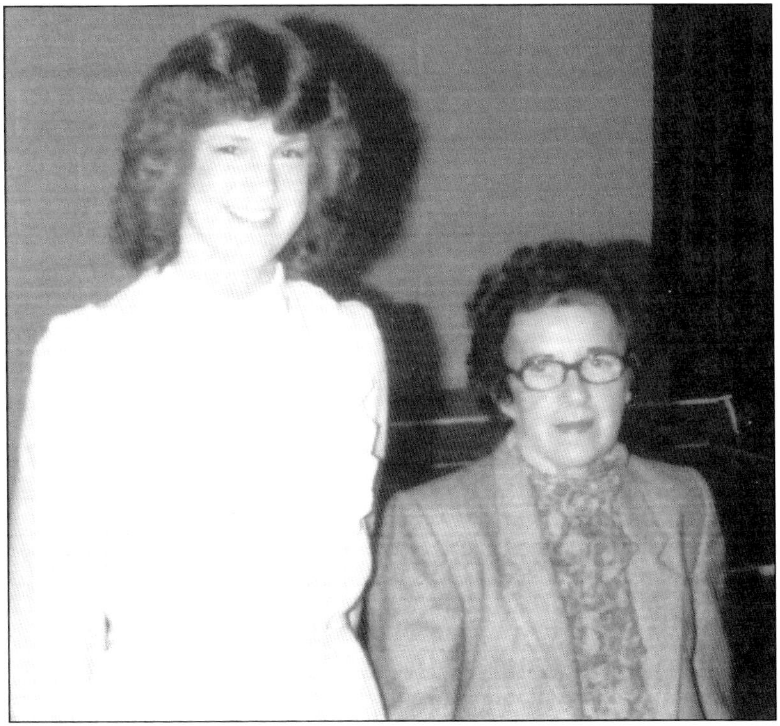

In 1984, Natalie Merz, a Sharonville resident, was awarded the first scholarship given by the Sharonville Fire Department in memory of Chief Robert "Bob" Yeager. Natalie went on to become a Clinical Nurse Manager at Children's Hospital. Pictured are Natalie Merz (left) and Jane Yeager, wife of Bob Yeager.

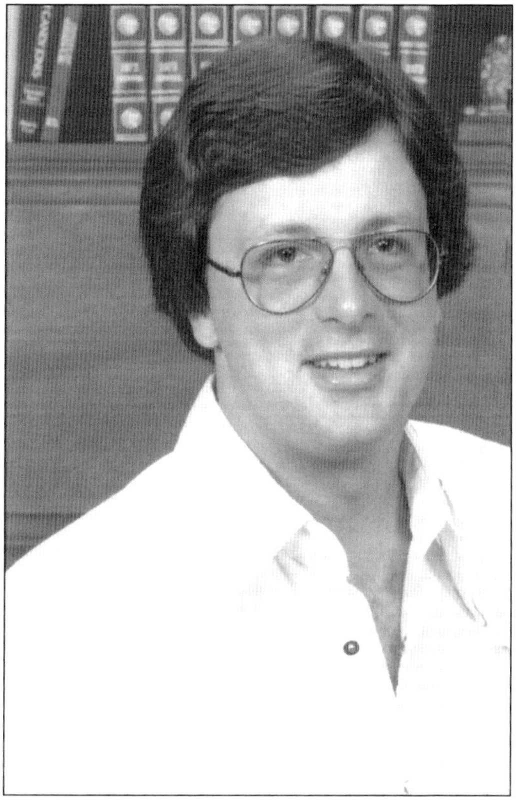

Sharonville firefighters' fundraising activities merit admiration today, just as they did in 1984. When Lt. Mark D. Hauenstein, then aged 29, required a heart transplant, firefighters got together on his behalf and held numerous fundraising events. The support of the people and businesses of Sharonville and neighboring communities helped raise more than $95,000 for living expenses in Houston, Texas, where the operation was performed, and medical expenses upon returning home. At that crucial time, Mark's insurance coverage had expired. The people of Sharonville gave him a second chance. Mark lived the life he loved, working for the Fire Department for five and a half years until his death on February 10, 1989.

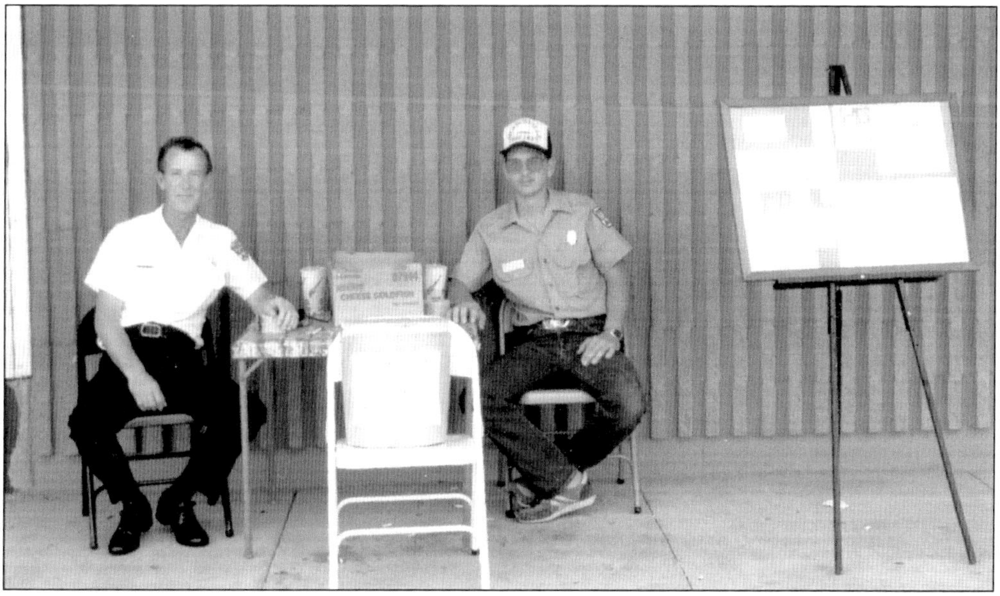

Members of the Sharonville Volunteer Fire Department found out how many friends they had as they held fundraisers to benefit Mark Hauenstein. Pictured are Lee Brown (left) and Gordon Henderer.

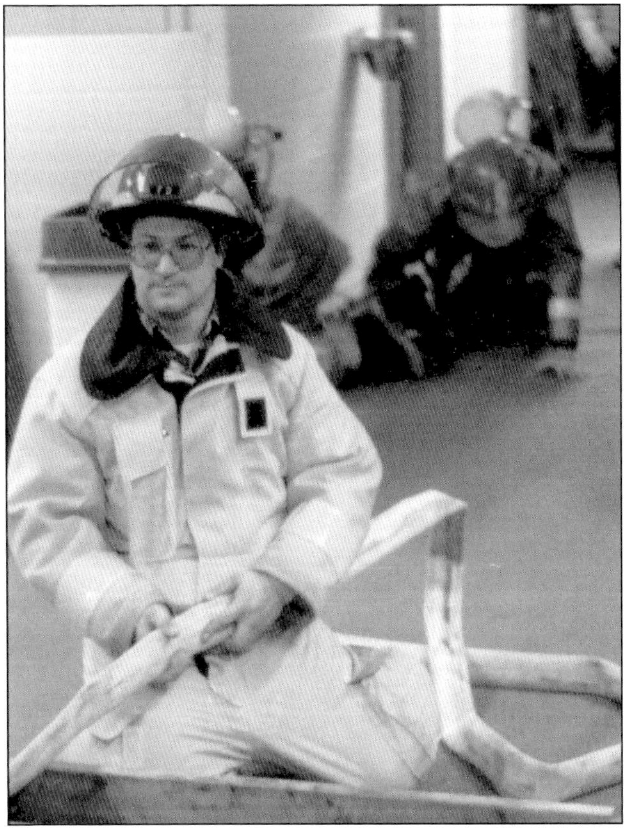

Joe Cherolis participated in hose training in November of 1985 at the Sharonville Fire Department.

John Mackey and Barry Conover conferred during a training session, c. 1990s.

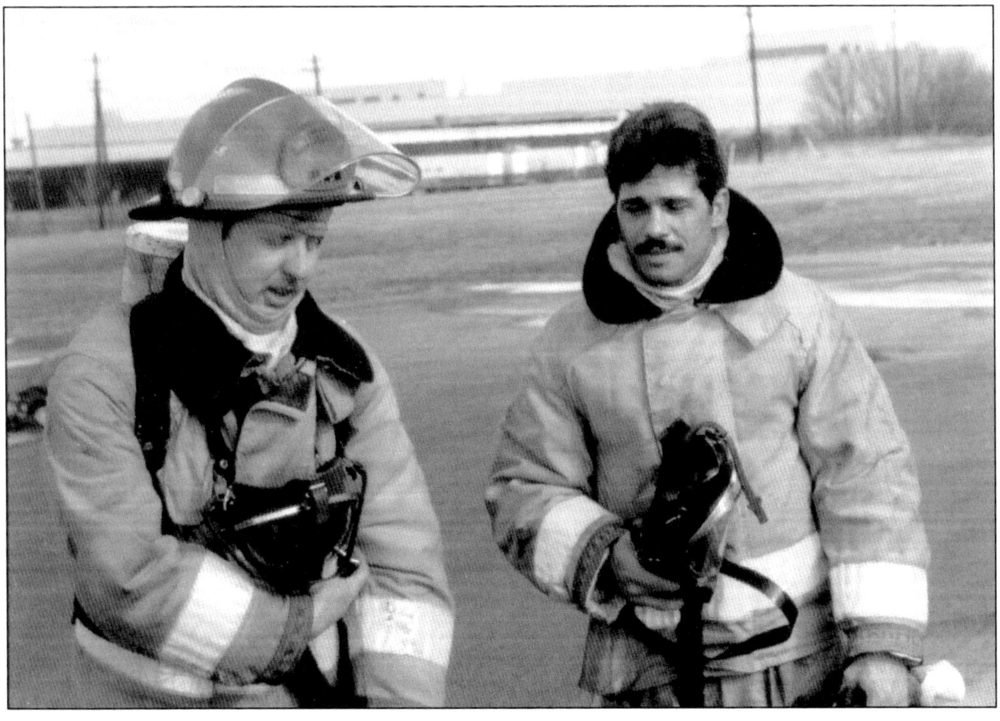

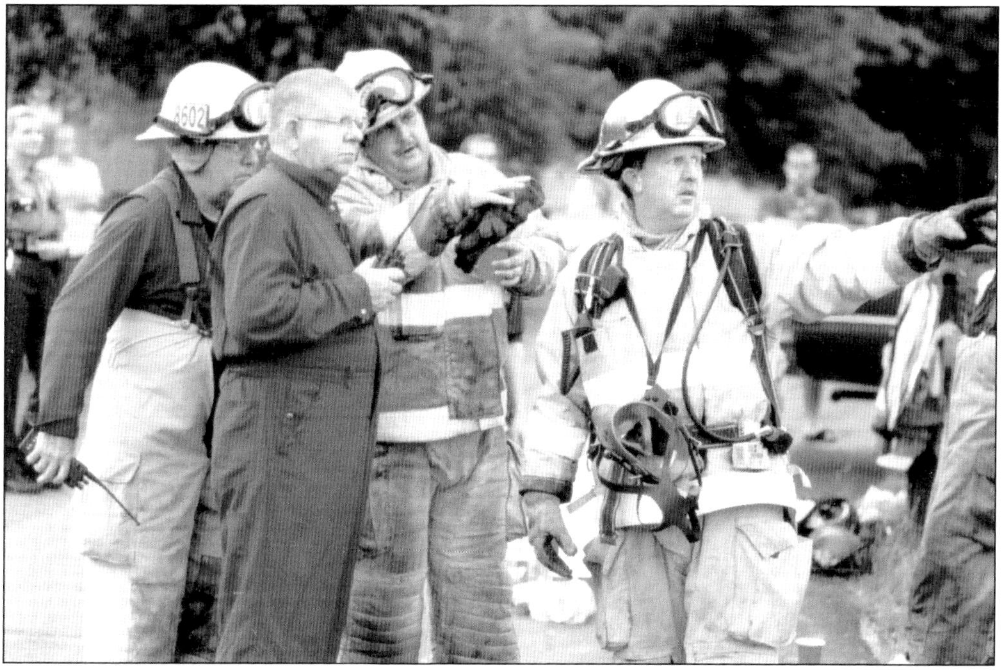

Sharonville Firefighters analyzed a situation during a training exercise, c. 1990s. Pictured, from left to right, are Assistant Chief Walt Hoppe, Chief Dale Duermit, Lt. Bernie Mackey, and Assistant Chief John Mackey.

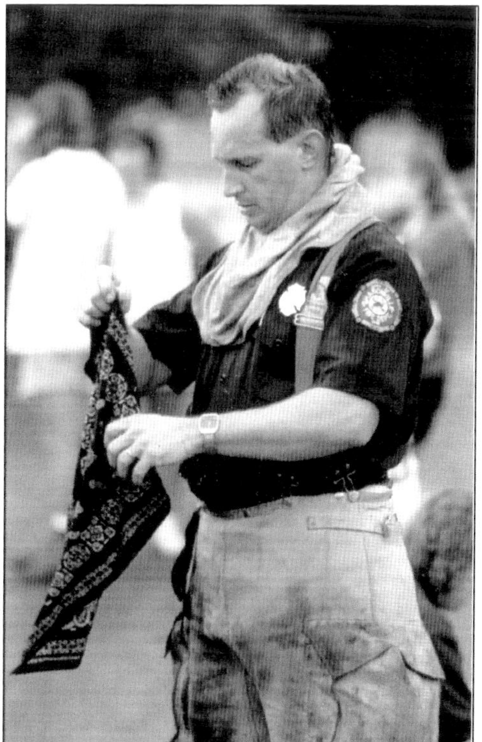

Firefighter Greg Klein took a breather after a training exercise with the Sharonville Volunteer Fire Department, c. 1990s.

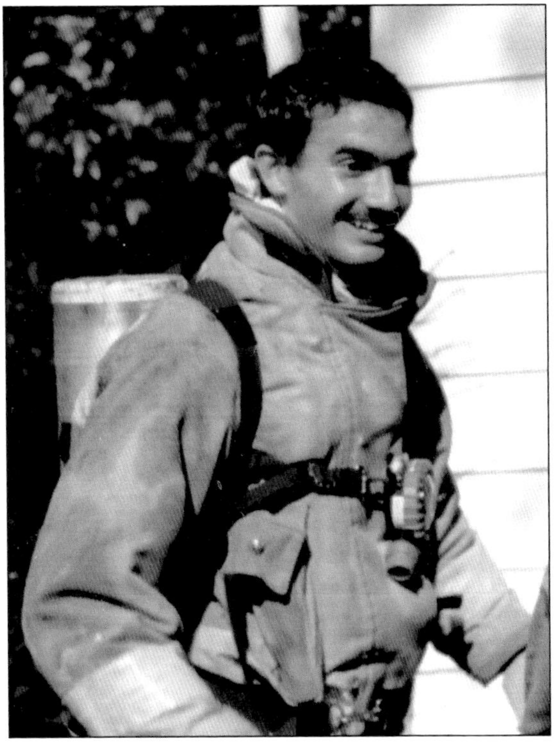

Frank Asbrock flashes a smile during a training session, c. 1990s.

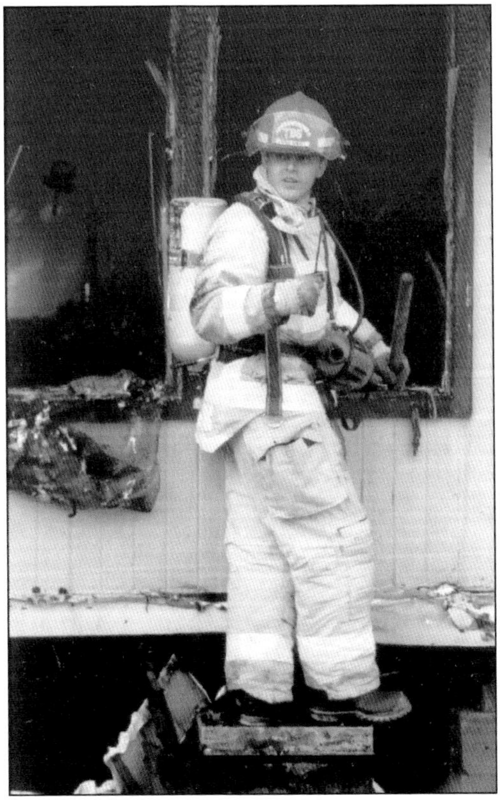

Firefighter Craig Robinson paused during a training exercise with the Sharonville Volunteer Fire Department, c. 1990s.

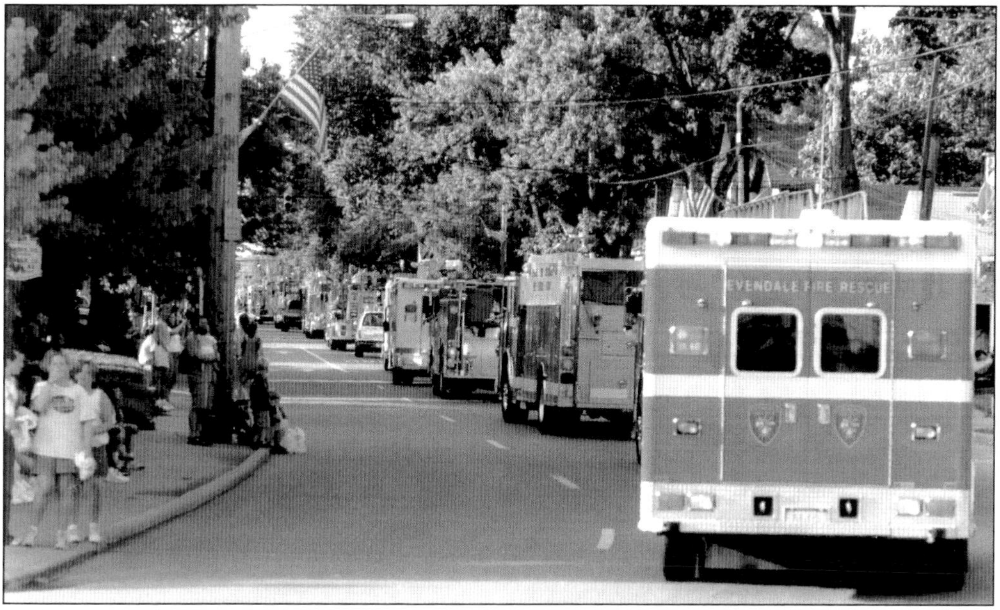

Each year the Sharonville Fire Department Club sponsors a festival to help raise funds for new equipment. The three-day festival begins the last weekend in July with the largest, loudest parade of fire trucks that a kid ever could imagine. Representatives from fire departments, the Cincinnati Fire Museum, and collectors drive their vehicles over the one-mile parade route to the festival grounds at Gower Park. Pictured are fire trucks and emergency vehicles heading north on Main Street.

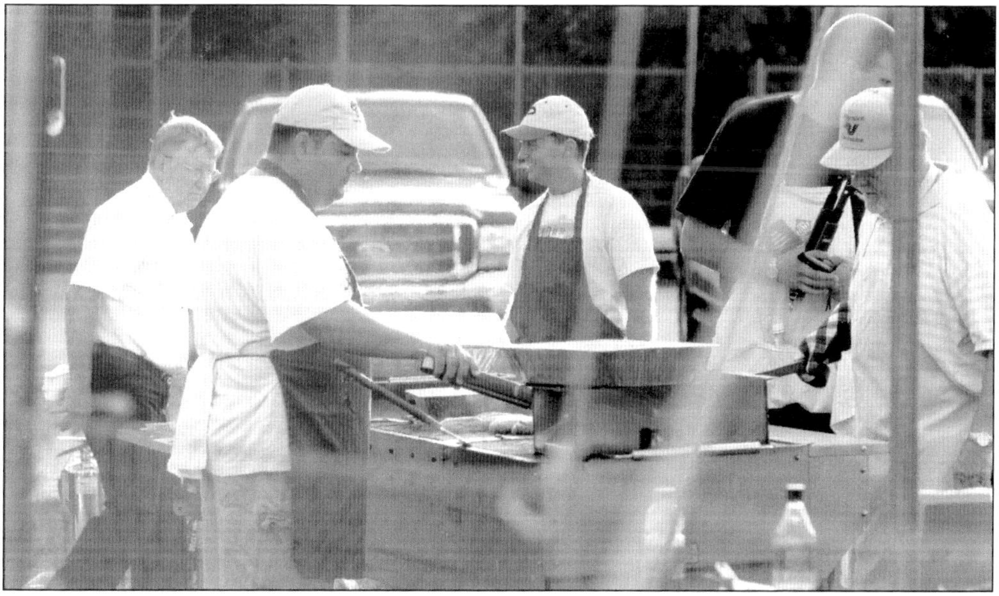

It's always a hot time by the festival grill. Members of the Sharonville Police and Fire Departments spend three sultry July afternoons and evenings serving up brats, metts, burgers, hot dogs, and corn on the cob with plenty of smiles. Pictured from left to right, on July 21, 2000, are: Assistant Fire Chief Walt Hoppe, firefighters Ed Gault, John Eichelbacher, Dan Sunderman, and former Police Chief Bill Nuss.

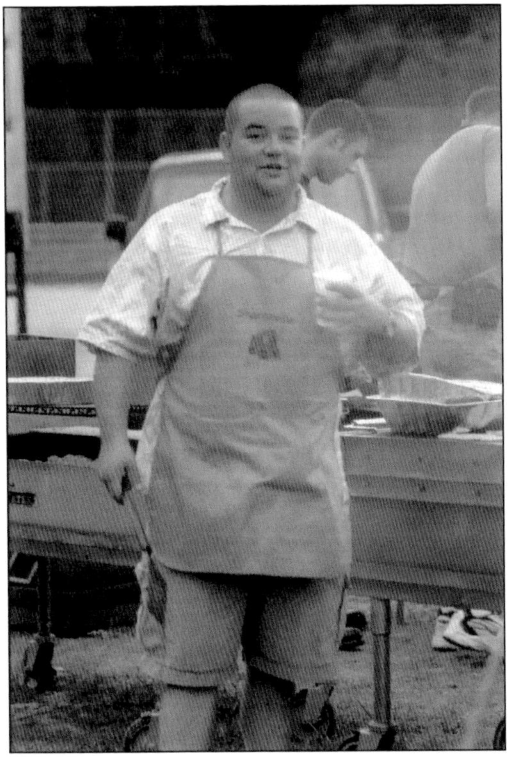

Eddie Gault is in charge of fire safety. Hey, you want a hot dog with that? There was plenty of food for everybody at the July 27, 2001 Fire Department Festival.

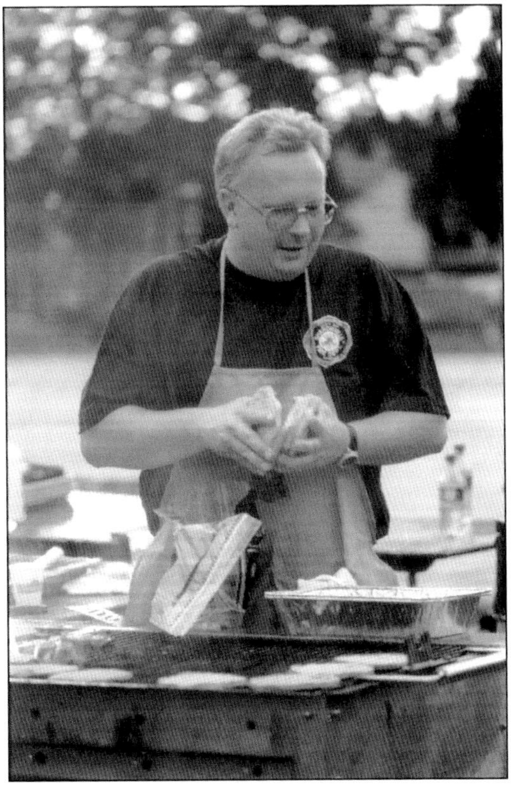

No grill is too hot for firefighter Kevin Willman. Even on a steamy July evening in 2001, he keeps those burgers coming.

Firefighter Ralph Hammonds is ready to sell the winning $1,000 ticket for the annual Fire Department Festival raffle, July 27, 2001.

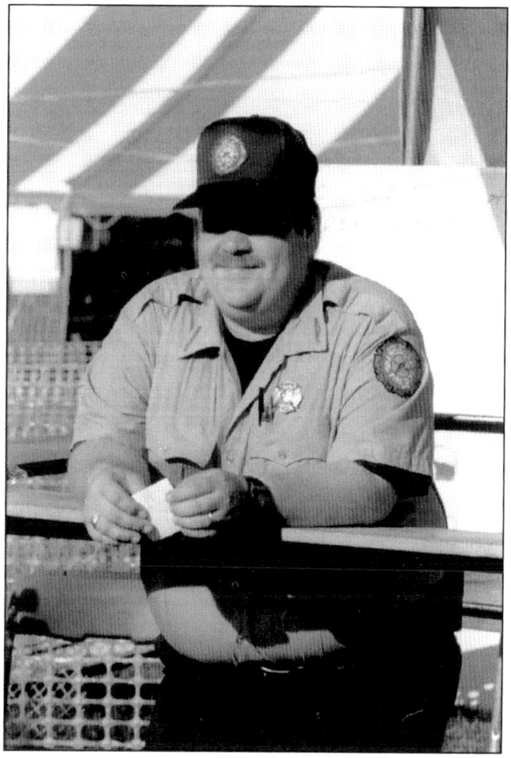

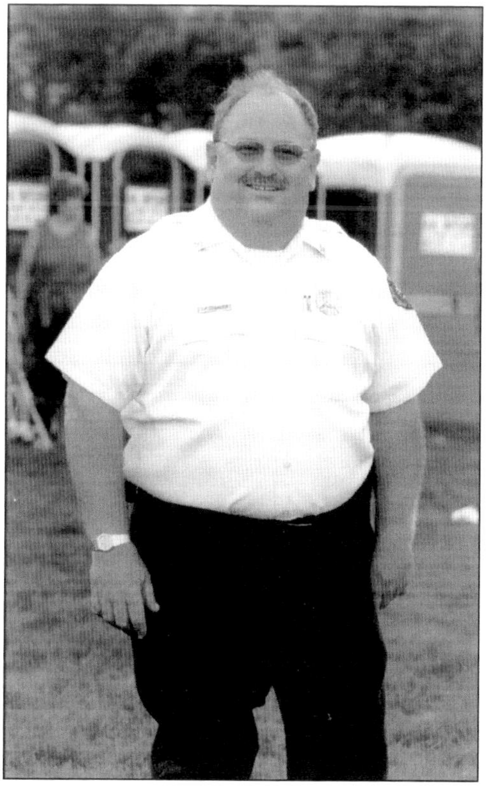

Firefighter Jim Edrington enjoys his evening at the Fire Department Festival, July 27, 2001.

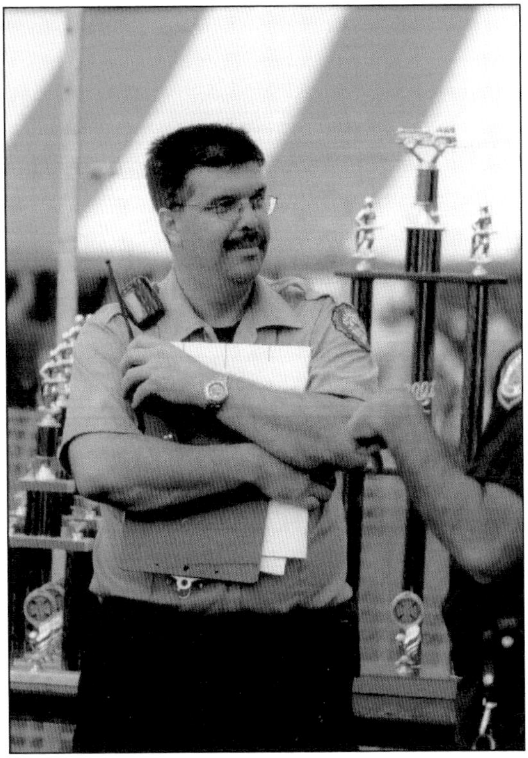

Sharonville fire lieutenant Scott Brooks seemed to have everything under control at the Fire Department Festival, July 27, 2001.

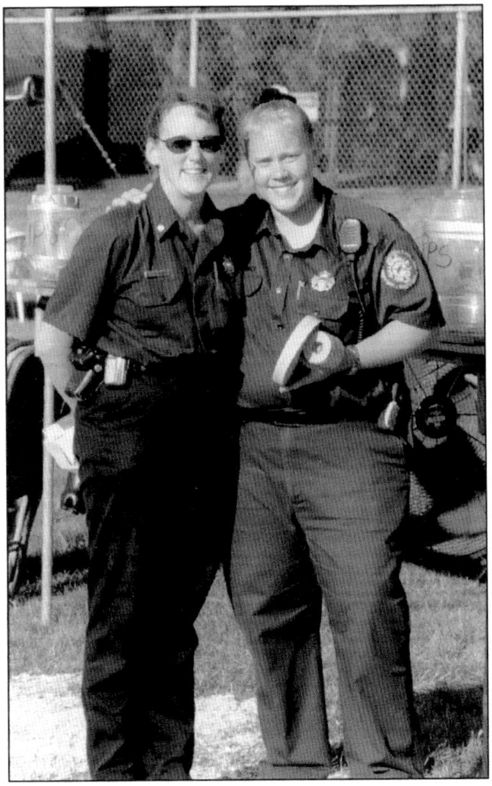

The annual Fire Department Festival is fun for everyone. Firefighters Bonnie Bobay and Amy Beatty smiled for the camera at the July 27, 2001 festival.

Seven

SHARON WOODS AND HERITAGE VILLAGE

Former Sharonville School teachers remembered that the whole community would go to Sharon Woods from the 1930s through the 1950s for fish frys and picnics. There was a lot of school spirit, and the Sharonville women were the best cooks for covered-dish dinners. Sharon Woods is the oldest park in the Hamilton County Park District, established in 1932. At that time there were 650 picnic tables and 150 stone grills, which were called "stoves" in the original literature. The Miami Purchase Association (and now, Historic Southwest Ohio, Inc.) began leasing space next to the creek and stone bridge in 1968, for the purpose of reconstructing buildings that reflect "significant educational, cultural, historical, and architectural attributes" and are in danger of being torn down due to development. Today, the Village consists of 13 structures that provide educational opportunities and many associated events.

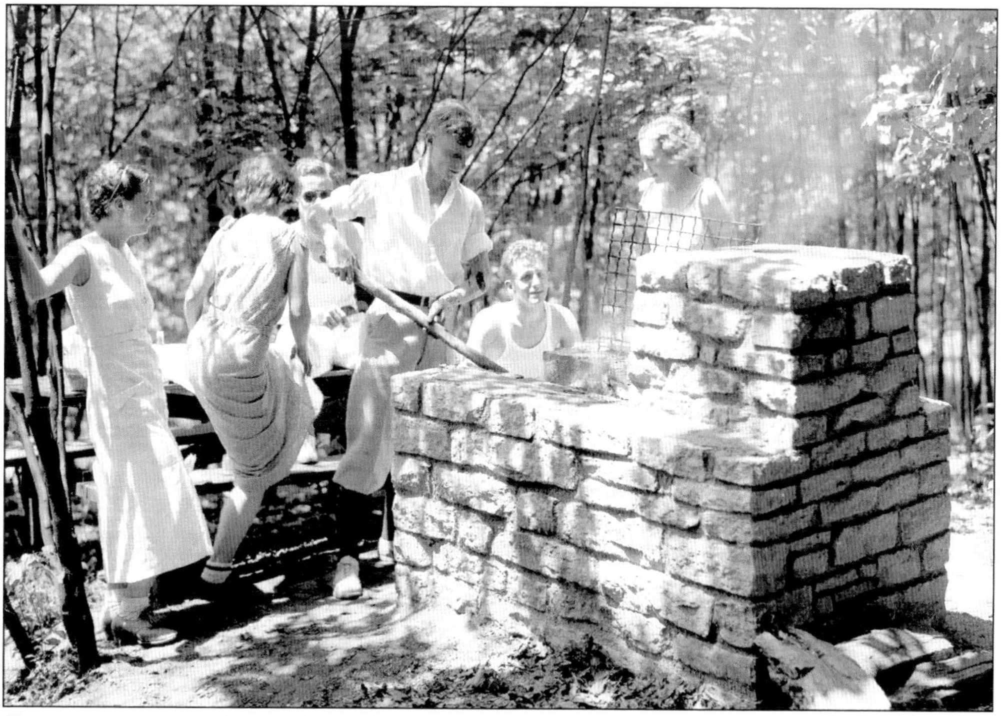

On a sunny summer day in the mid 1930s, these unidentified young people got together to try out the new stone grills at the Kemper Grove picnic area in Sharon Woods. Notice the knickers on the person tending the fire.

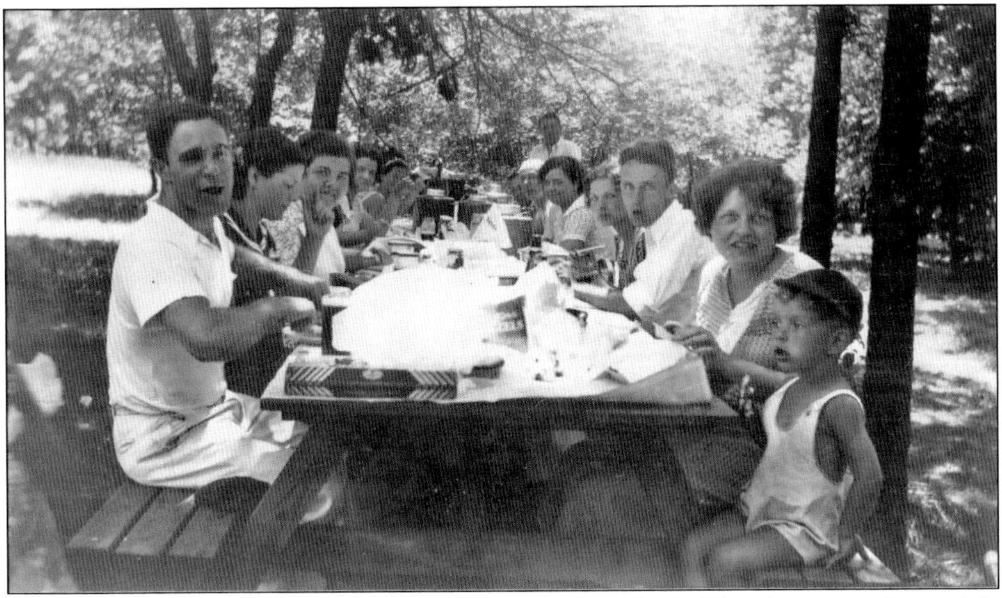

Over the years, many folks have enjoyed picnics at Sharon Woods. This photo was taken in July of 1935. Pictured, from left to right and front to back, are (left side of the table) Art Koenig and Charlotte Hanes (who would one day become the author's grandparents), and Loretta Hanes (Charlotte's sister); (right side of the table) young Jim Renner, Esther Hanes Renner, Osborne "Ozzie" Grever, Margaret "Maggie" Hanes Grever. The man standing at the far end of the table may be Elmer "Uns" Renner.

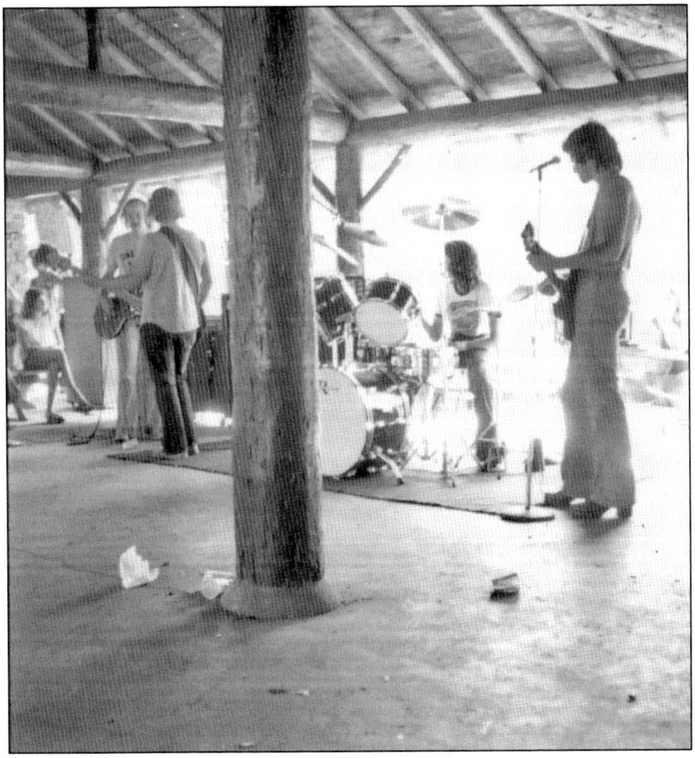

The Pavilion Grove shelter, built in 1932, served as a bandstand during the Cincinnati Technical College summer picnic on July 22, 1977. The Student Senate sponsored the outing for all in-term students, faculty, and staff. Organizers set up a volleyball net behind the shelter for some competitive afternoon exercise. Pictured is the local band "One Way Trip." The first guitarist on the left is Tom Collier.

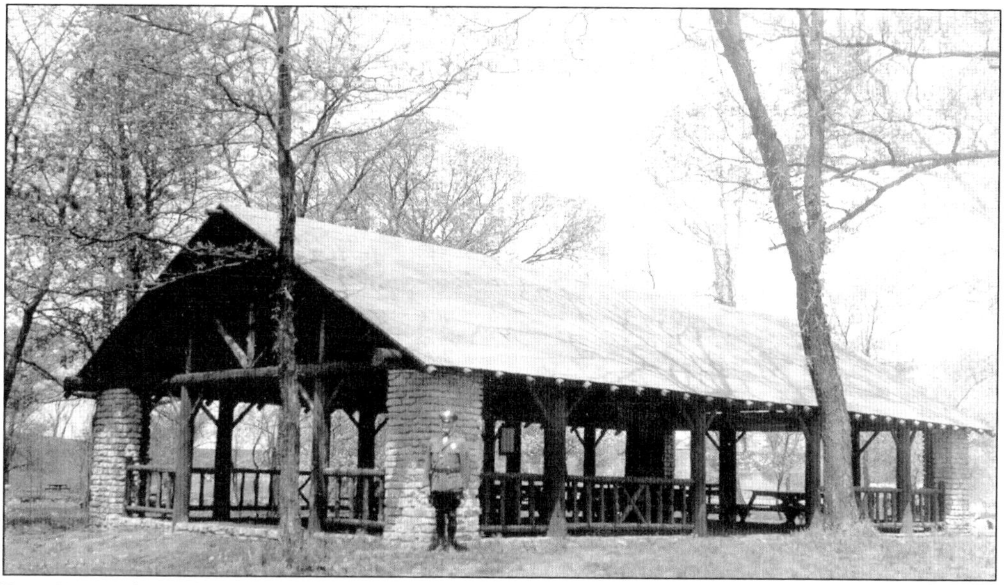

Dan Hines, first Chief of Police in Sharon Woods Park, stood in front of the first picnic shelter, Pavilion Grove, shortly after it was completed in 1932. According to park history, the first night watchman hired was Shell Parker, who was deputized by Sheriff Asa Butterfield and was paid $2.50 a night. A second watchman was hired in October of 1932. They were issued leather jackets and .38 caliber pistols.

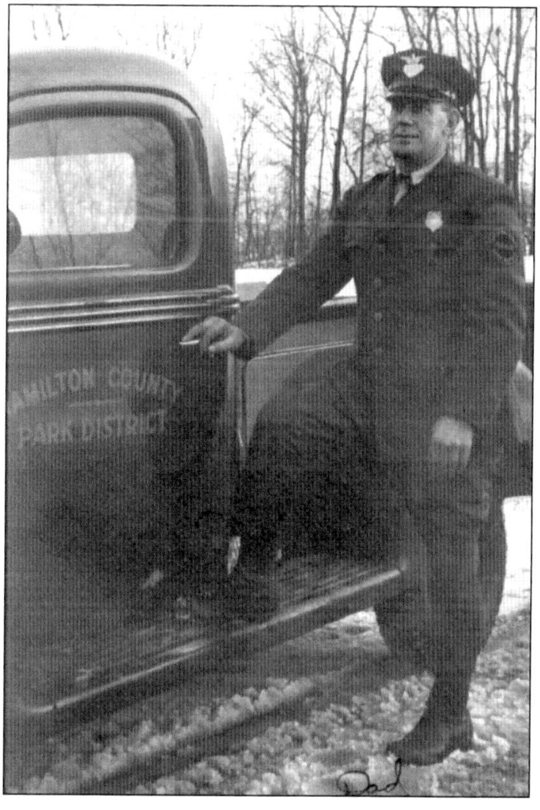

Dan Hines, the first Chief of Police in Sharon Woods Park, is pictured with his park vehicle. Hats, badges, and shirts were first purchased for the park policemen in 1933. By 1936, the staff had grown to include a police "captain" and three officers. It is assumed that Dan Hines was that "captain." Based on the dates on photos from the Hines family, he could have been the second watchman hired in 1932.

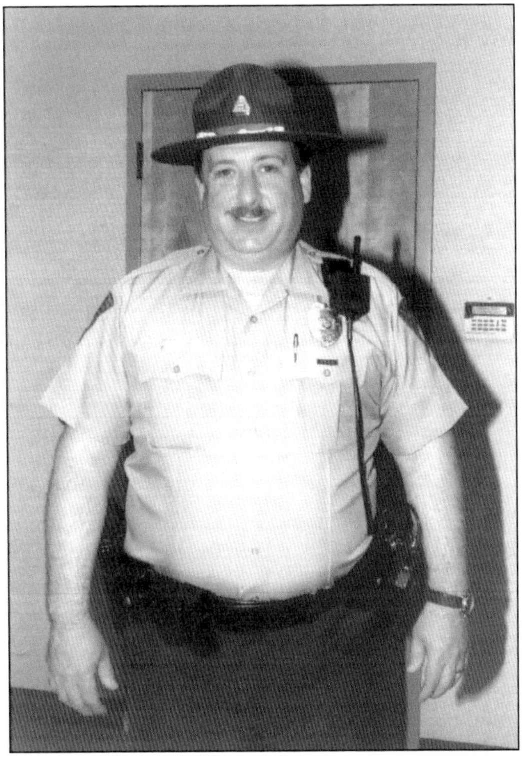

Today the Hamilton County Park District Rangers are state certified peace officers. They patrol by cruiser, foot, horseback, and bicycle. A nationally-accredited department, the Rangers are trained in all areas of police work, including emergency response and investigation. Pictured is Mark Adams, a Ranger since 1981, who is currently assigned to Sharon Woods. Mark's picture was taken on April 9, 2002.

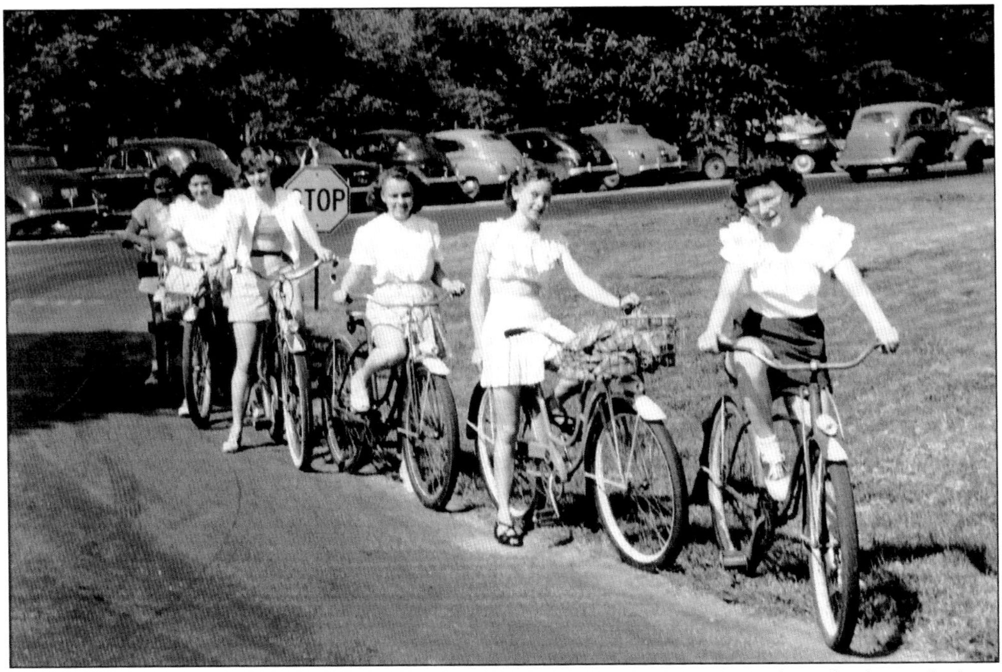

Bicycling on a summer day is always a fun pastime. These girls from nearby suburbs took their bikes to Sharon Woods in the early 1940s. They are, from left to right Virginia Kemmejer of Rossmoyne, Mary Englert, Jean Gassert, and Lucille Englert of Deer Park, Ruth Kemmejer of Rossmoyne, and Helen Gassert of Deer Park.

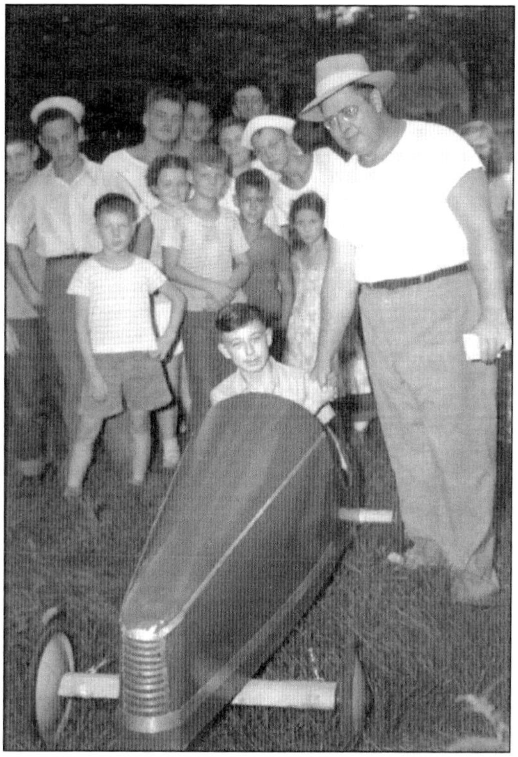

For three years, 1946, 1947, and 1948, a local Soap Box Derby race was held in Sharon Woods Park. It served as a test race for the metropolitan Cincinnati race. The local race was sponsored by the Sharonville Kiwanis Club, Dr. B.A. Schnell, president. Prizes were donated by local merchants. The winners, residents of Evendale, were Don Glaser, 1946 and 1948, and Bob Abbott, 1947. Pictured is Don Glaser, age 13, presented with a check by Myron R. Luke.

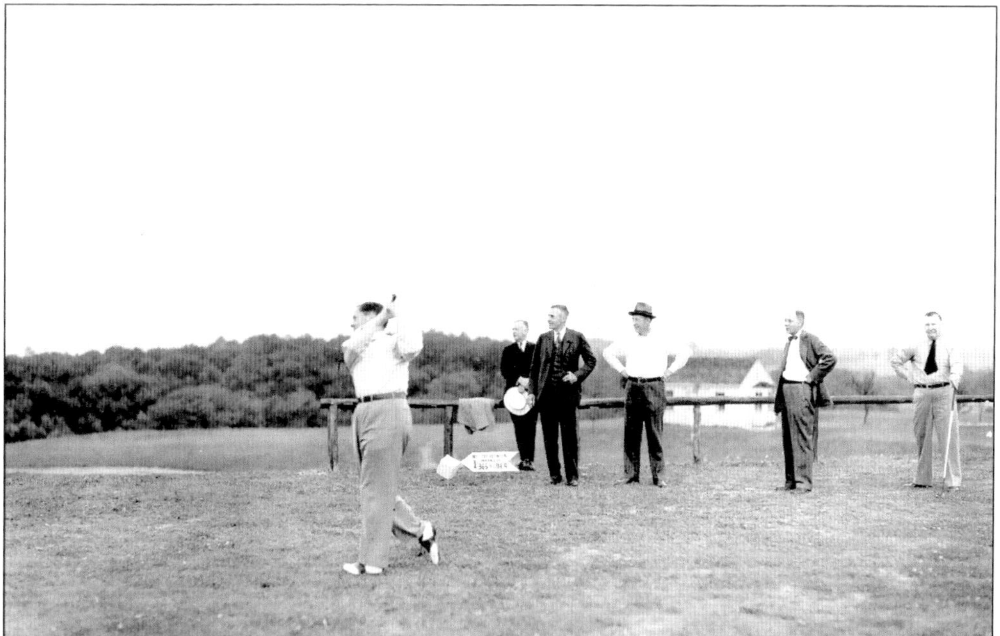

Judge Alfred Nippert and others look on as golf legend Bobby Jones drives the first ball to open Sharon Woods Golf Course, on Friday, May 27, 1938. Golf enthusiasts should know the sign at the first tee says: "365 yards, Par 4." Pictured, from left to right, are Bobby Jones, Judge Alfred K. Nippert, Ralph Rogan, Larry Schalk, Mr. Brutton, and William H. Albers.

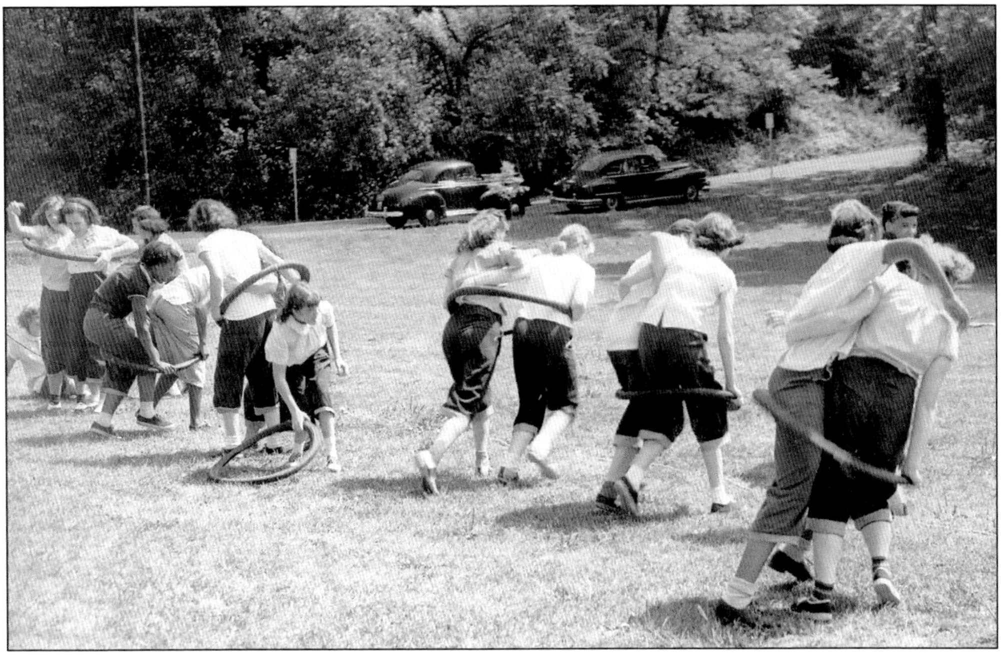

Negotiating bicycle tubes were part of the challenge in this relay race at Sharon Woods in the early 1940s. This outing was probably an end of the year event for one of the local girls' high schools.

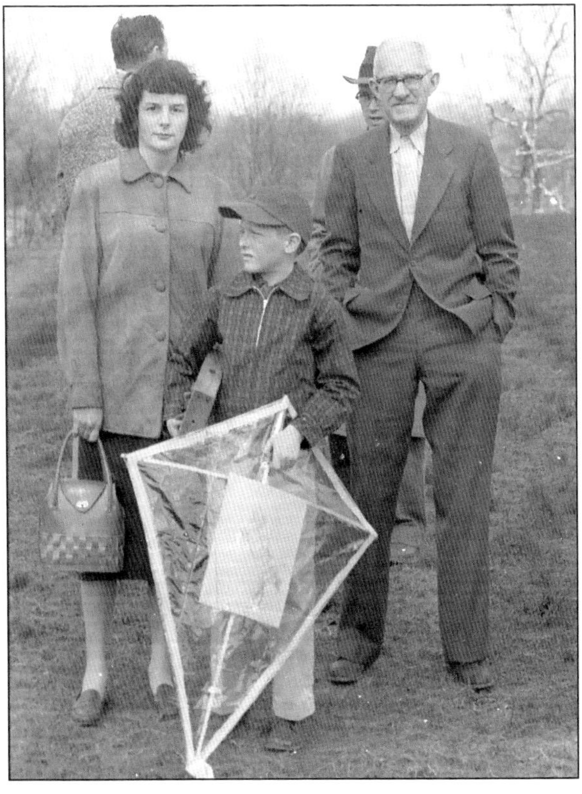

An old traditional spring event in Sharon Woods was a kite contest. Winners, who often constructed their own kites, were named in a variety of categories. On March 30, 1957, Glenn Mason of 3765 Malaer Drive in Sharonville, took the prize for largest kite. Pictured, from left to right, are Glenn's mother, Mrs. Clarence Mason, Glenn and his award-winning kite, and his great-grandfather, Mr. William Tate.

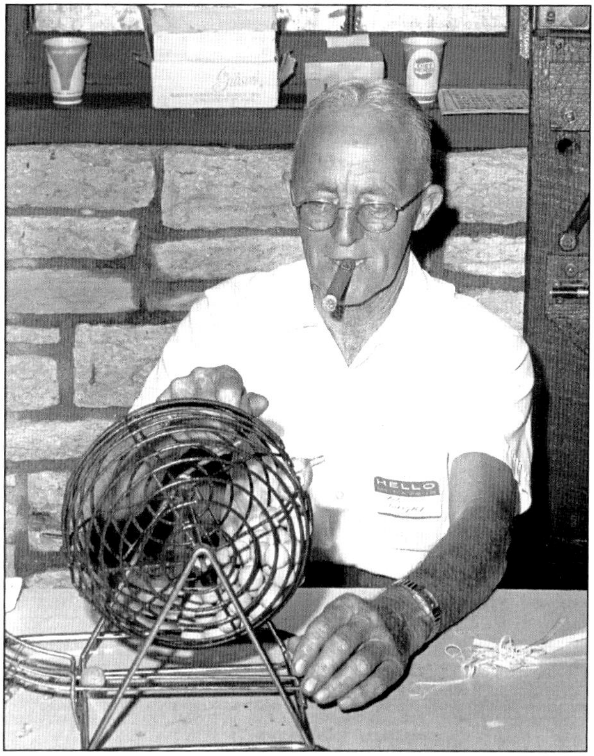

Al Wright spun the numbered balls for a bingo game at a function held at the Sharon Woods boathouse (now known as Lakeside Lodge), c. 1940s. Interestingly, the Park Board denied a request from Mr. Baron Orr to conduct a bingo game in the park in 1938.

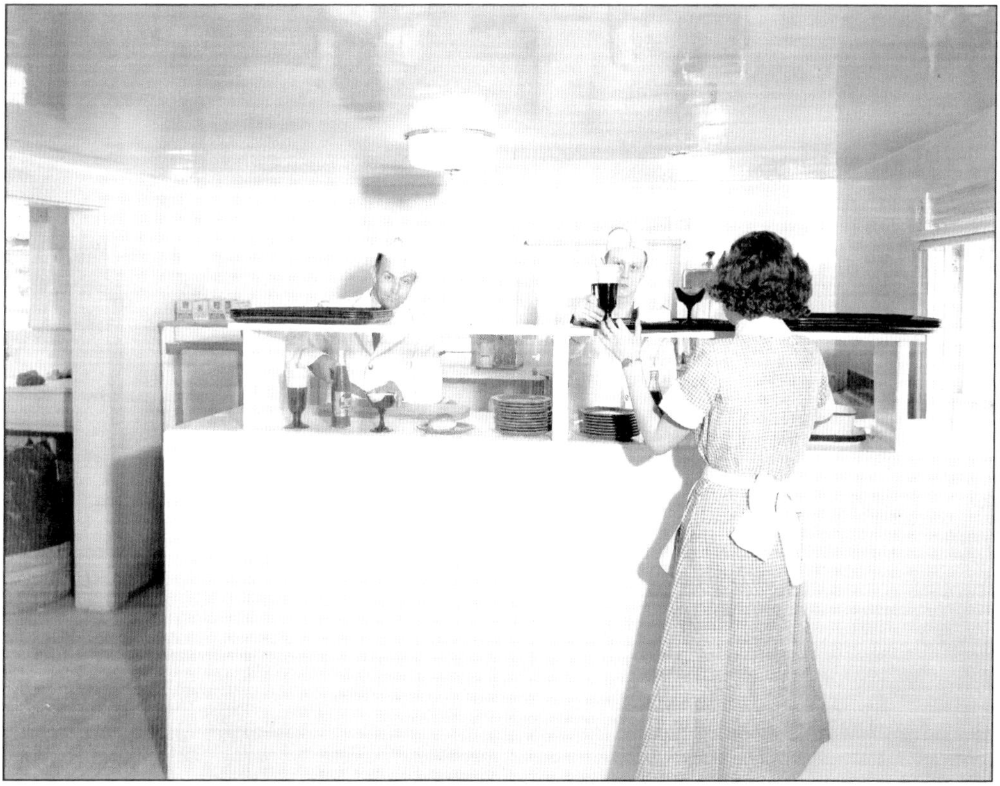

Cooks served up Hires Root Beer with lunch at the brand-new Sharon Woods Sandwich Shop, c. 1940s.

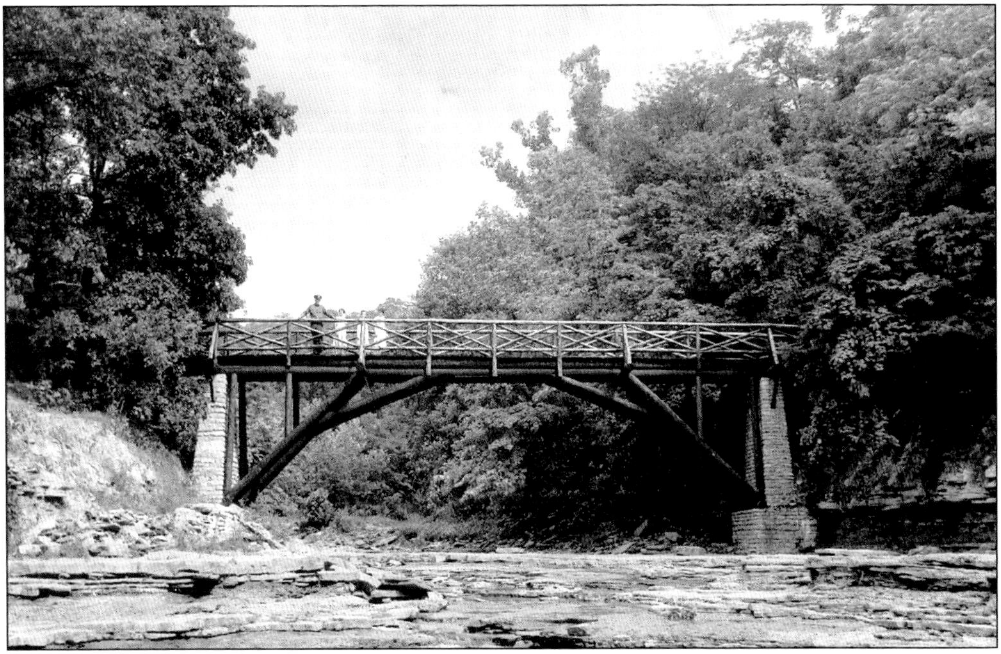

The Ranger captain and three girls stood on the wooden footbridge that spanned Sharon Woods Gorge. This photo was taken in the late 1930s or early 1940s when the bridge was new. Today only the stone piers remain and the gorge is cut a bit deeper, after the swift high waters raged through during a storm in spring of 2001.

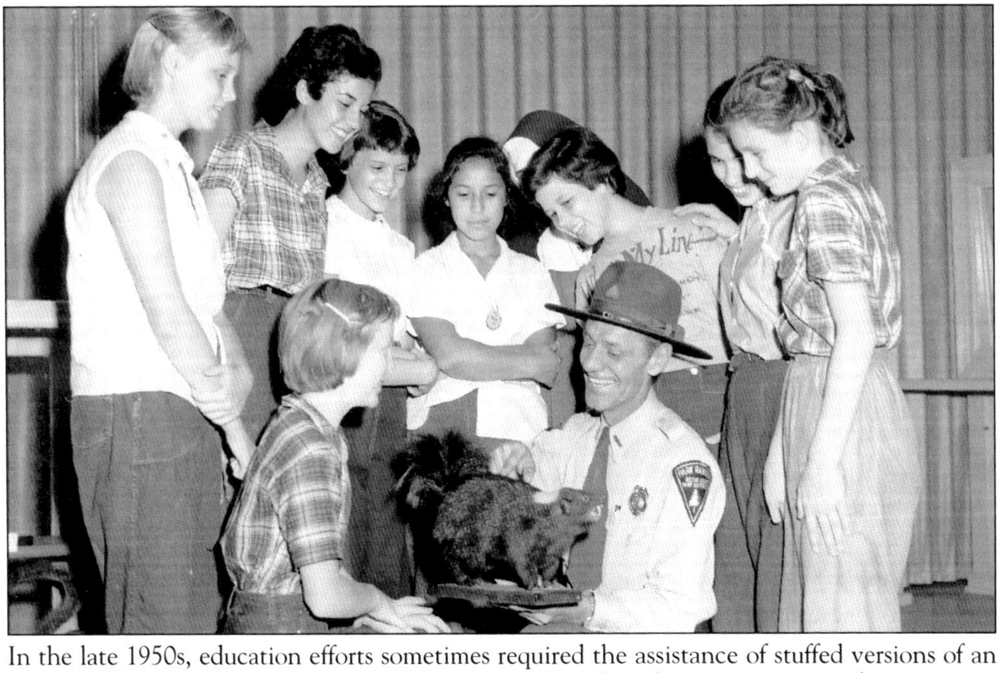

In the late 1950s, education efforts sometimes required the assistance of stuffed versions of an animal. Chester Pickering, Captain of the Sharon Woods park rangers, apparently is pointing out the finer points of a skunk to these schoolgirls and their teacher (the nun mostly obscured by the girl wearing the "What's My Line?" T-shirt).

Throughout its history, part of the mission of the Hamilton County Park District, and thus, Sharon Woods, has been educating the public. In April of 1972, veteran Naturalist Warren Wells took a group of fifth graders out for a lesson in conservation.

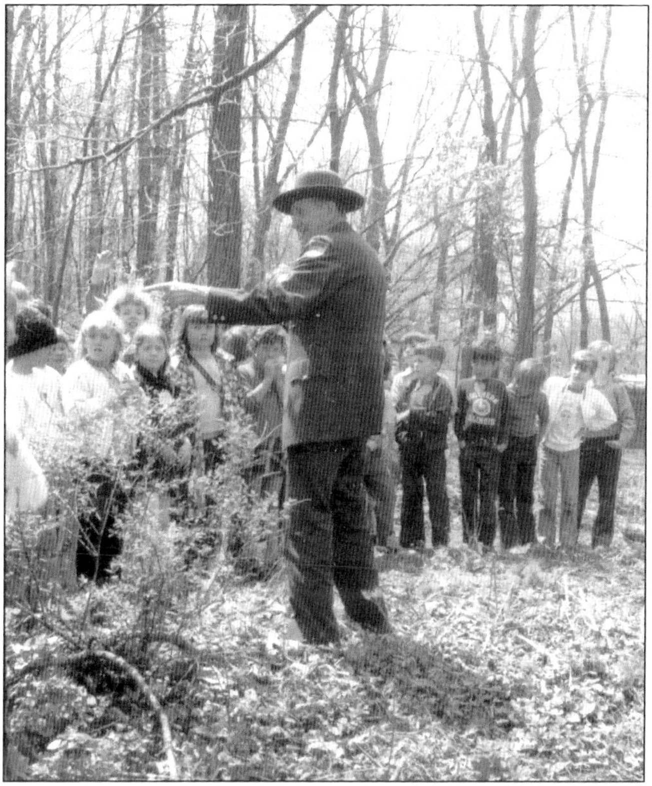

Day camps at Sharon Woods have always been a popular attraction for boys and girls. This group of boys seems to be learning about crafts and cooking outdoors with Mike Weber, July 2, 1957.

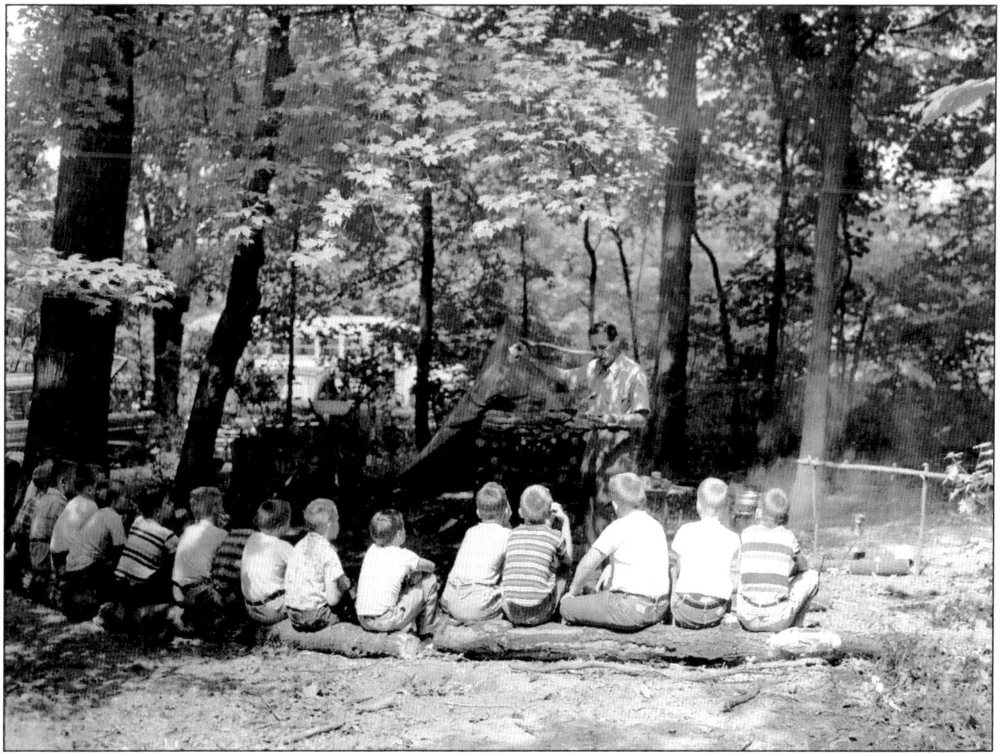

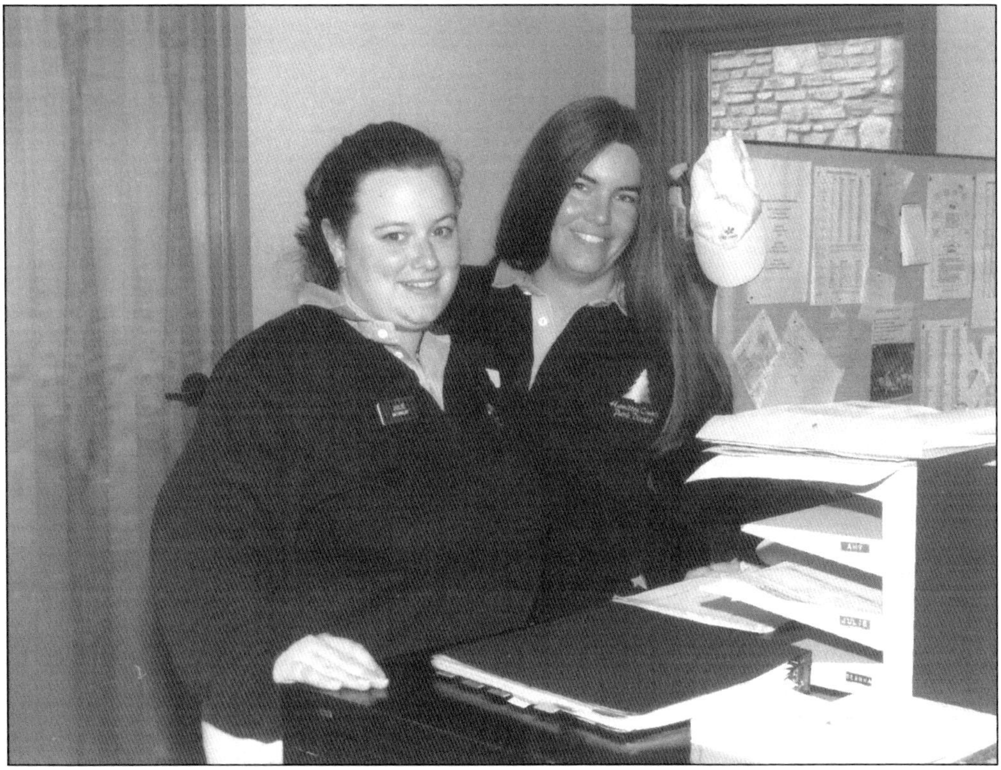

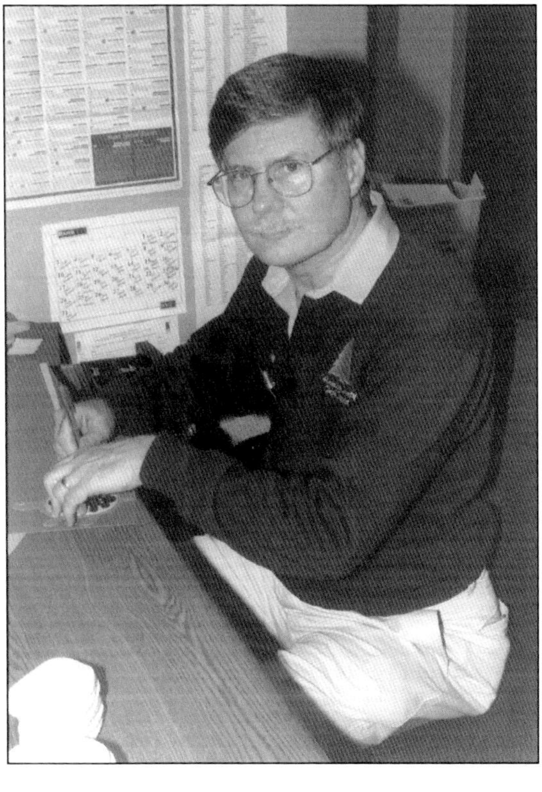

The Naturalist Department today offers a wide variety of nature-related programs. In Sharon Woods, you might participate in the Adventure Program for third graders, a fossil or owl hike, or many other indoor or outdoor educational activities. In April, 2002, naturalists Julie Herzog and Amy Smith check out the schedule before leaving the office.

Having a job as a park naturalist doesn't mean being in the woods all day. On April 9, 2002, Al Winstel, a district naturalist since 1977, was in the office working on a craft project for an upcoming children's program.

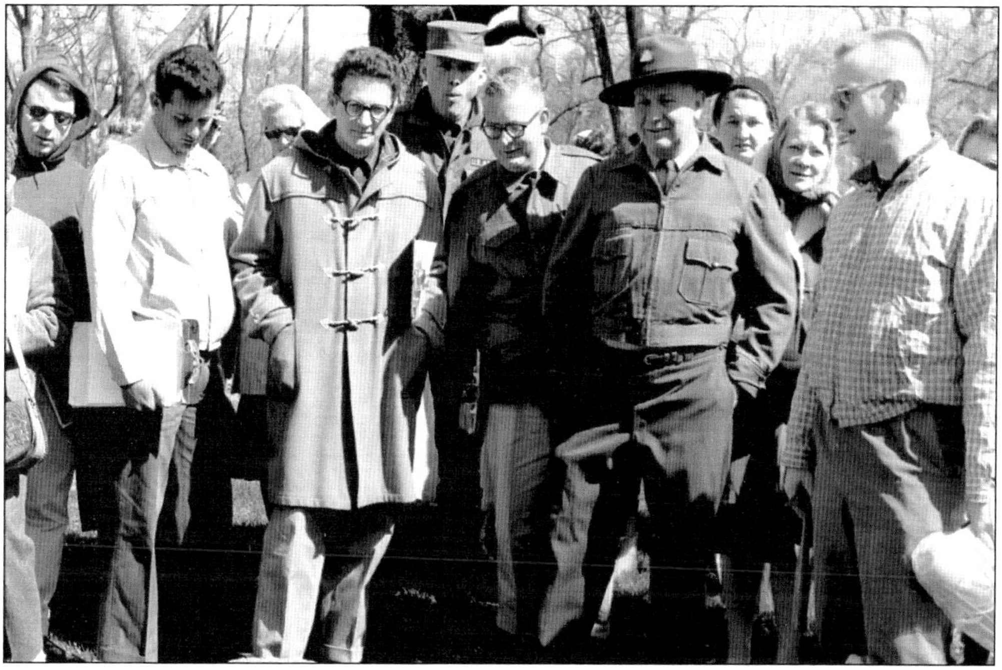

Sharon Woods has always been a great place for geology research, due to the impact three glaciers had on the area. Dr. Frank Koucky, Assistant Professor of Geology at the University of Cincinnati, conducts field studies in natural history on April 14, 1962. The class members were discussing an erratic boulder in front of them. Pictured, from the left to right at the extreme right of the picture, are J. Herbert Heger, Co-director of the Hamilton County Park District (wearing uniform), and Dr. Koucky.

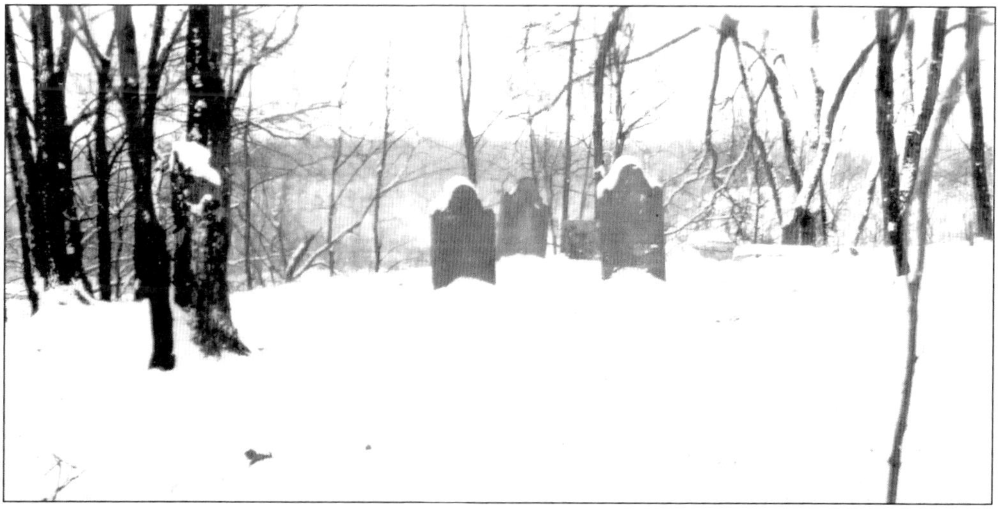

On the hill above Buckeye Falls sits Cummins Cemetery, established c. 1870. The WPA records at the Hamilton County Recorders office indicate that eight graves were present in the 1930s. Only parts of the markers have been found recently. They belong to William Senteny and John Cummins, a Civil War veteran. Riddle and Zind families once owned parcels of land near the cemetery. Naturalist Al Winstel and members of the Society of Historic Sharonville continue to research the cemetery.

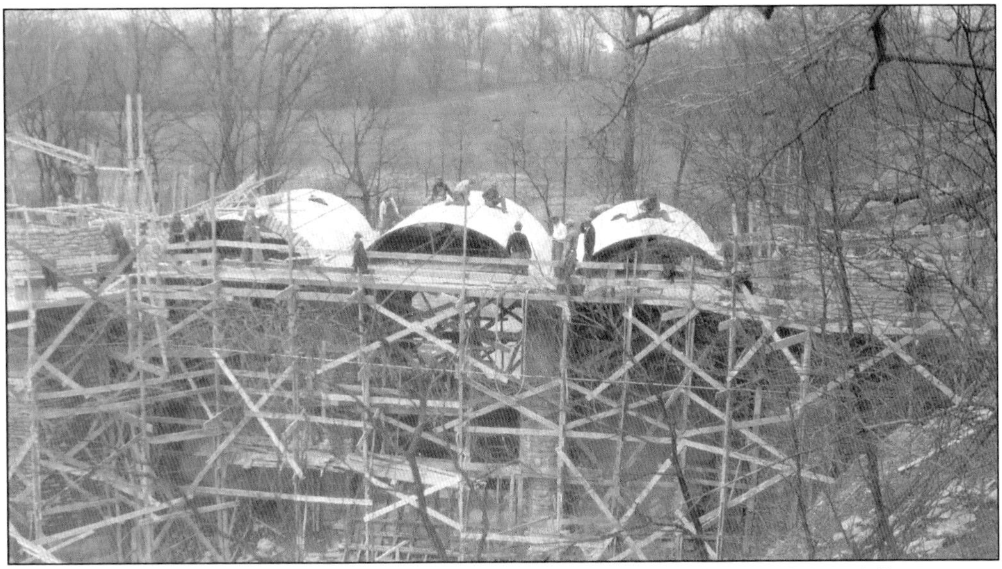

This picture of construction of the stone bridge was taken April 15, 1936. It fell victim to a damaging flood in the spring of 2001, when a rushing Sharon Creek left its banks. The tremendous force of the water pushed a tree into the bridge like an arrow to a target, separating some of the stone facing and buckling the roadbed. Studies are currently underway to determine how to repair the 66-year-old landmark.

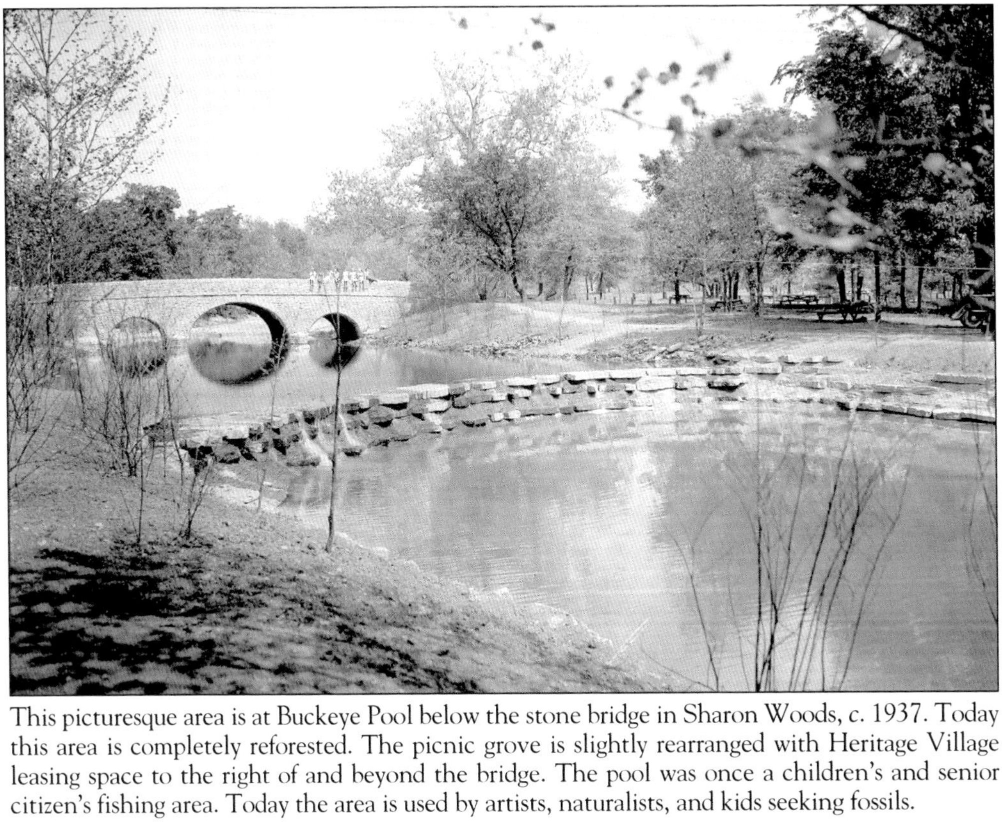

This picturesque area is at Buckeye Pool below the stone bridge in Sharon Woods, *c.* 1937. Today this area is completely reforested. The picnic grove is slightly rearranged with Heritage Village leasing space to the right of and beyond the bridge. The pool was once a children's and senior citizen's fishing area. Today the area is used by artists, naturalists, and kids seeking fossils.

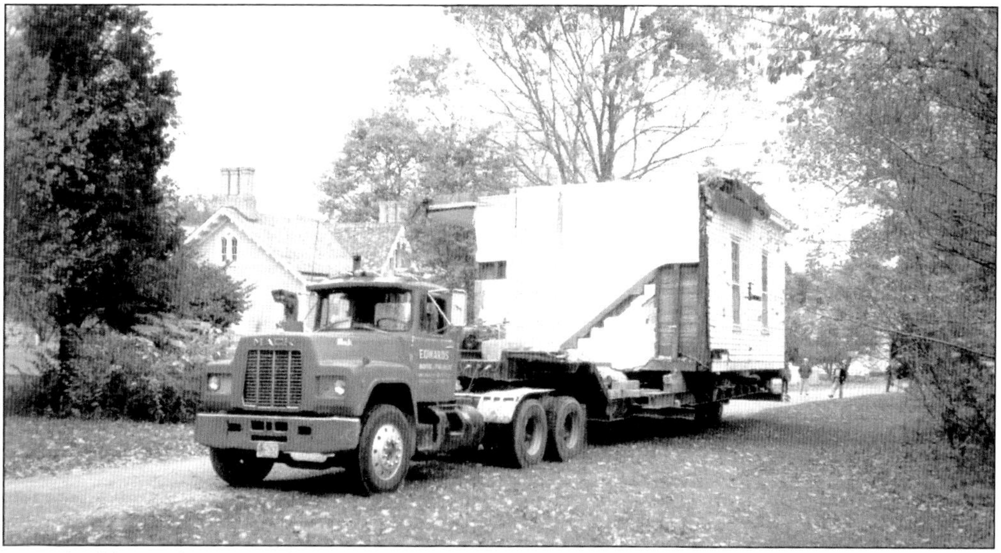

Most buildings that are relocated to Heritage Village are first dismantled and each piece is numbered for careful transport and reconstruction on site. However, the Benedict Cottage was moved in one piece on a large flatbed truck. Here the house slowly travels along the Village road to its future home. Sam Benedict was appointed to the park board in 1958, and in 1969, his family donated the 66 acres that became Trillium Trails Wildlife Preserve.

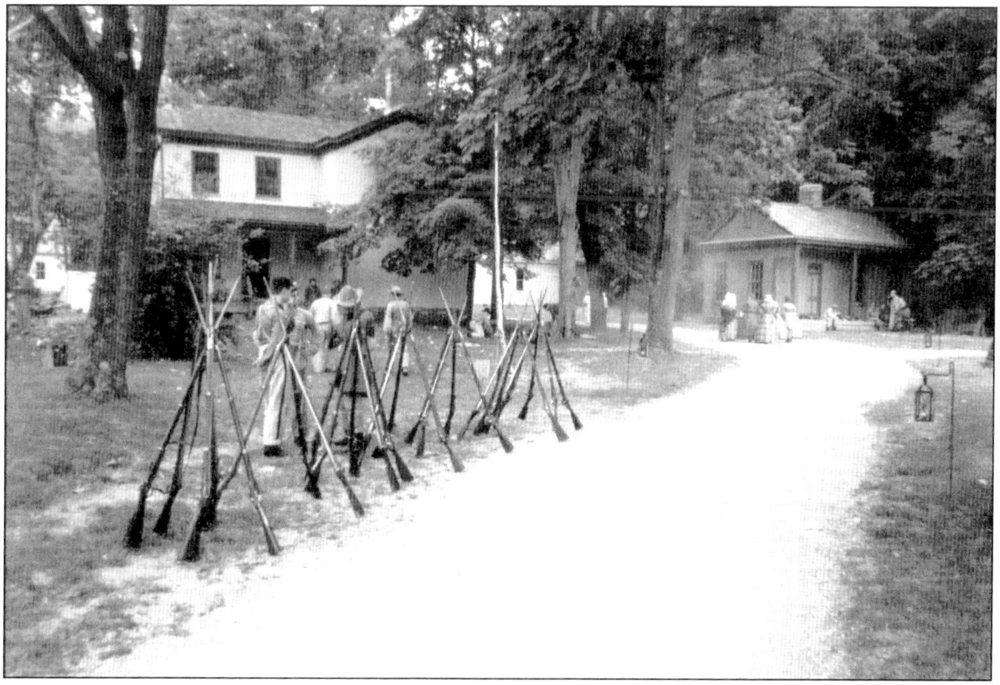

The Longknife rifles carried by the militiamen wait until they're needed as the men gather for private conversation in the Village "camp." Pictured is the main "road" through Heritage Village. At the end of the road, to the right, is the restored Benedict Cottage.

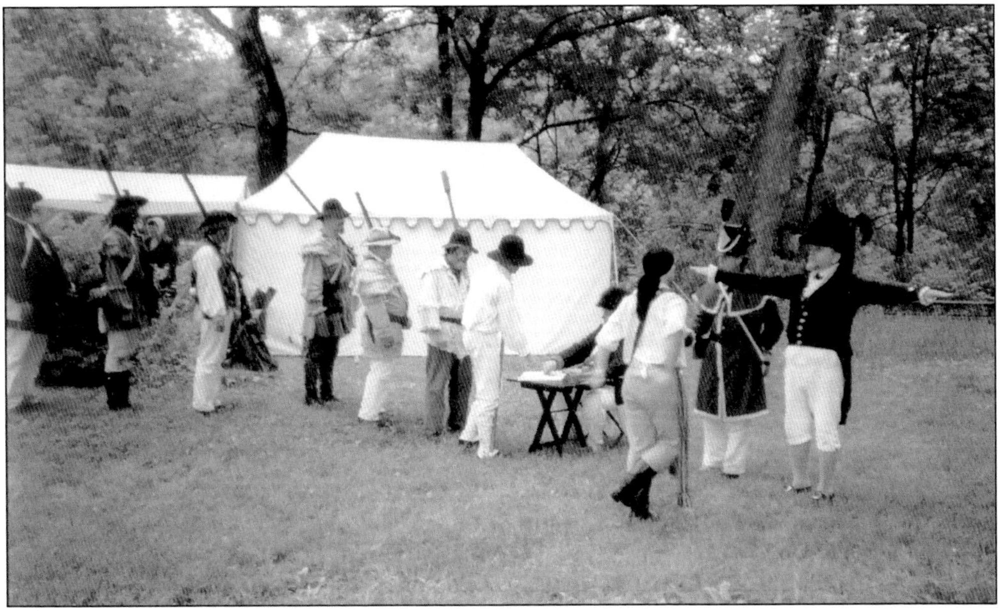

Pictured is the "enlistment" registration table for 1812 militiamen. During the 1812 Fair and Muster visitors can experience life as it was in the early days of Cincinnati, when a mixture of soldiers, settlers, Indians, and elegant ladies and gentlemen were creating a new city. Re-enactors show how soldiers lived and camped, and how people accomplished daily tasks.

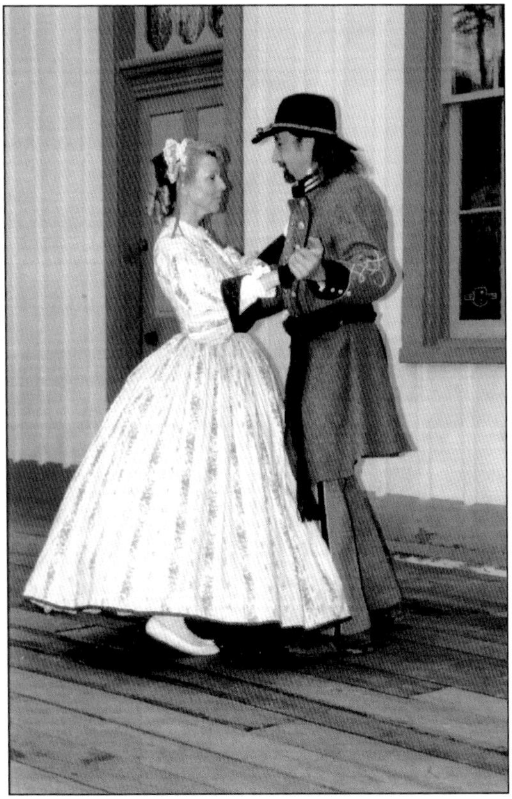

Civil War "musters" aren't just about Union and Confederate soldiers. At the Village, you might also find an officer in full dress uniform dancing with a lady attired in her 1860s best. These interpreters were dancing on the wooden platform outside the Chester Park Train Station.

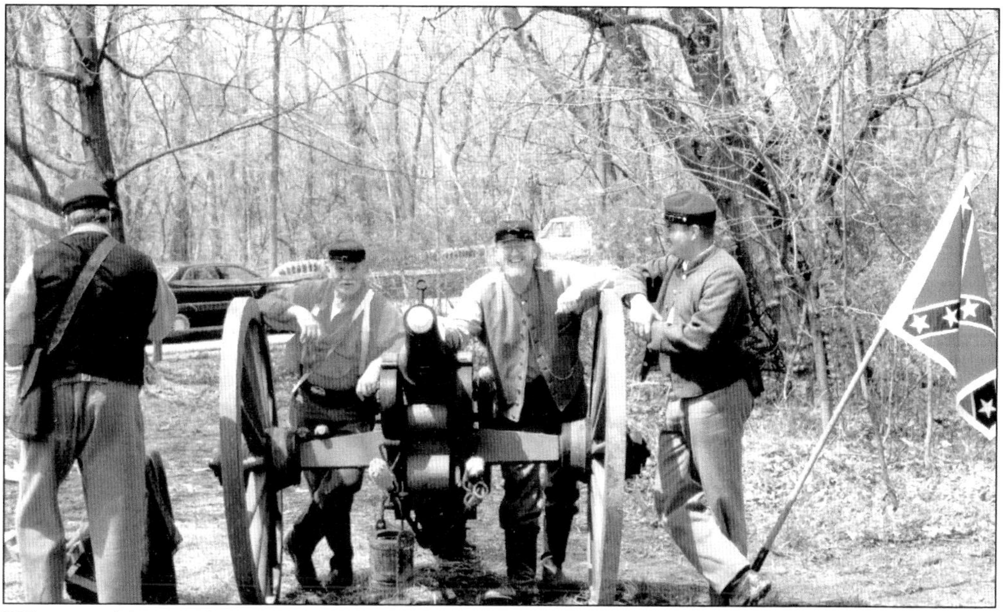

What would a Civil War reenactment be without a cannon? It's not unusual for the sounds of a summer afternoon to be broken by the loud volleys of the cannon that can be heard across Sharonville. Locals recognize it as a call to arms at the Village. "Confederate soldiers" posed for this picture with their pride and joy.

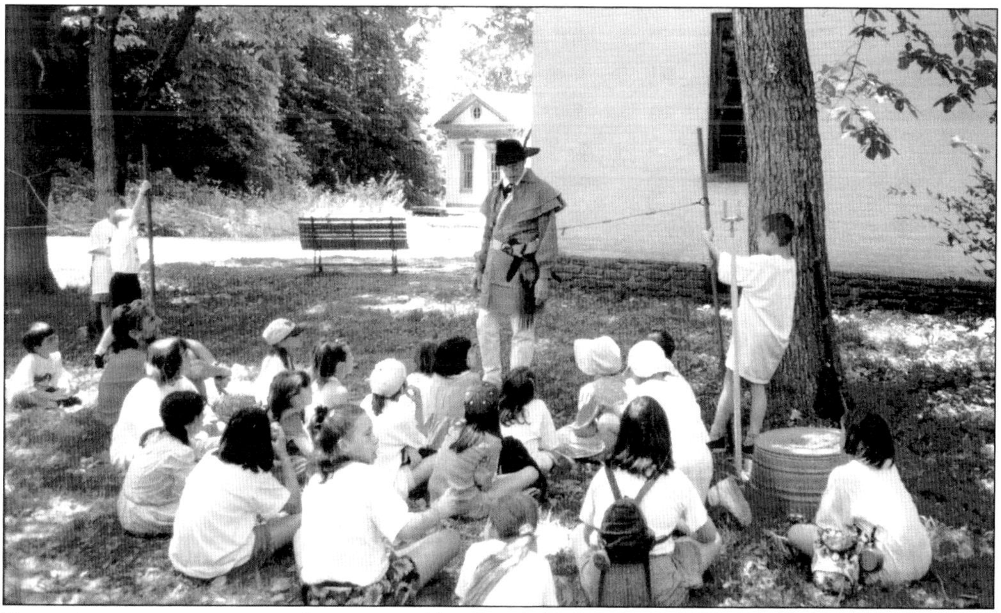

Trained interpreters present history as if they were living it. Countless school and scout groups have made trips to the Village an integral part of their history curriculum.

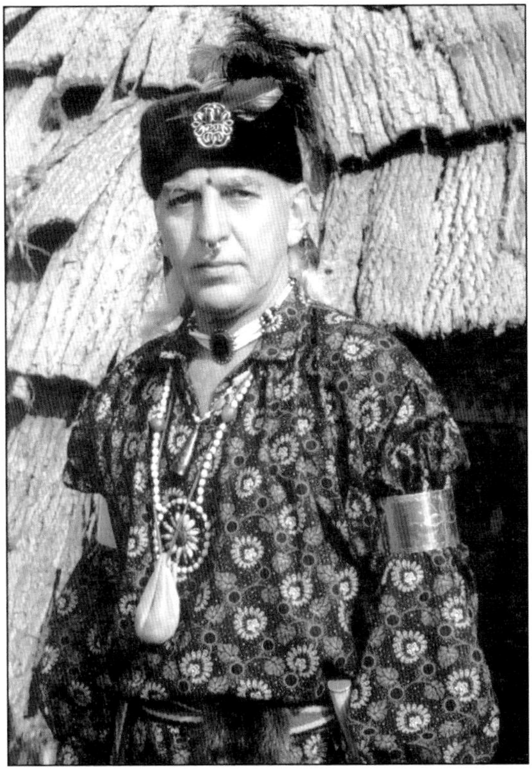

Heritage Village also makes sure to tell the story of the "other" people who were in Ohio long before the immigrant pioneers arrived. Often, visitors learn about Native-American culture via the stories and songs presented by Ayapia (Larry Eveland), a Shawnee storyteller and drummer. By teaching visitors about his ancestors, Ayapia dispels popular myths and shows us how to "walk softly upon the earth." He is living proof that the Native people are still with us today.

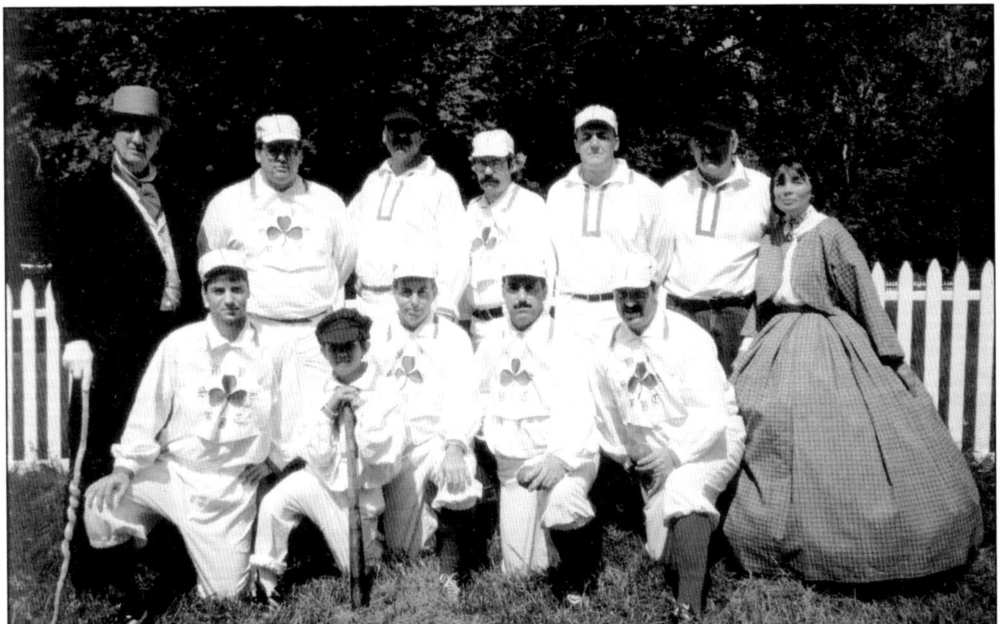

The Sharon Woods Shamrocks are an 1880s-style baseball team founded to teach visitors how they played the game in the days when it was "a gentleman's game" without big stadiums or high tech equipment. The Shamrocks (and now vintage Cincinnati Redlegs) play other historical teams on the Village lawn and at "away" venues during the summer months.

Eight

Sharonville Families

The soul of a town rests within the people who take up residence there. They rent apartments, buy homes, support the local businesses, attend the neighborhood schools, use the recreation facilities and libraries, volunteer their time with community and church events, and sometimes are even buried there. Of all the chapters in this book, perhaps this one best exemplifies the average Sharonville citizen: the neighbors next door; the teenagers who have part-time jobs or play team sports; the people who keep family traditions alive. The clothing and technology of the day might be a bit different, but at one time or another, they've all called Sharonville their home.

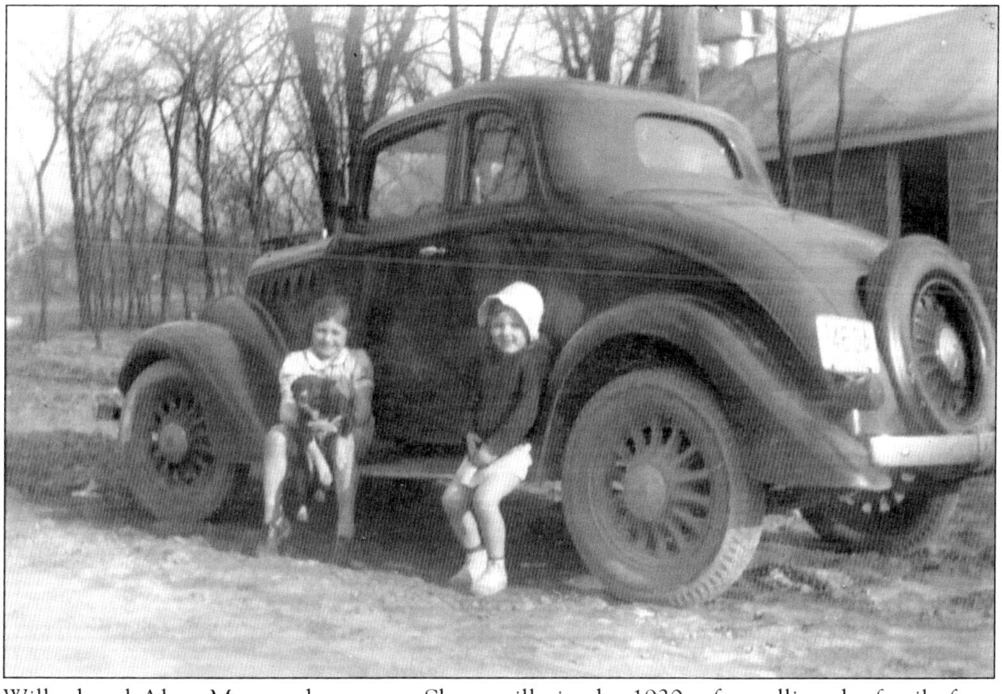

Willard and Alma Marquardt came to Sharonville in the 1930s after selling the family farm to the government so that the community of Greenhills could be established. Willard and his father George built the family home on 32 acres at the top of Cornell Road. Mary Marquardt, the pet dog, and Martha Jean Marquardt sat on the running board of the family Packard, a two-door coupe, at 4031 Cornell Road in 1939.

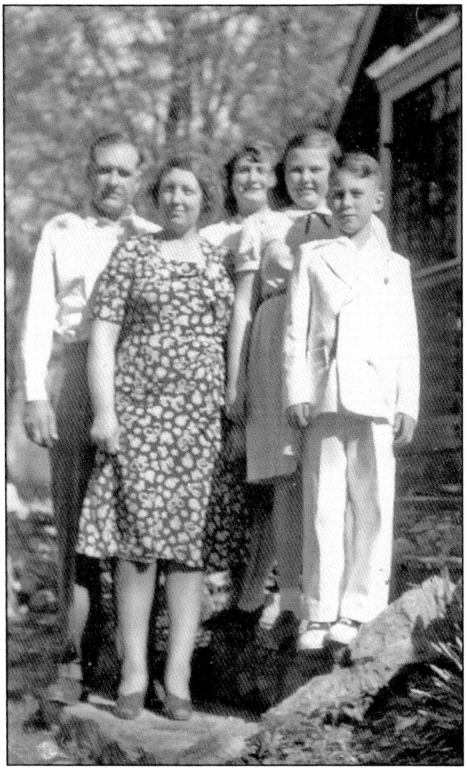

The Marquardt family moved into the new house and farm on Cornell Road in 1937. Willard farmed the property, in addition to holding down a job as an electrician, until the late 1940s, when he rented out the acreage for others to farm. Pictured, from left to right, are Willard, Alma, Mary, Martha Jean, and Don Marquardt in front of the house, *c.* 1940s.

The Whallon family posed for this *c.*1907 photo on the front steps of their home at the southeast corner of Spinner and Walnut Streets. The home still stands today, owned by St. Michael Church. Pictured, from left to right, are (front row seated) Jacob Whallon holding Herbert A. Beins, Elizabeth Drum Whallon, and Evelyn Beins; (back row) William Perkins, Stella Whallon Perkins, James T. Whallon, Edna Whallon Beins, and Doctor Herbert F. Beins.

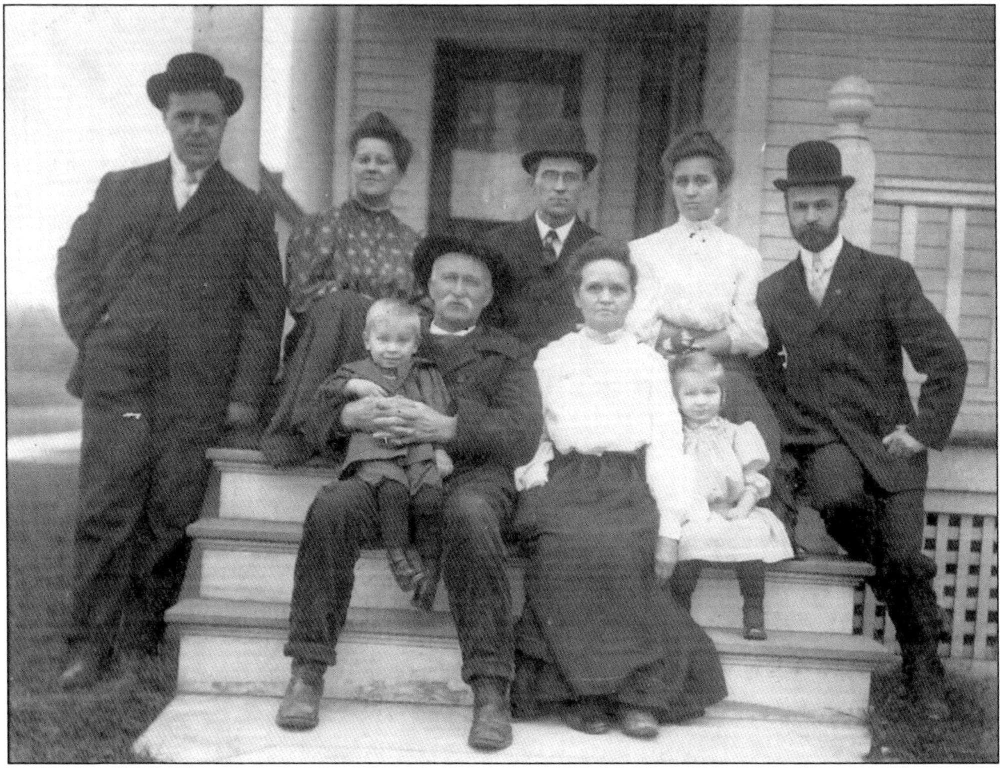

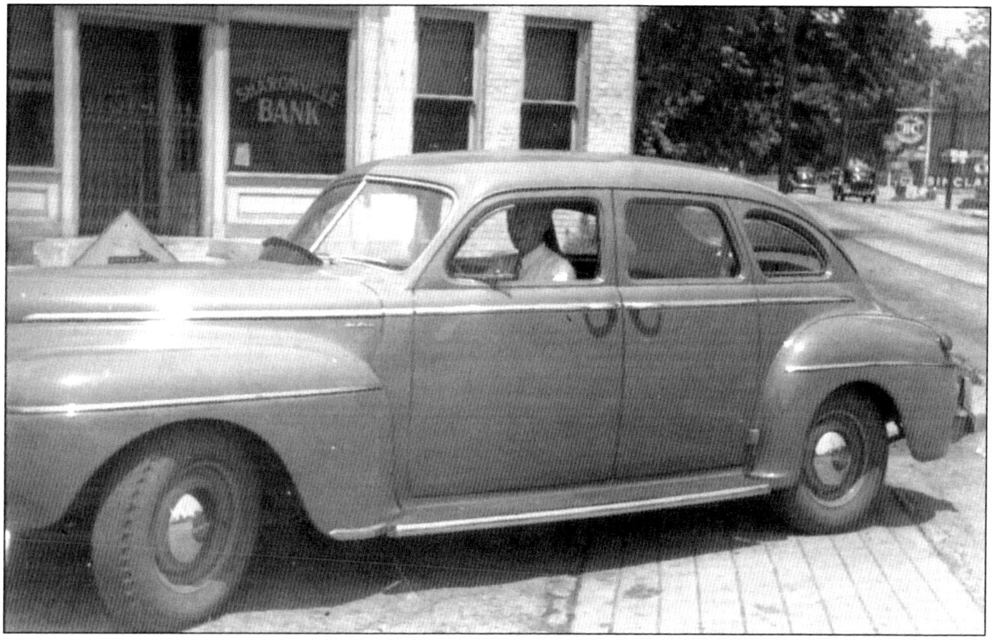

Mary Louise McWhorter Ferrell remembered that in 1943, Reading Road through Sharonville had only two lanes. Vehicles like G.H. McWhorter's 1941 DeSoto were all the rage. In this photo, Mr. McWhorter (Mary Louise's dad) is parked in front of the Sharonville Bank.

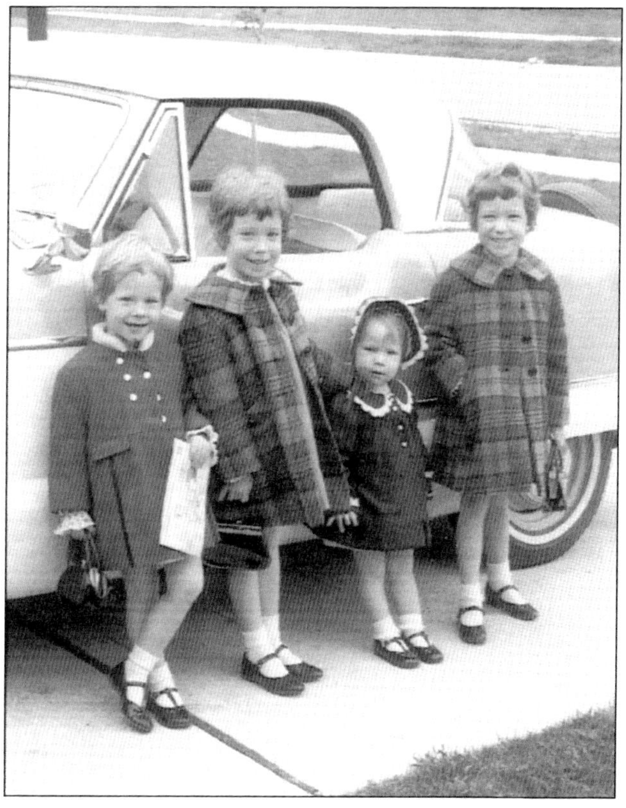

The young Houston girls, daughters of Bob and Ernestine, stood in front of their dad's 1956 Nash Metro and mugged for the camera in 1966. The Nash, affectionately called "Mr. Magoo," held the girls, one adult, and six bags of groceries. The Houston girls, from left to right, are Jennifer, Sandra, Coleen, and Robyn.

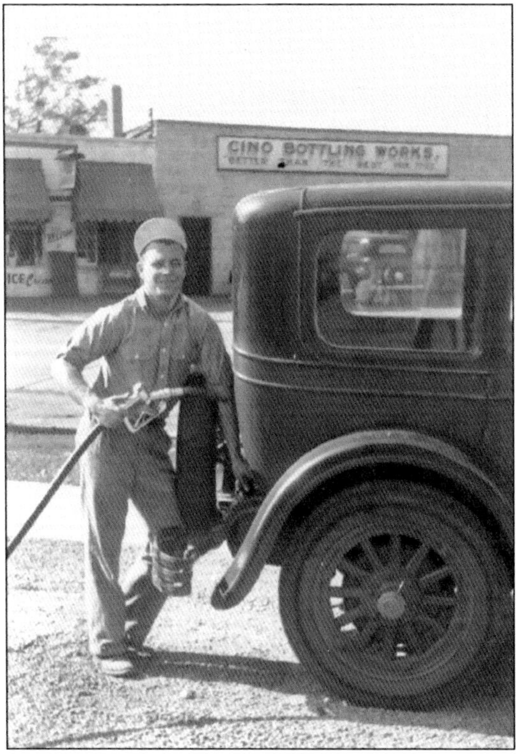

Eugene Flanigan pumped gasoline at a service station on Reading Road across the street from the Cino Bottling Works, c. 1940.

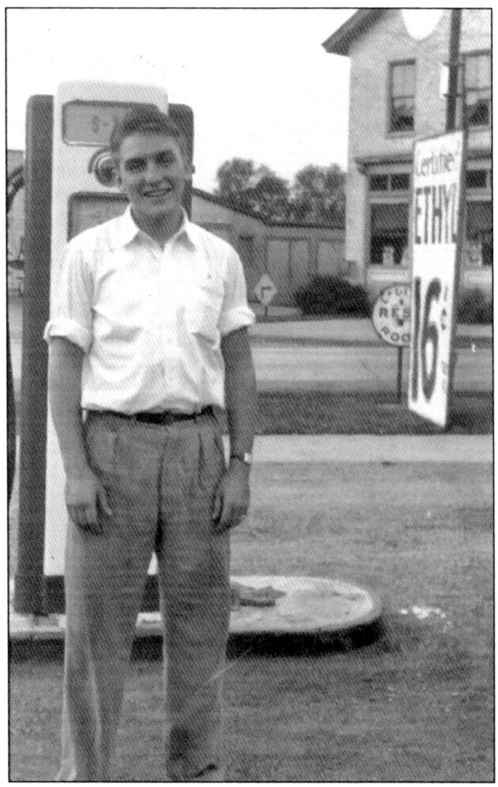

Paul Kuhlman, of the Sharonville High class of 1939, posed near one of the pumps at the Sinclair service station on Reading Road across the street from the Sharonville Bank, c. 1940.

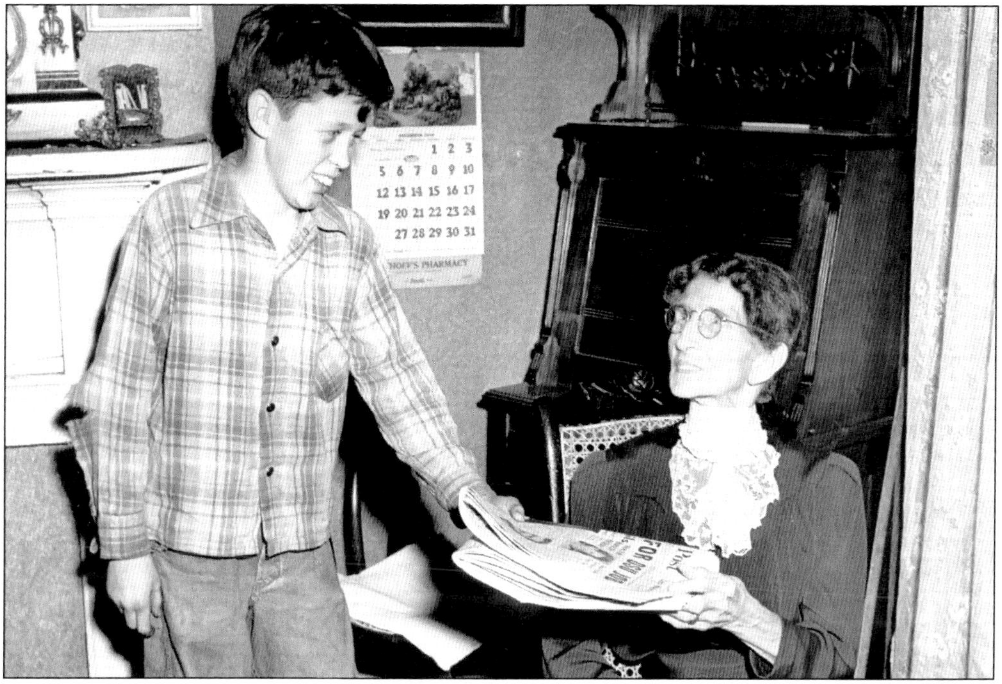

Young Don Clark was captured by a Cincinnati Post photographer while delivering the daily paper to Mrs. Nettie Streeter on her 100th birthday, December 26, 1949.

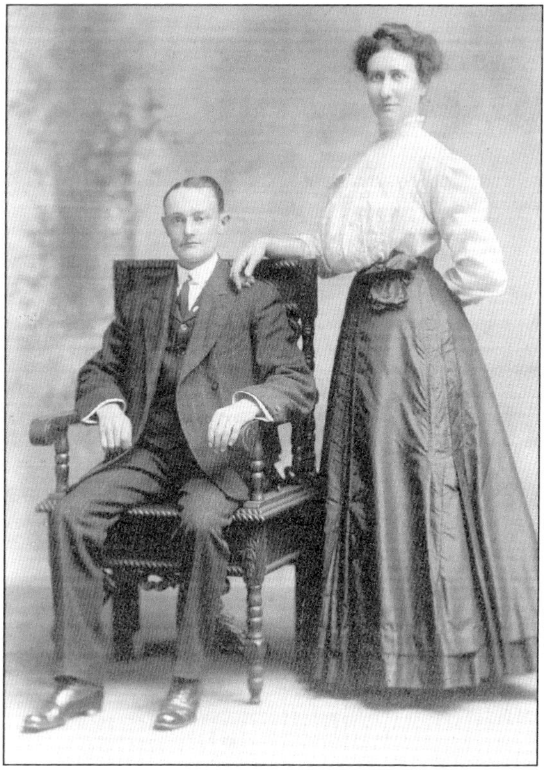

Frank Pence, former mayor of Sharonville, and his wife Blanche had their portrait taken by Young & Carl of Cincinnati in the early 1900s. Frank was married at age 17 and his wife died in 1923, after an illness of nearly nine years. He was known for returning his $350-a-year salary back to the village and to local churches. He came to Sharonville in 1907, with only $13.50 in his pocket. He lived to be nearly one hundred years old.

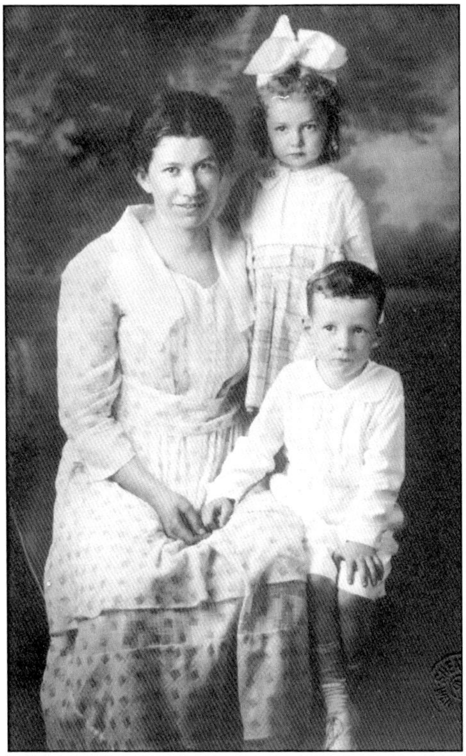

Louise Funk Vail and her children posed for this professional portrait in 1919. They are, from left to right, Louise, three-year-old daughter Marie Vail, and five-year-old son Jack Vail. Marie grew up and married into the Schwan family.

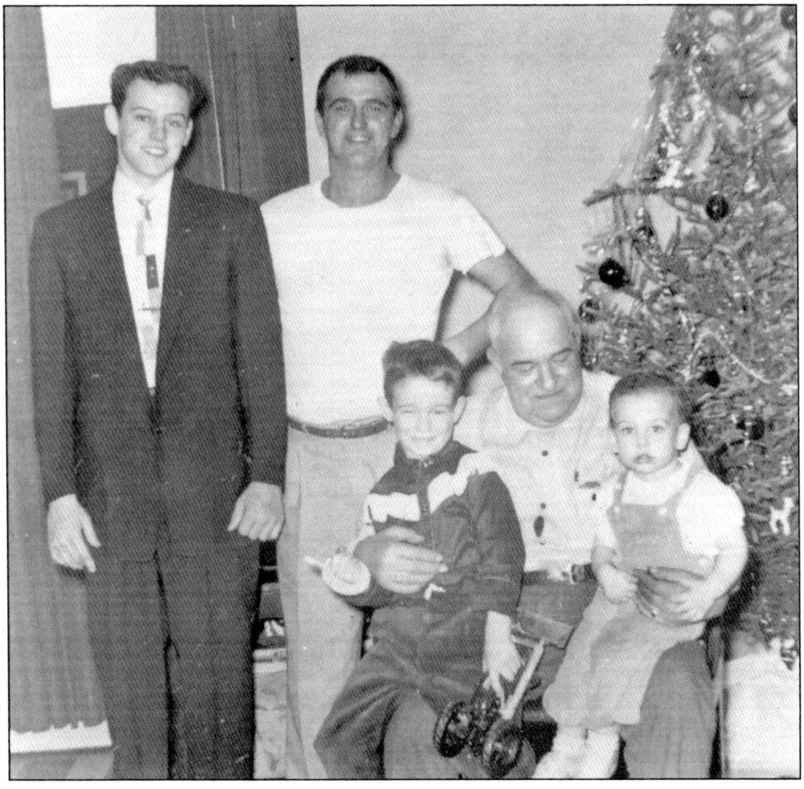

Three generations of Schwans gather at Christmastime in 1954. Pictured, from left to right, are 65-year-old Grandfather "Turk" Schwan, 40-year-old Wilbert "Turk" Schwan, 16-year-old Randall "Turk" Schwan, 5-year-old Paul Schwan, and 1-year-old Mike Schwan.

Elizabeth Frances Swink Prenatt posed for this photo on August 7, 1917. The wife of John Prenatt, born February 3, 1870, in Somerset, Kentucky, she was a member of the Red Cross and the Ladies Aid Society. Grandson Doug Prenatt remembers she made delicious blackberry dumplings.

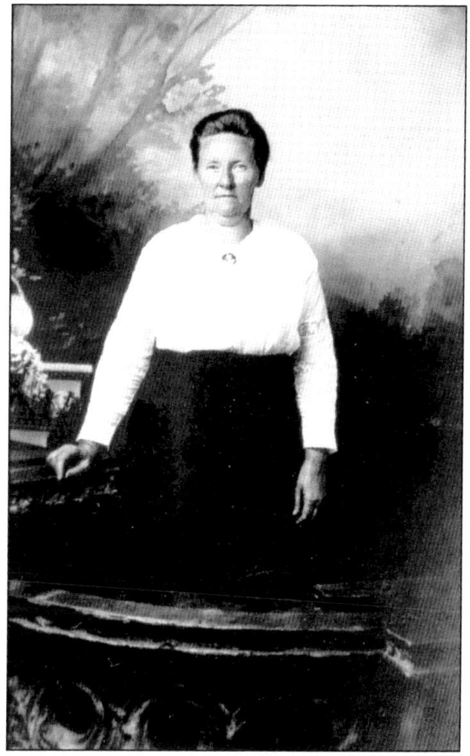

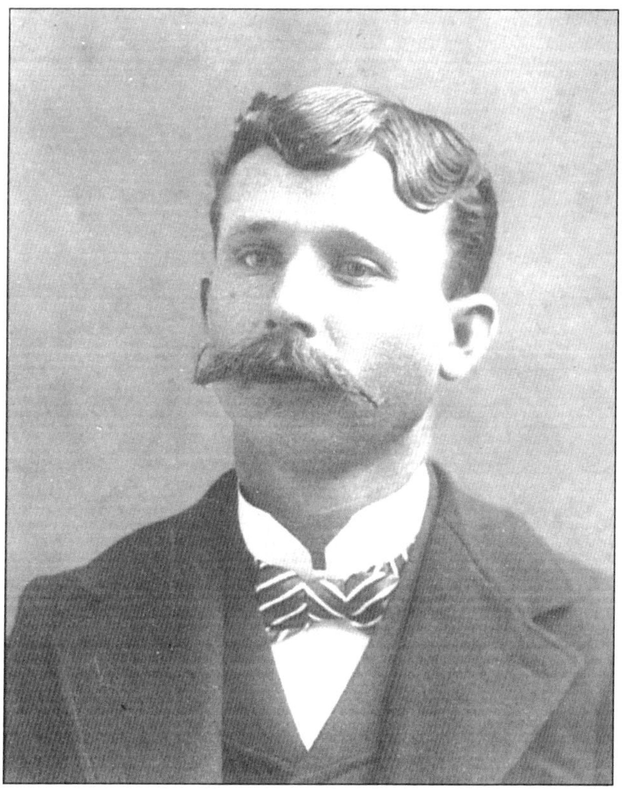

This portrait of John Prenatt was taken for his wedding, September 2, 1900. In 1906, John was transferred from Middletown to Sharonville by the New York Central and Big Four Railroads. He was a 36-year-old section boss who was born in Indiana. For a time, the family rented one of the three homes on Hill Street. John's job was to maintain the main line tracks for the passenger trains.

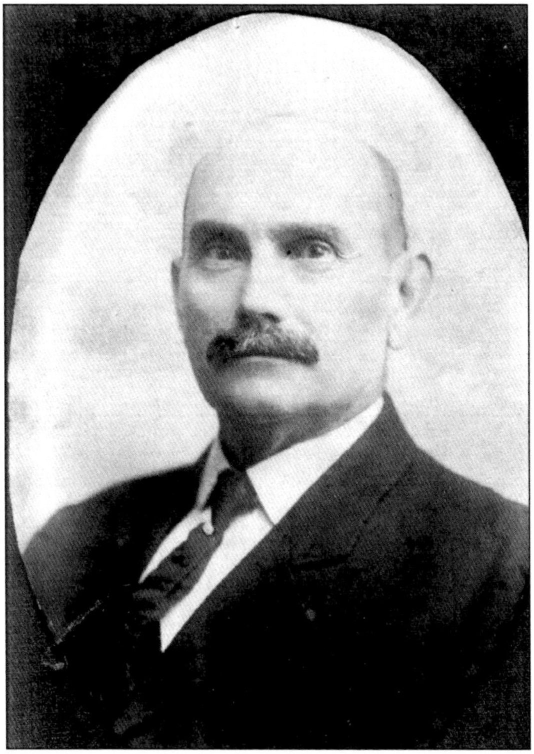

Frederick J. Breuleux (January 14, 1856–April 14, 1929) was born on a farm a half mile east of Sharonville. His parents, Philip and Susanne (Billiod) Breuleux, both immigrated to the area from eastern France. He attended Sharonville schools and the Presbyterian Church, and worked on his father's farm until 1880, when he went to the Hauck farm as superintendent. He married Etta Beeler on November 28, 1880.

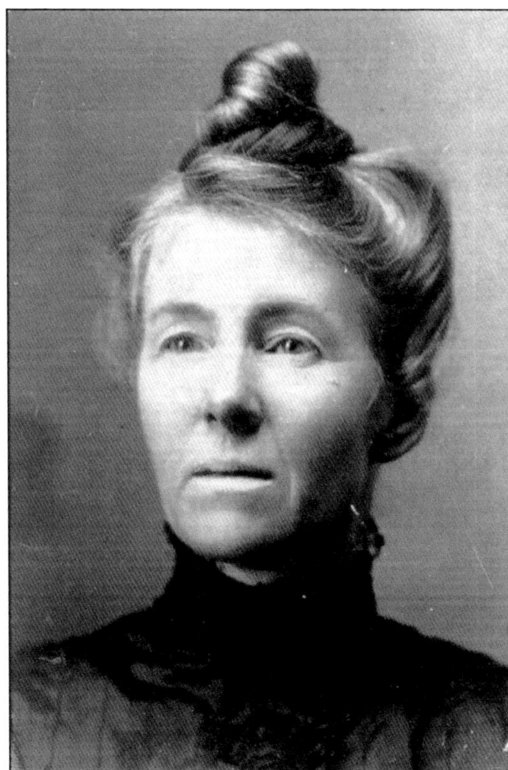

Etta Beeler Breuleux (November 22, 1858–December, 1930) was born on a farm east of Sharonville, the daughter of Samuel and Rebecca (Jenkins) Beeler. She was educated in the public schools of Sharonville. In 1880, she married Frederick Breuleux. They were parents of four children: Charles and Ina (both of whom died in childhood), Stanley, and Ruby. They made their home in the superintendent's house located next to the Hauck Mansion.

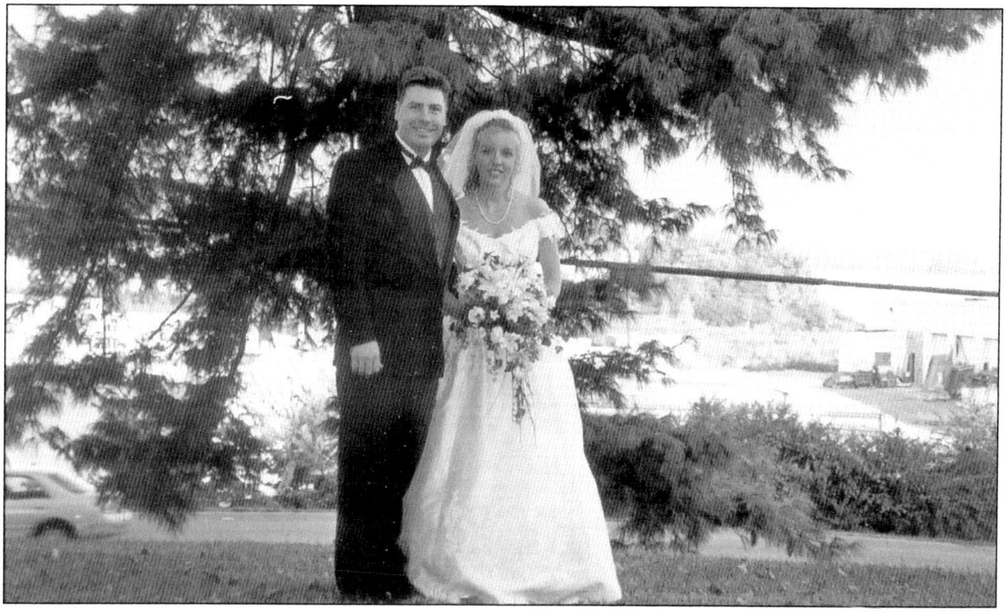

Michelle Rene Smith is the great-granddaughter of Ruby Breuleux Muchmore and Oliver Muchmore. On September 26, 1998, Michelle married Patrick Andrew Thompson at the old Hauck farm on Mosteller Road. This photo was taken at the same place the photo of Ruby and Oliver was taken 79 years earlier.

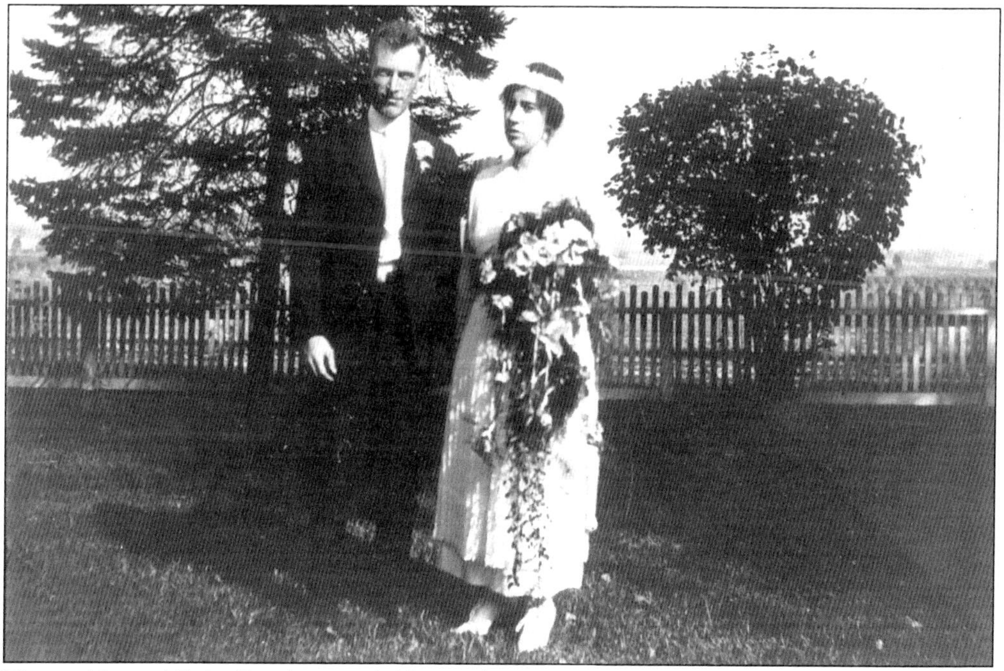

The wedding of Ruby Breuleux and Oliver Charles Muchmore took place October 1, 1919, at the home of Ruby's parents, next door to the Hauck mansion. The house, which still stands near the corner of Mosteller and Crescentville Roads, is currently the location for the Toedtman School of Music. The estate was part of Louis Hauck's summer home and farm, used for growing grain for his Hauck Brewing Company of Cincinnati, Ohio, and for boarding draft horses.

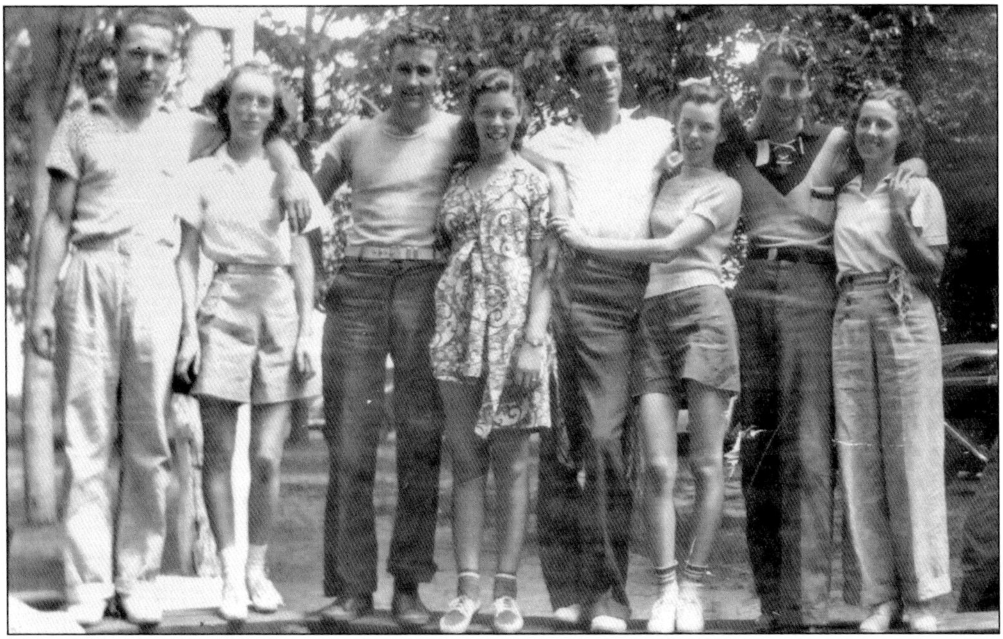

The 4-H Progressive Club was formed for teenagers who reached the age limit for 4-H but wanted to continue their association. This group gathered for a weekend at Camp Allyn in 1937. Pictured, from left to right, are Harold Gorman, Ruth Williams (later Gorman), Ken Morgan, Marian McGrew (later Morgan), Mel Burg, Gail Williams (later Burg), Dan Berssenbruegge, and June Gorman (later Berssenbruegge).

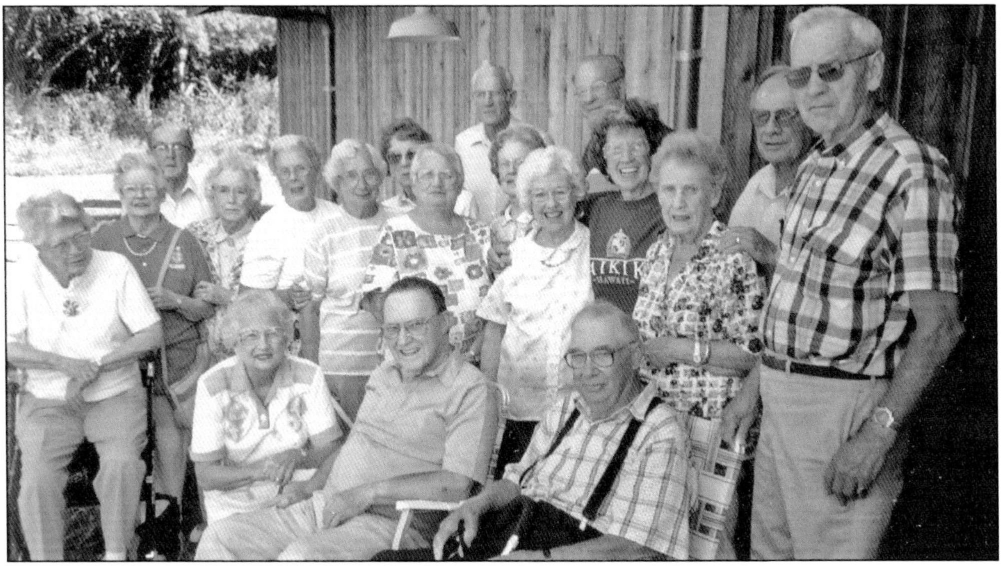

In 1997, the 4-H Progressive Club planted a buckeye tree at Gorman Heritage Farm in Evendale. This photo was taken September 2, 1998. Pictured, from left to right, are (seated) Merle Cradler, Ina Greene, Harold Gorman, James Gorman; (second row) Thelma O'Sullivan, Ruth Gorman, Marian Morgan, Dorothy Gorman, Jean Geist, June Berssenbruegge, Jean Sandy, Harold Baxter; (third row) Dan O'Sullivan, Flo Robinson, Gail Burg, Ann Boehm, Don Sandy; (back row) Ray Baxter, and Mel Burg.

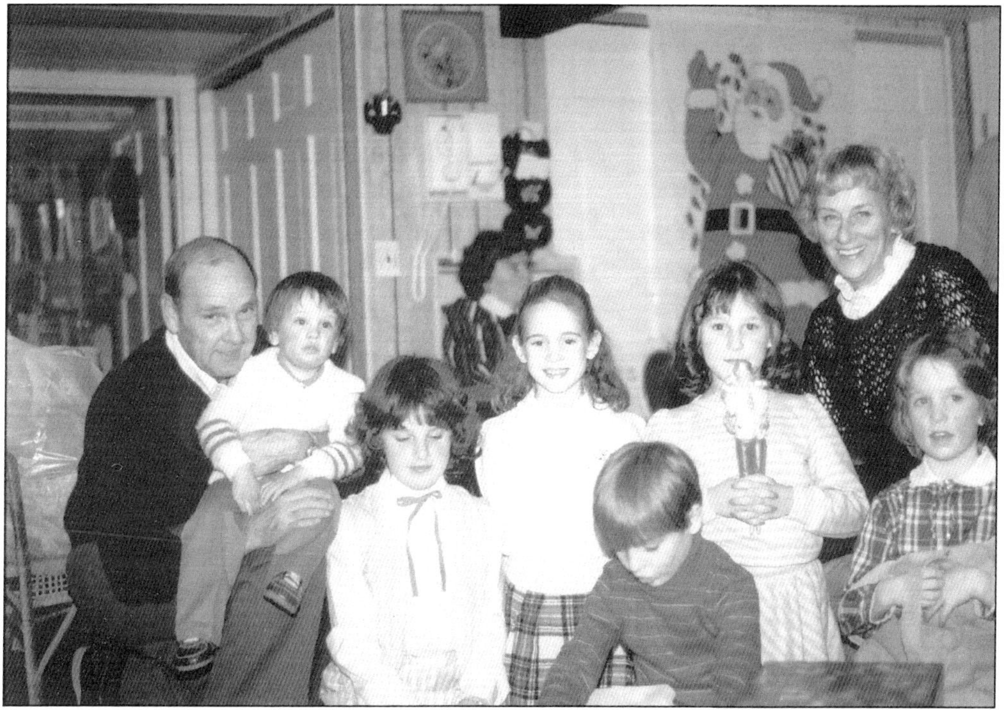

Holidays at the Robertson's house were always fun. Everyone enjoyed Christmas at Grandma and Grandpa's home on Parfour Court in 1983. Pictured, from left to right, are Don Robertson, Brent Robertson, Angela Robertson, Jennifer Crown, Ryan Robertson, Amy Robertson, Rita Robertson, and Kimberly Crown. Betty Davis Robertson is sitting under the telephone in the background.

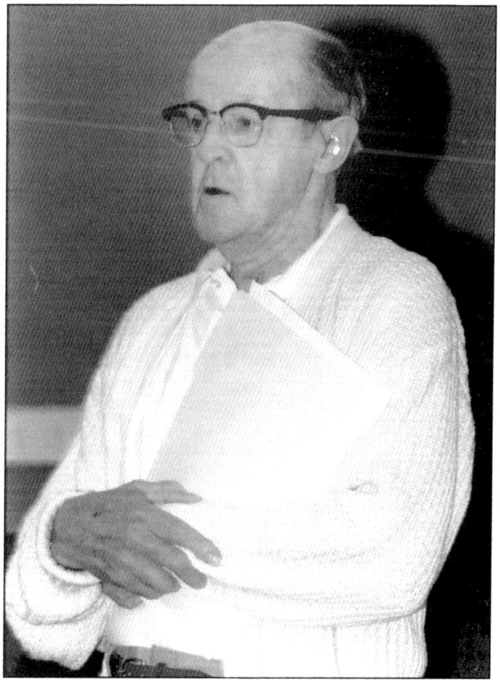

Dan O'Sullivan was a "call boy" as a child. He'd wake up the railroad crew when it was time for a train to leave. Dan was the last postmaster for the Sharonville post office. When the local office was restructured as part of Cincinnati, he became the local superintendent. Dan is pictured at a June 23, 1990 Society of Historic Sharonville program reminiscing about the town as he knew it.

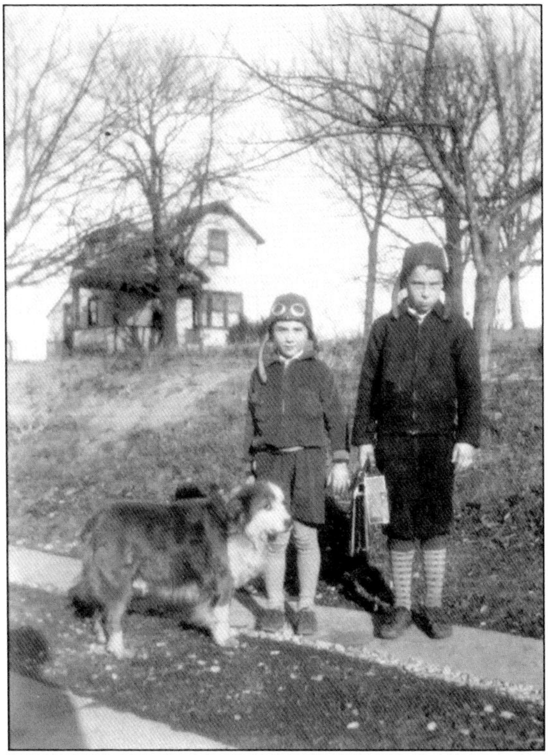

The Hagee boys, Robert J. and G. Richard, took a moment to pose with their pet collie "Queenie" in front of their home on Symmestown Road (now Kemper Road) in 1936. The Emmons' house is in the background.

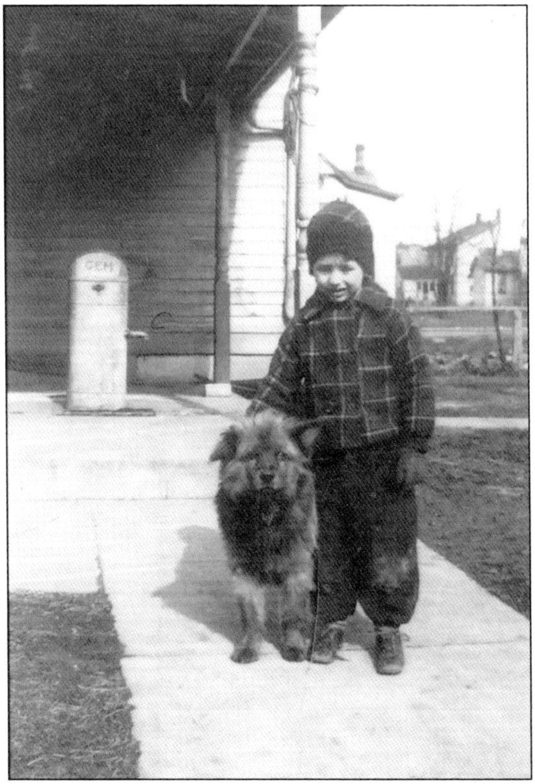

This photo of young Marts Beekley was taken by the back porch of 108 (11080) Reading Road before 1939. The house and the dog were owned by Mike Burk. The Burks lived in the upper flat and the Beekleys lived downstairs. The pump behind Marts went to a cistern that was removed when the new kitchen was built.

Loretto E. and George J. Hagee, the parents of G. Richard and Robert J. Hagee, are pictured in front of their home at 5361 East Kemper Road in 1958. This was the first and only home owned by the couple.

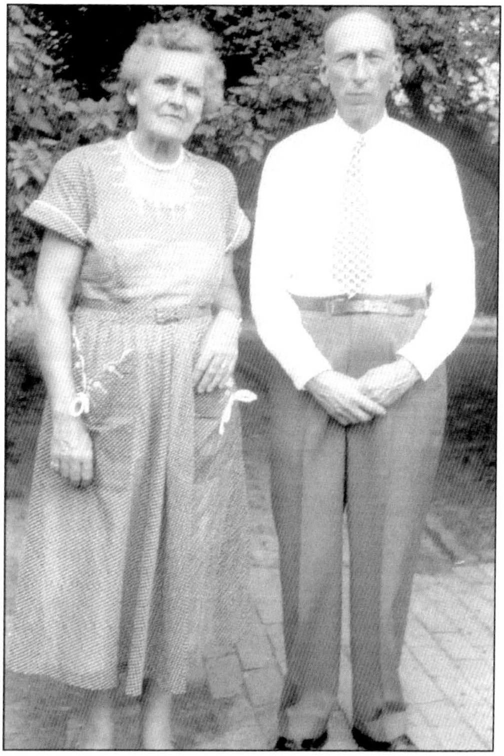

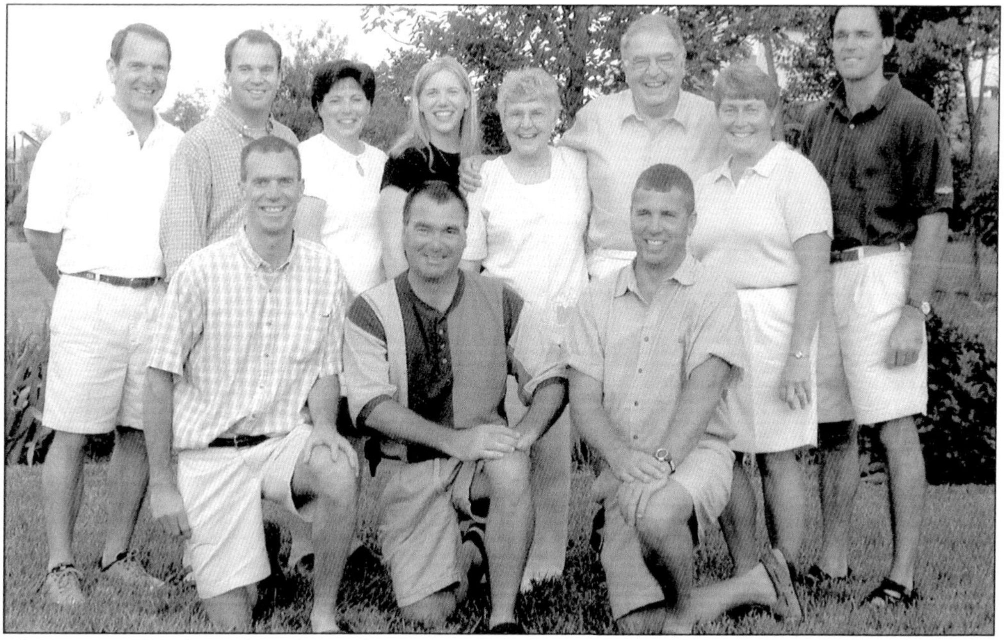

The Haines family gathered for this group photo while everyone was in town for a surprise celebration of Bill's 70th birthday in early June, 2001. Pictured, from left to right, are (front row) Tom Haines, Jim Haines, and Mark Haines; (back row) Mike Haines, Steve Haines, Karen Haines Durchholz, Lynne Haines Mick, Mary Haines, Bill Haines, Jean Haines Lamping, and Dan Haines.

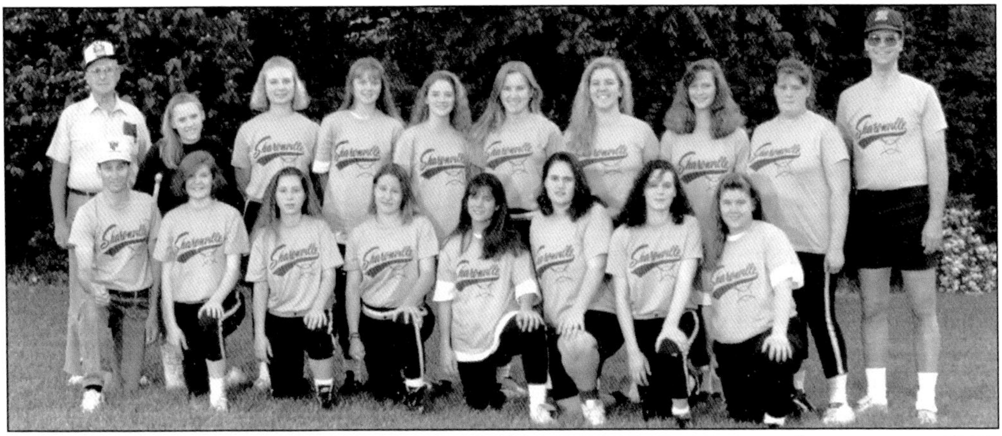

These girls were the Tri-City Class A Softball league and tournament champions in 1993. Pictured, left to right, are (front row) Manager Patrick Schehr, Heather Gaines, Erin Schehr, Courtney Pelz, Terri Ulland, Amy Roelker, Shanna Bales, Melanie Rader, (back row) Norm "Grandpa" Kerrison, Mary Ann Margeson (on crutches), Rachel Dehner, Carey Vonderhaar, Krista Leist, Kim Scharding, Joy Settlemayer, Amy Bartholomew, Jamie Hacker, and Coach Tony Leist.

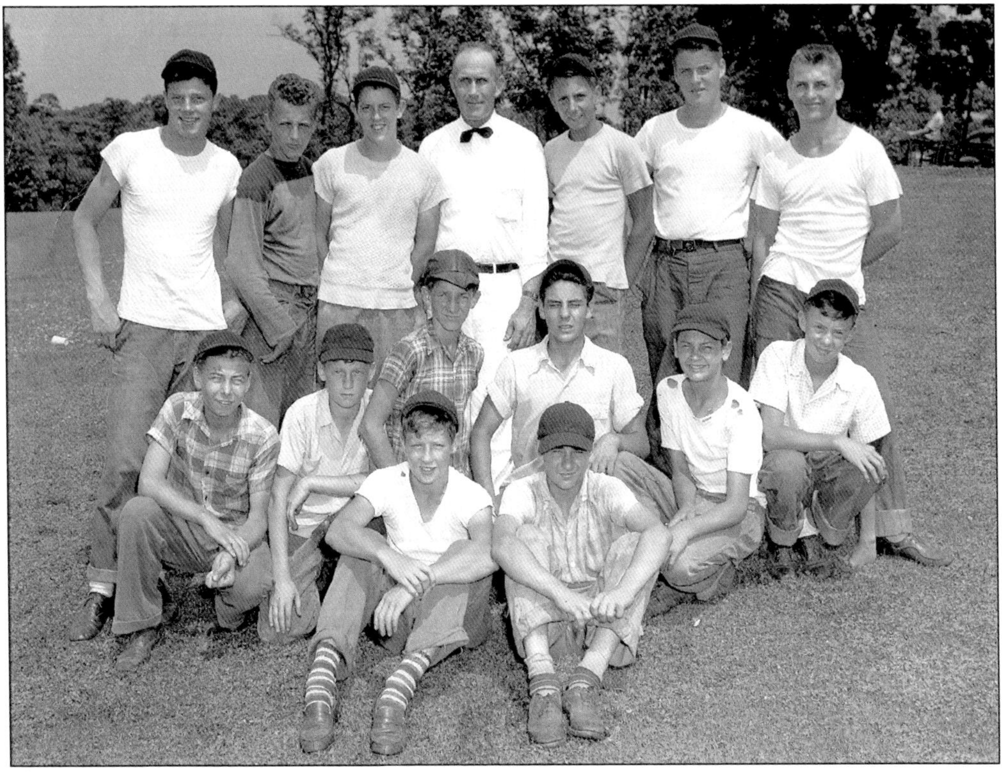

Over the years, Sharonville has fielded teams in a variety of leagues. In July, 1946, the Sharonville Knothole team was managed by Mr. Cork. Pictured, from left to right, are (front row) Larry Kolesar and bat boy Frank Celenza; (middle row) Ralph Berger, Moise Greavu, Dan Danbury, Joe Celenza, Jim Lautenslager, and Raymer Atha; (back row) Cleve Rush, Kenneth Cork, Bob Ballew, Mr. Cork, Bruce Flickenger, Tom Powers, and Marts Beekley.

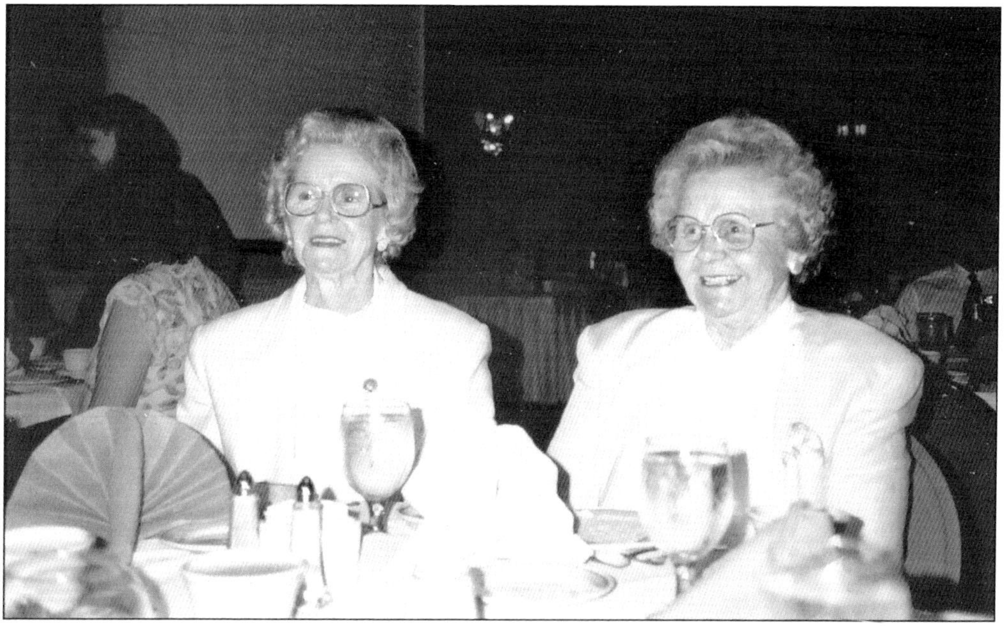

Everyone looks forward to the annual Sharon High School reunions. Pictured at one of the 1980s reunions are Mary Louise McWhorter Ferrell (left) and her sister Margaret McWhorter Ryan.

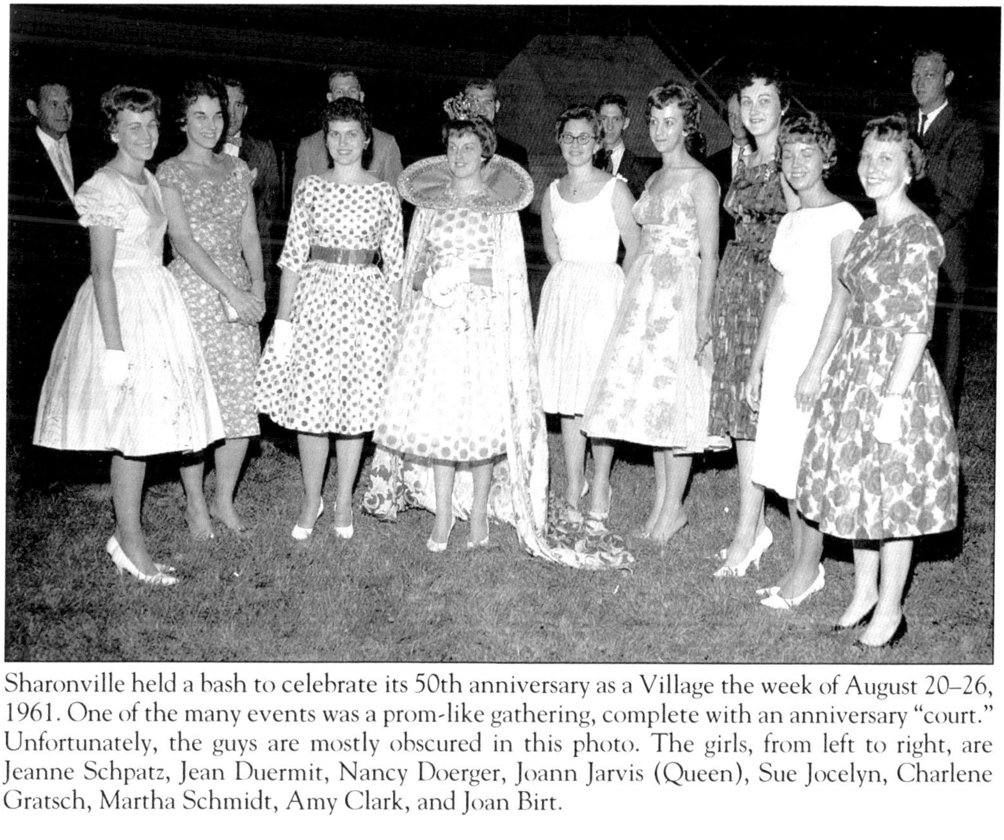

Sharonville held a bash to celebrate its 50th anniversary as a Village the week of August 20–26, 1961. One of the many events was a prom-like gathering, complete with an anniversary "court." Unfortunately, the guys are mostly obscured in this photo. The girls, from left to right, are Jeanne Schpatz, Jean Duermit, Nancy Doerger, Joann Jarvis (Queen), Sue Jocelyn, Charlene Gratsch, Martha Schmidt, Amy Clark, and Joan Birt.

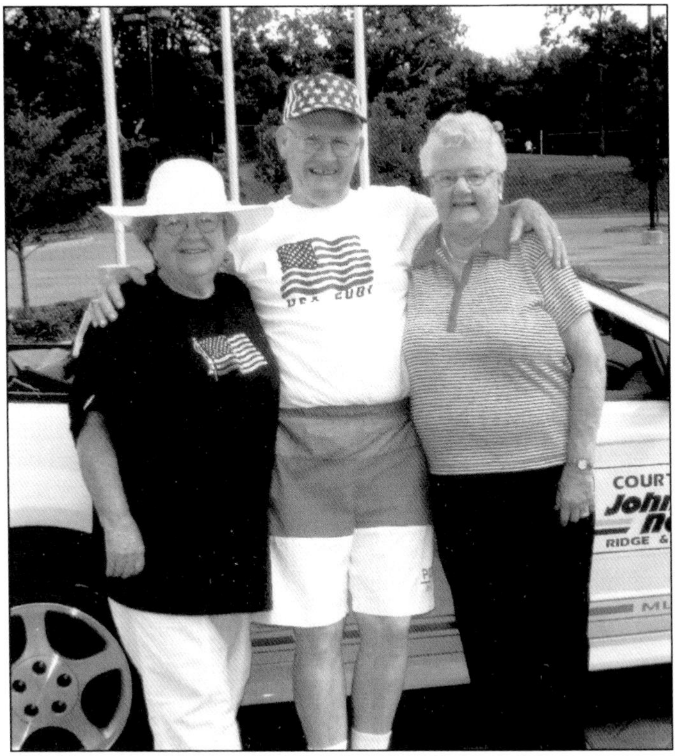

Sharonville's 2001 Independence Day Parade Grand Marshals "came of age during the Great Depression and Second World War." They are everyday heroes and ordinary citizens whose lives are about giving back to their community. Pictured, from left to right, are Elaine Krick (Sharonville resident for 50 years), Bo Boham (9 years), and Kay McCarty (31 years). All have been active volunteers in a variety of community organizations.

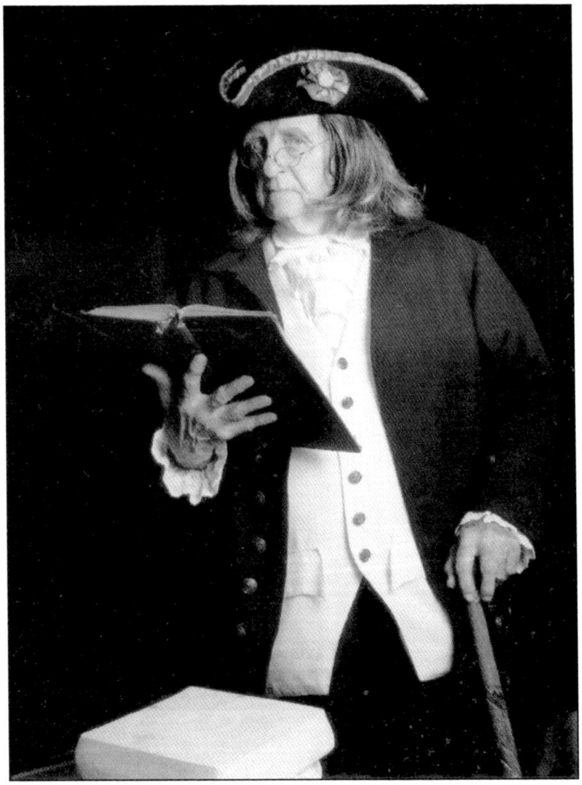

Ben Franklin paid a visit to the 150th Anniversary Spring Fete at Maple Knoll Village in Springdale in 1998. Ben, the father of the modern post office, is portrayed by Robert C. "Bucky" Walters, a resident of Sharonville and a retired postal worker, since 1989. He regularly travels to conventions, schools, and meetings around the country to share Franklin's observations of life in the 18th century.

Nine

Society of Historic Sharonville

The Society of Historic Sharonville was formed in 1988 to collect and preserve historical materials, sites, and structures, to disseminate historical information pertaining to Sharonville and the area surrounding it, and to encourage people to learn about the history of the town. The city administration provided the vacant license bureau building, coincidentally the first town firehouse, to the Society for use as a museum and office. Wonderful persons donated memorabilia, and other talented people helped set up the original exhibits. Membership currently fluctuates between 80 and 100 people, and occasionally a new and ambitious volunteer will come forward to help the Board of Directors follow through on projects. We are fortunate to have the continued support of the city council and other city personnel.

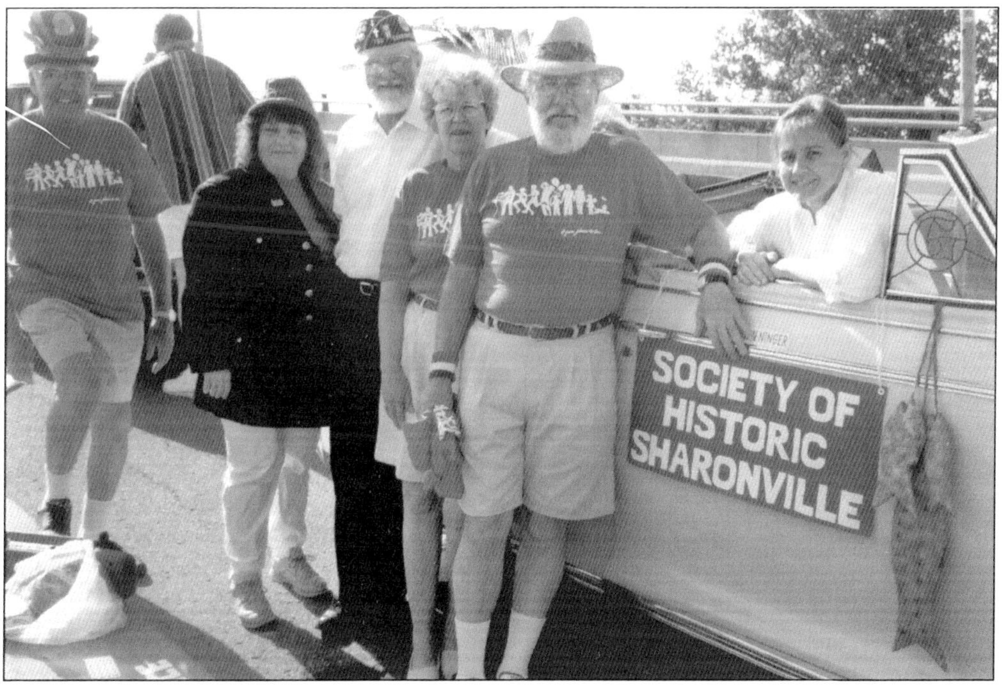

Our Board of Directors likes to participate in the annual Sharonville Independence Day parade. Stopping for a pre-parade photo in 1996, from left to right, are Stan Gruenninger (Glendale resident and owner of the historic vehicle), Karen Shaw, Bill Lewis (who was riding with the VFW unit), Ernestine and Bob Houston, and Maria Eckhoff.

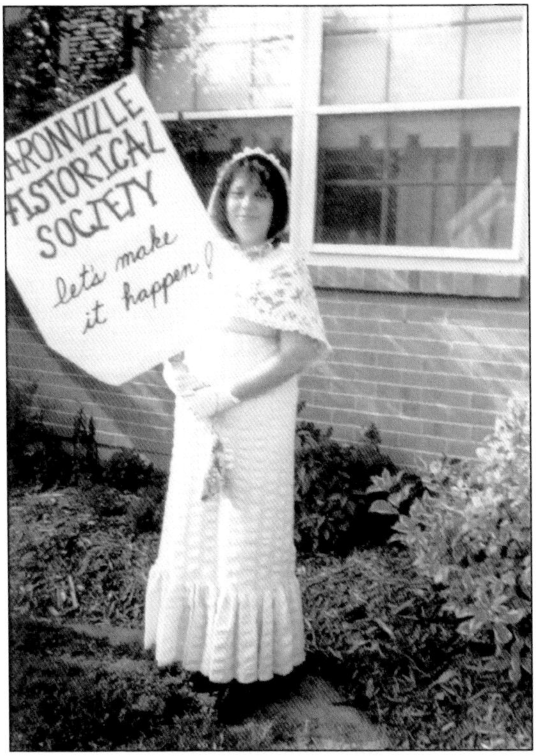

Sharonville resident, Karen Shaw, helped get the historical society off the ground. Inspired by a former Mayor, Myron Luke, a life-long resident of the area, Karen put together a proposal urging the establishment of a local organization to preserve Sharonville's long history. Here she is pictured with the sign she carried in the Sharonville Bicentennial Parade in 1988.

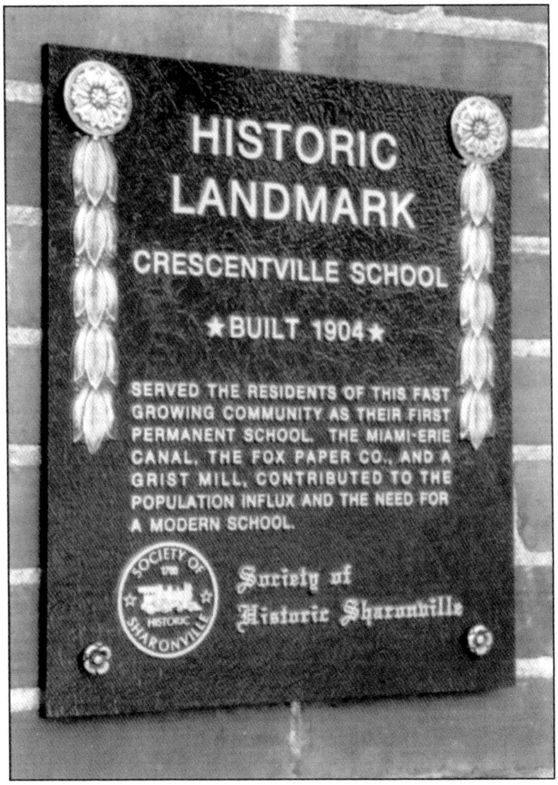

One of the first projects undertaken by the Society of Historic Sharonville was the recognition of significant buildings around the city. This plaque was dedicated in August of 1994, and is located on the old Crescentville School, built in 1904, which now serves as the West Side Recreation Center.

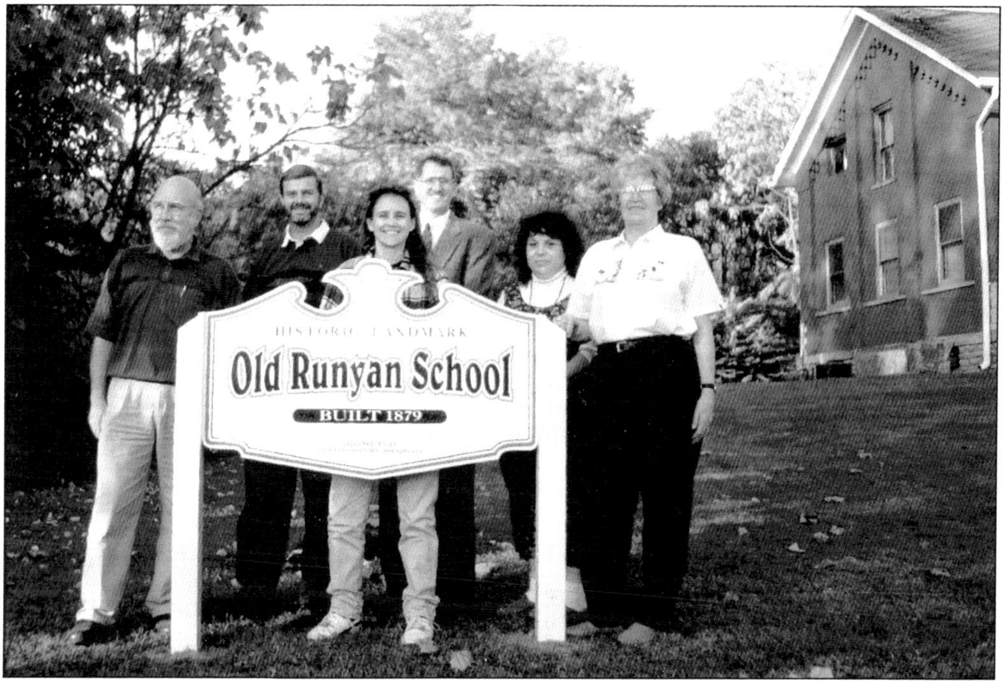

In September of 1996, the Board gathered to dedicate a sign marking another Sharonville landmark. The Old Runyan School was built in 1879 on land once owned by local pioneers, Isaac and Henry Runyan. Pictured, from left to right, are board members Bob Houston, Virgil Lovitt II, Maria Eckhoff, Al Ledbetter (Sharonville City Manager), Karen Shaw, and Ernestine Houston.

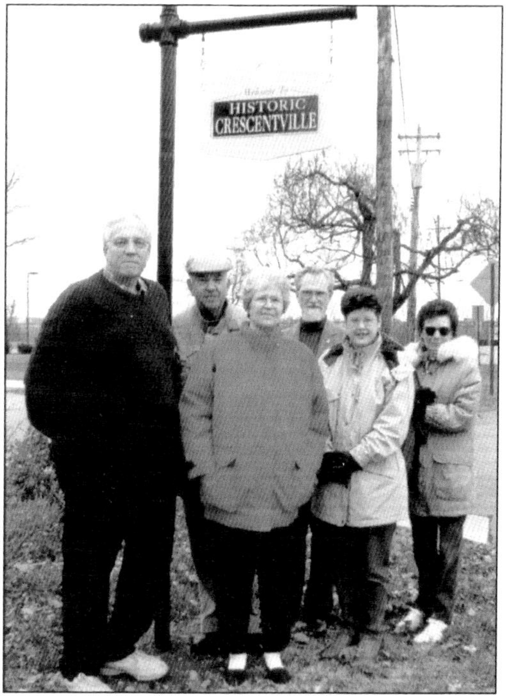

The Crescentville area of Sharonville, which includes Circleville Road, was built near the old Fox Paper Mill for the families of employees. The mill was located across Crescentville Road. The Society of Historic Sharonville thought it fitting to recognize the historic area with a new sign in December of 1995. Pictured, from left to right, are Mayor Paul Kattelman, Virgil Lovitt, Sr. (a Crescentville School alumnus), and board members Ernestine Houston, Bill Lewis, Kim Webster, and Audrey Privett.

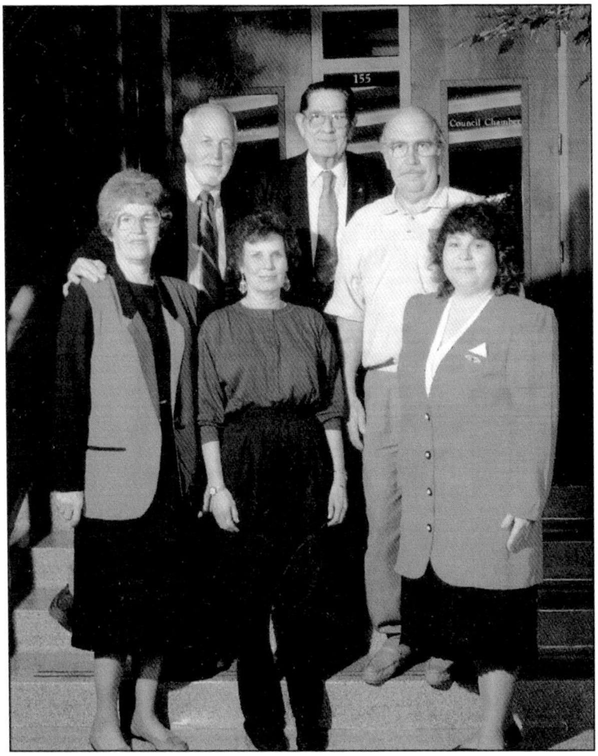

The founders of the Society of Historic Sharonville gathered for this picture with photographer John Payne, who contributed his talents to help produce the bicentennial book, *Sharonville, Then and Now*, c. 1988. Pictured, from left to right, are (front row) Ernestine Houston, Audrey Privett, and Karen Shaw; (back row) John Payne, Myron Luke, and Bob Houston.

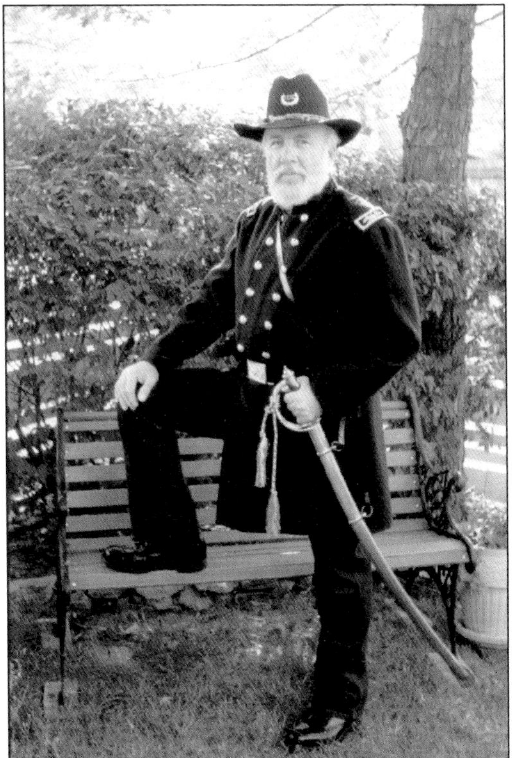

Robert W. Houston was a member of the Sharonville City Council for 18 years and a founding member and former President of the Society of Historic Sharonville. A Civil War buff, and reportedly a descendant of Colonel Sam Houston, Bob had this photo taken in Bowling Green, Kentucky, by former Cincinnati photographer John Payne in the 1990s. The Historical Society Museum was named for Bob at the time of his retirement from the city, in December of 1999.

Jonathan Shuff was 20 years old, five-foot-eight, sporting shining blue eyes and light colored hair, and a light complexion not yet hardened by the sun and wind encountered during life as a farmer. The son of Jacob and Nancy Shuff lived only a fraction of their years. He was a young man in the prime of his youth whose fate was cast in the Civil War. He enlisted on August 9, 1862, and was assigned, like many of his neighbors, to Company E of the 83rd Regiment, Ohio Volunteer Infantry (OVI). He mustered in at Camp Dennison for what was supposed to be a three-year tour of duty. Instead, he received a gunshot wound at the Battle of Vicksburg on May 22, 1863. He died the next day. In Sharonville, on a grassy knoll around which a subdivision grew, Jonathan Shuff was laid to rest. Pictured is one page from Jonathan's military pension record.

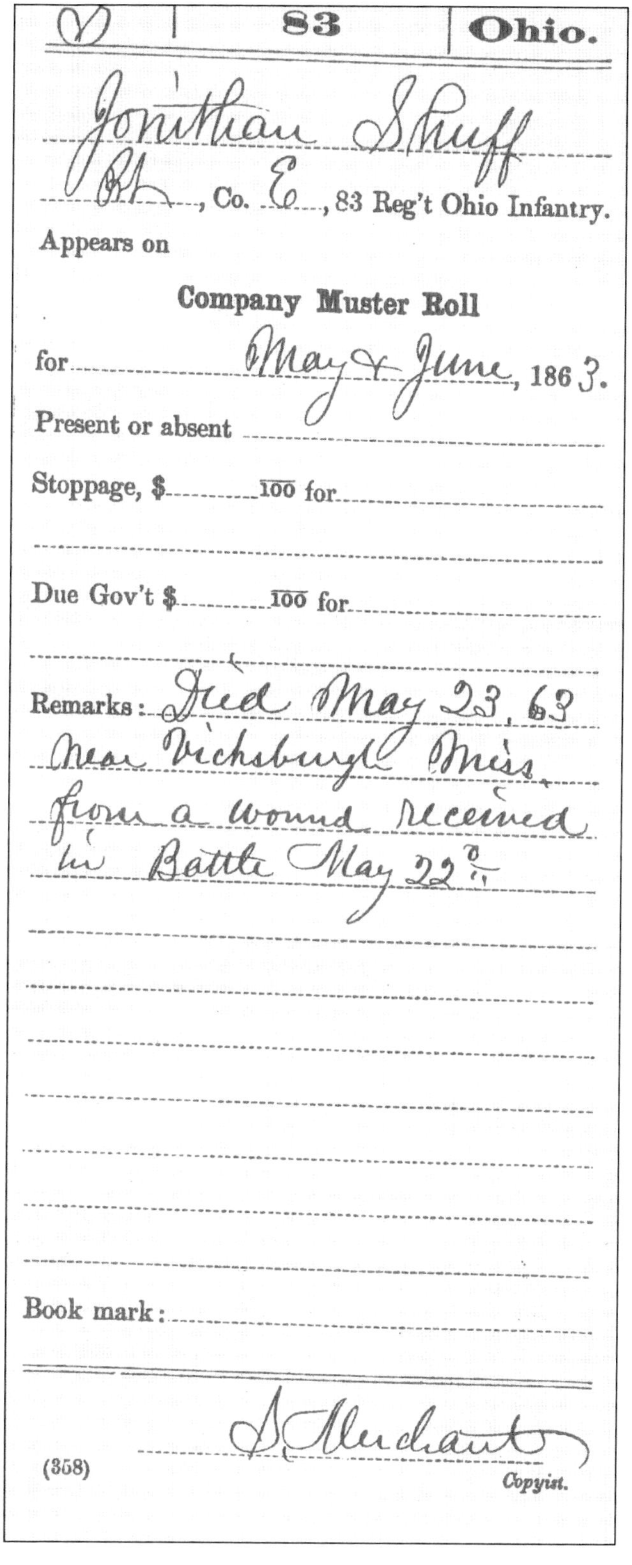

S | 83 | Ohio.

Jonathan Shuff

Pt, Co. E, 83 Reg't Ohio Infantry.

Appears on

Company Muster Roll

for May & June, 1863.

Present or absent

Stoppage, $ 100 for

Due Gov't $ 100 for

Remarks: Died May 23, 63 near Vicksburgh Miss. from a wound received in Battle May 22d.

Book mark:

(358)

Copyist.

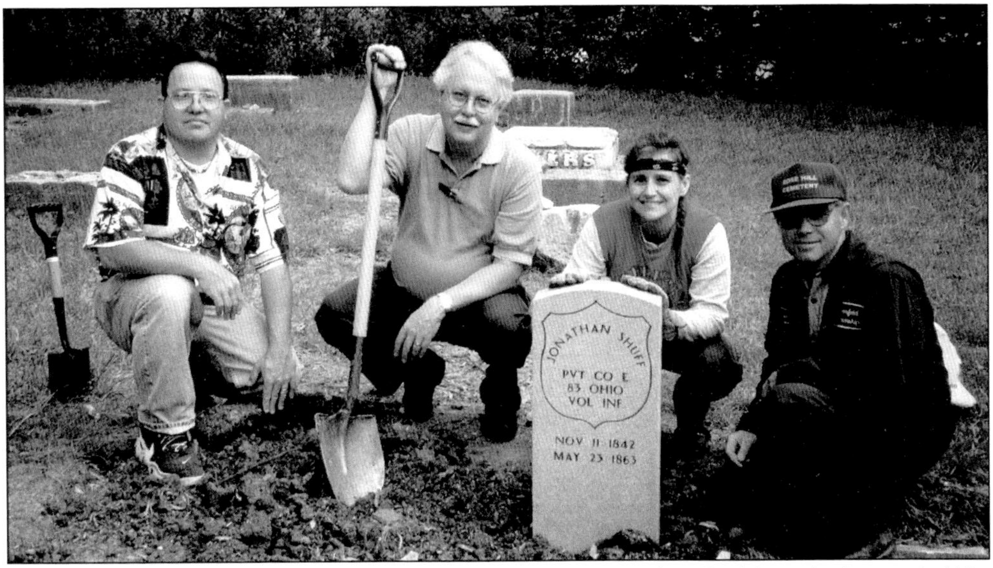

The 4-foot marble slab that marked Jonathan Shuff's resting place had been broken in half by unthinking fiends. Today, thanks to the efforts of many people, Jonathan has a new marker, and the resting places of his relatives are more respectable. Setting the new marker at Shuff-Myers Cemetery in May, 2000, from left to right, is the "cemetery team" of Darrin Upp, reporter Walt Schaefer, Maria Eckhoff, and Carl Muennich. The other "fixer," Bob Houston, took the photo.

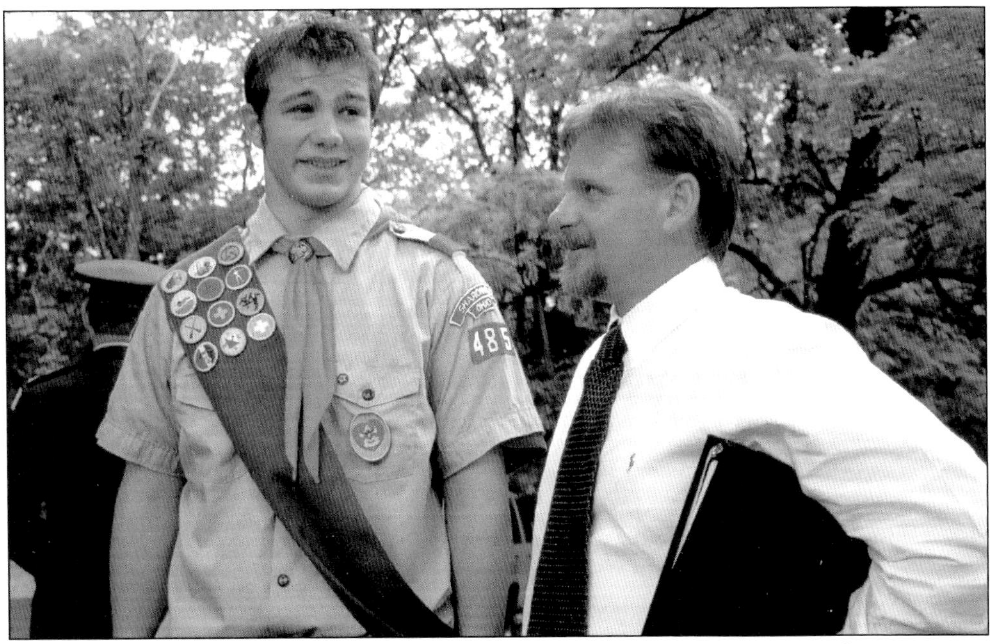

It was a former resident, Bill Elmore, who approached the historical society about restoring the cemetery. Though attending school out of state, Bill ordered military records and the new government-issue marker. Glen Lovitt, an Eagle Scout candidate, handled negotiations for a driveway, light pole, shrubbery, and dead tree removal, and got his troop-mates to help spread mulch chips. Pictured are Glen Lovitt (left) and Bill Elmore at the dedication ceremony, held on May 29, 2000.

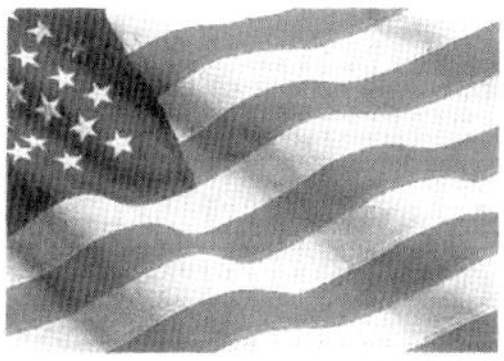

Memorial Day
May 29, 2000

12:00-1:00 p.m.
Sharonville, Ohio

The Society of Historic Sharonville
Rededication of Shuff-Myers Cemetery
and
grave site of
Private Jonathan Shuff, 83rd Regiment, Co. E, OVI

Program

Presentation of the Colors: Boy Scout Troop 485
Ohio National Guard
Ohio Valley Volunteers, Civil War Interpreters

Introduction: ....Sharonville Mayor Virgil Lovitt, II

Invocation: ....Col. Ken Daft, Ohio National Guard

How it Started: ....Bill Elmore, Sharonville, OH and Davenport, IA

Society of Historic Sharonville: ....Bill Lewis, President, Board of Directors

Eagle Scout Project: ....Glen Lovitt, Troop 485

Ohio Valley Volunteers, Civil War Interpreters: ....Walt McVicker

Ohio National Guard: ....Lt. Colonel Kevin Bennett

Keynote Speaker: ....Honorable Rob Portman, Ohio Congressman

Rededication: ....Col. Ken Daft, Chaplain

Levi Worster Chapter, Daughters of the Union 1861-1865: Place a flower on Jonathan Shuff's grave on behalf of the descendants of all men who served in the Civil War

Taps: ....Marine Staff Sgt. Christopher Gilstrap

Rifle and Cannon volleys: ....Ohio Valley Volunteers

Closing: ....Mayor Virgil Lovitt, II

1:00 Military fly-over: ....Ohio National Guard, F-16

(Please see other side)

The rededication ceremony at the Shuff-Myers Cemetery was attended by several hundred residents. Pictured is the dedication program.

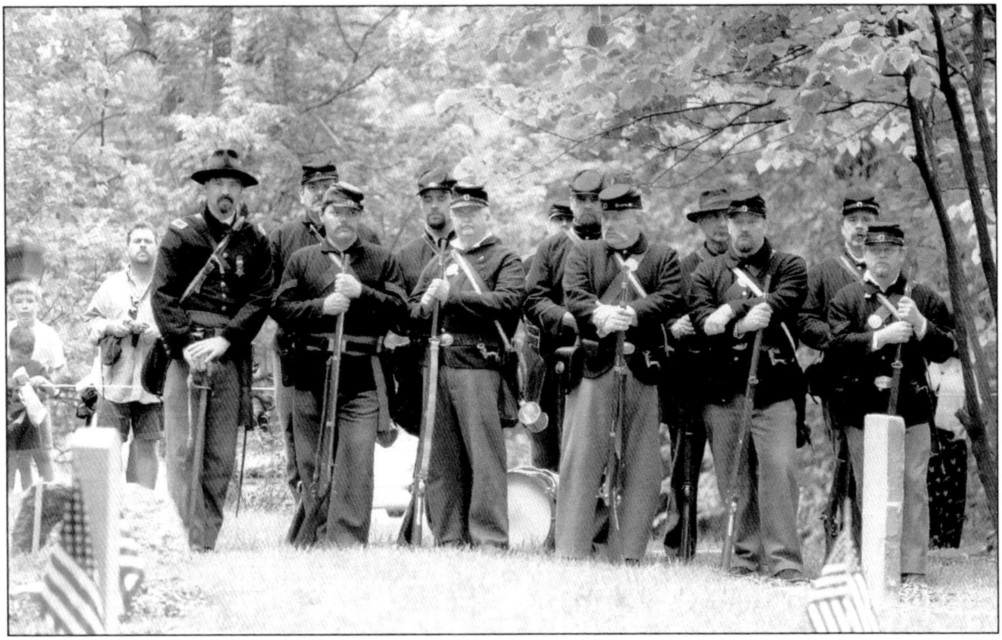

Ohio Valley Volunteers, a group of local Civil War Reenactors, were present at the dedication of Shuff-Myers Cemetery. They fired a 21-gun salute with their vintage firearms and also set off volleys from the cannon.

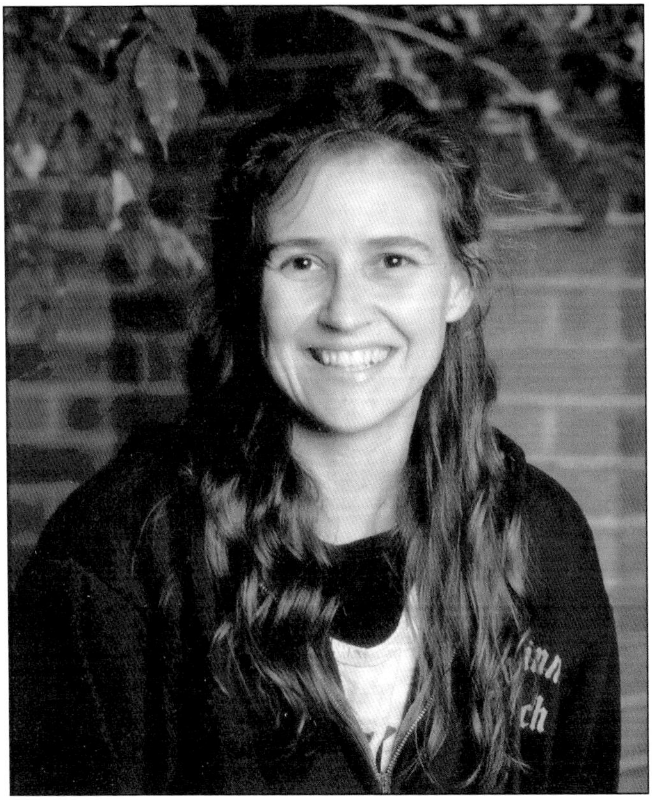

Young historian, and now curator and author, Maria Eckhoff, often sandwiched Sharonville historical society meetings in between volleyball matches played in a league at GE Park in Springdale. Photographer John Payne coaxed her to pose for this picture even though she was still dressed for a game in the mid 1990s. Her hectic schedule often includes two jobs, volunteer work for the Park District and Sierra Club, weightlifting, bicycling, and genealogical research.